# Natural Spirituality

BOOKS BY JOYCE ROCKWOOD HUDSON

*Long Man's Song*

*To Spoil the Sun*

*Groundhog's Horse*

*Enoch's Place*

*Looking for De Soto: A Search Through the South
for the Spaniard's Trail*

*Natural Spirituality:
Recovering the Wisdom Tradition in Christianity*

*Apalachee*

*The Church of Divine Wisdom* (Hagia Sophia), founded in Constantinople
in the fourth century by Roman Emperor Constantine, who was
converted to Christianity by a dream.

Joyce Rockwood Hudson

# NATURAL SPIRITUALITY

## Recovering the Wisdom Tradition in Christianity

JRH PUBLICATIONS   Danielsville, Georgia

Published in 2000 by JRH Publications
Danielsville, Georgia 30633-0942
Telephone 706-789-3400

Designed by Sandra Strother Hudson
Set in Centaur with Centaur display by G&S Typesetters, Inc.
Printed and bound by Thomson-Shore, Inc.
The paper in this book meets the guidelines for permanence
and durability of the Committee on Production Guidelines
for Book Longevity of the Council on Library Resources.

Printed in the United States of America
9 8 7 6 5 4 3 2 1

Publisher's Cataloguing in Publication Data
(*Provided by Quality Books, Inc.*)

Hudson, Joyce Rockwood
Natural spirituality : recovering the wisdom
tradition in Christianity / Joyce Rockwood Hudson.
— 1st ed.     p.     cm.
Includes bibliographical references and index.
LCCN: 99-95304     ISBN: 1-893383-55-5

1. Spirituality.   2. Wisdom—Religious aspects—
Christianity.   3. Jungian psychology—Religious aspects—
Christianity.   4. Individuation (Psychology)—Religious
aspects—Christianity.   I. Title.

BT590.S65H84 2000     248
QBI99-1107

Cover illustration: *The Flight into Egypt* by Duccio di Buoninsegna (c. 1255–1319),
Museo dell'Opera Metropolitana, Siena, Italy. This image depicts the dream
which prompted Joseph to take Mary and Jesus to safety in Egypt.
Reproduced by permission of Scala/Art Resource, NY.

Frontispiece: Engraving by G.J. Grelot, 1680. Photograph used with permission
of the Byzantine Library at Dumbarton Oaks.

*In memory of*

SUSAN CARDWELL HURT

1946–1984

*Her death brought us not only sorrow
but also the saving grace that
set all this in motion*

*When the Lord has given you the bread of suffering and the water of distress,*
*he who is your teacher will hide no longer, and you will see your teacher with*
*your own eyes. Whether you turn to right or left, your ears*
*will hear these words behind you, "This is the way, follow it."*
ISAIAH 30:20-21


*Nature is the mistress, the soul is the disciple;*
*what the one has taught, or the other has learned, has been delivered to them by God.*
TERTULLIAN, CHURCH FATHER, C. 200 AD

# Contents

Figures, *xiii*

Preface, *xv*

Acknowledgments, *xvii*

PART ONE: *Nature and Spirit*

1. Beginnings, *3*

2. Nature and Spirit in the Christian Tradition, *15*

PART TWO: *Jungian Spiritual Tools*

3. Consciousness, *31*

4. The Unconscious, *49*

5. The Language of the Unconscious, *63*

6. Dreams, *79*

7. Synchronicity, *99*

8. Carl Jung and Christianity, *110*

PART THREE: *The Individuation Journey*

9. The Opposites, *129*

10. Masculine Wholeness, *141*

11. The Beatles and the Masculine Quaternity, *160*

12. Feminine Wholeness, *190*

13. Psyche and Eros and the Feminine Quaternity, *204*

14. Individuation as Church Mission, *233*

15. Natural Spirituality as Church Program, *252*

*Appendices*

*Appendix A.* Natural Spirituality Sources, *269*

*Appendix B.* How to Use the *I Ching, 282*

*Appendix C.* Scriptural Reflections by Members of a
Natural Spirituality Dream Group, *286*

Notes, *293*

Index, *299*

# Figures

FIGURE ONE. The Four Functions, 38

FIGURE TWO. Stages of Life, 44

FIGURE THREE. The Unconscious, 50

FIGURE FOUR. Mother World–Father World Duality, 144

FIGURE FIVE. Mother World–Father World Quaternity, 145

FIGURE SIX. Human Wholeness, 147

FIGURE SEVEN. The Masculine Quaternity, 148

FIGURE EIGHT. Poet Quarter, 149

FIGURE NINE. Soldier Quarter, 151

FIGURE TEN. Wise Man Quarter, 154

FIGURE ELEVEN. King Quarter, 157

FIGURE TWELVE. The Feminine Quaternity, 191

FIGURE THIRTEEN. Eve Quarter, 192

FIGURE FOURTEEN. Scarlett Quarter, 194

FIGURE FIFTEEN. Athena Quarter, 198

FIGURE SIXTEEN. Sophia Quarter, 200

FIGURE SEVENTEEN. Guidelines for Dream Work, 261

# Preface

THIS BOOK is meant to help Christians, Protestant and Catholic, claim for themselves the natural spirit of God that comes to them every day and night through the meaningful events of their waking lives and through their dreams. The holy men and women of biblical times recognized the natural spirit and were guided by it. Their theologians called it wisdom. The recognition of natural spirituality was also carried by the people of the early Church, who knew very well that all of life, waking and sleeping, unfolds with divine wisdom in it. It is only in recent centuries that the natural spirit of God has been lost to our awareness. Now in our day it wants to be known again, and it is springing up in many contexts, more often outside established religion than within it. But in order for the natural spirit to be received in the safest and most effective way, it needs the context of a traditional, God-centered, religious life.

Natural spirituality is in no way antithetical to the traditional Christian life of prayer, praise, and caring community. It is a complement to it, a room to one side of the main room, available to those who need it and seek it, a place for deepening and centering, for refining the energies of life and turning them ever more toward God and the service of the greater good.

# Acknowledgments

I WISH TO THANK Miriam Chaikin for the close reading she gave to this work in manuscript form and for the benefit of her editorial wisdom. Likewise, I thank Karen Orchard for her editorial advice and for her encouragement and support for the project from the beginning.

I am grateful to Charles Hudson, Martha Harris, Gabriel Clark, and Ann Clark for reading the manuscript and offering helpful suggestions and reactions.

The vision of natural spirituality as a church program that is presented in this book has been developed in joint enterprise with the members of the Natural Spirituality Program of Emmanuel Episcopal Church in Athens, Georgia. I thank them every one for their dedication to God's way in their lives and for their enthusiastic participation in this pioneering experience. They are the ones who have shown me that this kind of program is possible. I especially thank Agnes Parker, Frank Farrar, and Heidi Simmonds for their steady companionship.

To those members of our program whose scriptural reflections appear in Appendix C, I offer thanks for letting me use their work. They are, in alphabetical order: Sara Baker, Mary Jo Brown, Frank Farrar, Tim Kennedy, Suzanne Reamy, Helene Rhodes, and Janet Robertson.

I thank Hadley Morris for sharing with me what she learned in instituting a natural spirituality program based on a preliminary version of this book at All Saints' Chapel at the University of the South in Sewanee, Tennessee. Her advice was instrumental in perfecting the format for the introductory study group, as described in Chapter Fifteen.

I wish to thank the past and present members of the clergy of Emmanuel Church who have given our natural spirituality program such a receptive and supportive environment, especially Jim Yeary, Barry Griffin, and

Eddie Ard. I thank two other men of the Church, Nick Johnson and Cecil Hudson, for crucial early support in my journey, before its destination was clear and its fruit had been born. And I offer deep gratitude to Mary Jo Brown, whose companionship was crucial in those early years when there was no program, nor any thought of one, but only the two of us struggling together to make sense of our inner experience within the context of our life with God.

I am grateful to Robert Johnson and John Sanford for their attention to this book in its preliminary form and for their much appreciated words of encouragement. And to Annette Cullipher, Jim Cullipher, and Sandra Perkins at Journey Into Wholeness, I offer thanks for kindness and support.

Janet Williamson directed me to the cover illustration for this edition, for which I am most grateful. And finally, I offer special thanks to Sandy Hudson for her beautiful design work and for her help in bringing *Natural Spirituality* through its final stage of production.

*June 1999*
*Danielsville, Georgia*

# PART ONE

# NATURE
# AND SPIRIT

CHAPTER ONE

# *Beginnings*

THIS WORK does not proceed from a career in ministry, theology, or psychology. It proceeds from the experience of a layperson, from life lived on the ground in Christian community. It is fitting, then, that I give its background in personal terms.

In the fall of 1991, I offered to teach a course on natural spirituality at the Episcopal church that I attend in the university town of Athens, Georgia. Though the content was to be based largely on Jungian psychology, I coined the term "natural spirituality" to distance the subject matter from clinical and secular contexts and to emphasize its rightful place in the life of the Church. Natural spirituality refers to a manifestation of the divine in creation that in biblical times was called "wisdom." It is an aspect of the Holy Spirit that has been neglected in Christianity in recent centuries, and yet, though neglected, it has always been with us, an ever present reality in every human life, whether noticed and attended to or not.

I am the daughter of an Episcopal clergyman. By nature and upbringing I have always been positively oriented toward the Church, finding nourishment for my soul in liturgical rites, hymns, and the rich imagery of the biblical tradition. When I was in my late thirties, seven years before I offered to teach this course, a series of events overtook me which shook the foundation of my rational and religious understanding of the very nature of life. At the time, I was a successful writer, with four published books. I had just completed a long historical novel, for which I did not yet have a publisher. My husband of sixteen years, a university professor of anthropology, was also a writer, renowned in his field. We were satisfied with our lives and had no idea that we had come to a turning point.

The turn began with a visit from family friends: two women, who were around my own age, and their three children, ages five to eight. They were

3

from our close circle of friends in Kentucky, where we had a summer home. It was now early February and our friends had driven together to Florida to visit the two women's respective parents. Our home in northern Georgia was their overnight stop on what was supposed to be their return trip.

We had a pleasant visit, lingering long around the dinner table, catching up on news. One of the women, whose name was Susan, was an actress of considerable accomplishment. What she especially wanted to talk about that evening was what had happened between her mother and her on the last day before she left Florida. She had a history of strained relationship with her mother, whose strong spirit was powerfully oriented toward church and family. As a successful actress, Susan was living a life very different from her mother's. She felt estranged. Her work required her frequent absence from home, sometimes for months at a time, during which time her two children remained behind in the care of their father. Although her family was doing well, Susan felt guilty and assumed negative judgement from her mother.

So it was that she was especially pleased about the time the two of them had spent together just the day before. She had taken her mother to the movies to see *Terms of Endearment*, the first time in years her mother had been to a movie theater. *Terms of Endearment* was about the relationship between a grown daughter and her mother. The daughter, who is herself the mother of two young children, learns that she has incurable cancer. Together with her mother, husband, and children, the heroine faces her death and takes her leave of life, knowing that her family is strong and will be able to carry on without her. Much of the film's drama is centered about the heroine's mother as she comes to terms with the death of her child.

This movie inspired a conversation of deep healing between Susan and her mother. In telling us about it, Susan kept reiterating that they had never before had such a satisfying conversation, that they had never before met each other with so much understanding and love. Her mother had told her that a mother always loves her child as tenderly as if it were a babe in arms, no matter how old the child becomes. Susan told her mother that she felt guilty about her own mothering of her children, because she was away so much. Her mother told her that she must not feel that way, that her children were turning out beautifully, a joy to their grandmother, and that Susan was a fine and worthy mother. This blessing from her mother was for Susan an especially precious treasure. Throughout that evening and the next morning she kept bringing it out and looking at it again.

The February day on which our friends arrived had been warm and pleasant, but in the evening rain began to fall. Later, while we slept, the temperature dropped and the rain turned to snow, and beneath the snow the rain-drenched ground became a field of ice. The morning dawned clear and cold—much colder than we had expected. Our water pipes were frozen. The roads were covered with several inches of snow, with ice beneath. But the sun was bright, and by midmorning the road in front of our house was completely clear. Traffic was moving again. Our friends loaded up their car, and we waved them off toward home.

Twenty minutes later the phone rang. There had been a wreck. Another car had slid on a shaded patch of ice and collided with our friends head on. Susan had serious internal injuries, though everyone else was only shaken up. Susan had been taken to the large hospital near the university, the others were in a small hospital closer to where the wreck had occurred.

My husband went to be with Susan. I went to bring the others home. Susan was taken into surgery. Back home, we waited, not knowing if she would live or die. For several hours we clung to hope. But then I began to think about what had happened between her and her mother—the two of them watching that particular movie and the reconciliation that had followed. It was too perfect. I could see that the end had already been arranged. Susan was going to die.

That realization caused a major shift in the ground of my being—a veritable earthquake. This did not come simply from the fact that my friend was dying. That was a tremendous shock, but even more of a shock was the realization that life could be this way—that Susan and her mother could live their last day on earth together as meaningfully as such a day could possibly have been lived, and yet neither of them had had the slightest idea that she was about to die.

As I reverberated from this stunning recognition and began to let go of my hope that Susan would live, a second powerful inner event took place. I suddenly saw vividly in my mind's eye a newspaper page, more than half of which was taken up with an obituary for Susan, including her picture. It was very clear, no mistaking what it was. I began to cry. At this same time my husband called with news that Susan had just died.

This tragedy marked the end for me of the world I had always known and that everyone around me seemed only to know—a world in which human consciousness is the highest source of knowledge and human will is the greatest purposeful power, religious statements ascribing higher knowledge and power to God notwithstanding. That world of ordinary consciousness did not allow for purposefulness in such events as Susan's last day with her mother. In the modern intellectual world, that day would be defined as a coincidence, an amazing one, perhaps, even a blessed one, but only a coincidence. Since no human consciousness had designed it, it had not been designed. It just happened to turn out well.

Similarly, in that world I was leaving behind it would be said that my vision of Susan's obituary just happened to coincide with the time of her death. By what mechanism could it be otherwise? The explanation from that world would probably be that the vision was my imagination at work, along with a repressed realization that she was too badly injured to live. This despite the fact that through several previous hours of anxious wait-ing, I had *not* imagined her death, much less her obituary, and it was only right at the time she actually died that the image intruded itself into my mind's eye.

As for myself, I knew more absolutely than I had ever known anything that these events were not merely coincidental. And so I was left stranded alone on the shore of a new world, a world in which a reality greater than any human reality orchestrates mercies to accompany tragedies, a world in which spiritual gifts flow copiously from death, not simply in a vague, ethereal way, but in a real, embodied way. On that tragic and transforming day, I realized that I was standing more directly in the presence of God than I had ever thought possible, that all of us were, and that the meaning of God's presence in our lives was more all-pervasive than even the Church had ever taught me it could be. I knew on that day that I had been changed forever by my experience of this truth and that I could never go back to the old world of more limited vision and understanding. And yet at the same time I wanted to go back, because I did not know how to go forward into the new world.

## A New Way of Thinking and Perceiving

THUS BEGAN a profoundly unsettling time for me. For a year I struggled alone to get my feet back under me, to return "to normal," which to me at that time meant the life I had been living before the wreck. But that life was never to return. I was caught in the throes of a spiritual transformation, and I was as helpless against it as Paul was helpless on the road to Damascus.

Although my traditional religious background did not help me *understand* the spiritual transformation that overtook me, it did prepare me to meet it in the right way. Because of my deeply-rooted spiritual heritage I was able to stand strong in my trust that this storm was in fact coming from God and that God would not abandon me. I knew also that wherever this experience was leading me, I would have to go there, however terrified I was of what God's intentions for me were. In that year following the wreck, every area of my life became unsettled and seemed to be called into question. What did God want of me? Was I supposed to leave my marriage? Give up my writing? Those were my greatest fears. Although neither outcome came to pass, I did have to open myself to major adjustments in both those areas and in every other aspect of my life.

The greatest change asked of me, however, was a change in *thinking and perceiving*. If the world is such that Susan's last days could be orchestrated as they were, how is a modern mind to grasp that reality and think about it? It was here that the Church itself failed me. No clue came from that quarter. It was only when I stumbled across the autobiography of Carl Jung, about a year after the wreck, that I began to gather up the tools I needed to make the fundamental change in my understanding of the world that was necessary to regain my footing.

The problem with which I was struggling was what to do with the increasingly unshakable realization that physical life in this world has more behind it than simple cause and effect. There is *meaning* woven into it. There was meaning in Susan seeing that particular movie with her mother, meaning in the inner image of the obituary. Ever since the day of the wreck, I had continued to see meaning in the world itself, and by this I do not mean merely general and abstract meaning—as in, God made the world and loves it and works in mysterious ways—but very personal and specific meaning. A door would slam as certain words were being spoken. What were those words? I would notice them and think about them and see that something of importance to my own life was being emphasized. An image would arise in my mind as I was driving down the road, or perhaps a line from a song. What was that image or that line? I would catch it and think about it and understand that something was being hinted at. Dreams would come tumbling darkly in the night, punctuating the patterns of meaning I was struggling to patch together in waking life.

What to do with all this? I knew I was not losing my mind. I was not hearing voices or having hallucinations or saying irrational things. Nor was I becoming dysfunctional in my outer life. But inside myself I was having a terrible time. I had no cognitive framework for this new way of perceiving. Neither the ordinary intellectual world in which I lived with my university-professor husband nor the traditional religious world in which I participated as an active church member was broad enough to include this expanded reality.

What I found in Carl Jung's autobiography was a man with a powerful intellect and a deep religious awareness whose frame of reference took in the kind of experiences I was beginning to have. He too lived with height- ened meaning. Here at last was someone who would have been able to understand me, had he been alive and accessible. Carl Jung had words and concepts for the new world I had entered. He himself was one of its earliest modern explorers and had led the way in describing its features in modern terms. He was both scientific and religious, intellectual and soulful, rational and nonrational, without contradiction. I immediately searched out more of his writings and read them intensely, gathering up his concepts to equip myself for my new spiritual journey.

Carl Jung was my mentor and guide for this journey. Most people have a more embodied guide—an analyst or some other person who has made the journey ahead of them. But in my ability to navigate those dark waters alone, with only a man's printed words to help me, is indication of the fact that this spiritual journey is indeed a natural one. It unfolds from the human psyche in a generally predictable way, although in its particulars and in its outcome it is altogether different in each individual life.

I did, however, have a flesh-and-blood counselor for a very brief period of time—for six weeks to be exact. After I had been reading Jung's writings for a few months, my inner experience intensified, bringing with it a gripping anxiety. One night as I was getting into bed, I thought to myself that I had better make an effort the next day to seek some outside help. Immediately the name of the priest at the Episcopal church I was then attending flashed into my mind. I did not *think* it—I had not had time to. It came of its own accord, with its own energy, and I was glad to accept it as a suggestion of a person who might be helpful. Although the anxiety attacks made me worry that I could actually lose my sanity, I was very reluctant to turn myself over to a psychiatrist, fearing that my experience would then be dealt with in purely psychological terms. I felt that at the heart of my struggle was the challenge to open myself to God and the new direction He was trying to give me, and I needed to be able to talk about it that way and have it understood in those terms. Jungian psychology would not have precluded this, but there were no Jungian analysts nearby.

It is to the credit of the modern Church in the 1980s that the priest I went to see had some psychological training and was familiar with the fundamental concepts of Freud and Jung. He understood the terminology I was using and the basic nature of my crisis. He was comfortable with giving value to dreams and was also willing to puzzle with me about how much meaning there might be in the intensified outer events that were surrounding my inner journey. He was frank in acknowledging that he had never been through a similar "confrontation with the unconscious," as Jung might have phrased it, but he recognized from the literature the nature of my experience and knew that it was good.

He knew I was going through a psychological process that is comparable to a shaman's initiation and which in the literature of analytical psychology is called a "creative illness." It is a serious event, but if the ego is not shattered by it, this life-changing process provides a rite of passage into the healing world of psyche and spirit and imparts to those who are called upon to endure it a significant gift for the healing of souls. Because of the ego strength my counselor perceived in me, he was able to assure me that I was not going to lose my sanity and that I would come out on the other side of this crisis changed and more solid. He was a great help to me as a steadying presence in this most tumultuous passage in my journey, a time I look back on as "when I was in the abyss."

It seemed at the time most unfortunate that this priest was in his last weeks in our parish. He had accepted a call to a church in another state, and after I had seen him for six weeks of regular sessions, he was gone, and I was on my own again. I had come through the worst of the swirling passage, however, and was back on firmer ground, learning now to live in this new world of perception into which my journey had led me.

## A New Room in the Church

AS I LOOK BACK, I can see that it was a good thing that I had no more outside help than I had—no other Christian clergyperson nor any Jungian analyst to lay words and explanations over my experience. I had to put together for myself a new cognitive framework, shaping it from my inner material, using Jung's writings as my primary source of intellectual understanding and the Judeo-Christian tradition as a touchstone to keep me grounded. Whatever new truth I was coming to, I knew it had to be congruent with the old truth of my world. It had to fit with town and country life in the American South, where churches and synagogues are the centers of religious life. These institutions of traditional religion carry the wisdom of the ages, conserving it and passing it on to each new generation, however imperfect that effort might be. It is to these centers that one goes to talk forthrightly about matters of the soul and to participate openly in religious activity. These religious centers in the modern world preserve an ancient discourse, and my new discourse had to mesh with that. Otherwise my spiritual life would be disconnected and irrelevant, too airy and grand, or too dark and submerged, to be lived in the outer world.

In the early years of this journey I had a difficult time fashioning a correspondence between my private spiritual experience and life in the community. My most persistent error was to try to interject my new understandings into traditional discussions and activities, both in the university community and in the Church. That this was not effective in secular life is not surprising, but neither was it useful in church life, not even in study groups, where issues of all sorts were open for discussion. I never met any hostility in the Church: people were always polite, sometimes interested, and now and then intrigued. But they were unable to take in what I was trying to say. It took a long time for me to become reconciled to the fact that this new way of seeing is not for everyone, at least not in its full measure. The fact is that for the majority of people there are other valid spiritual paths that are sufficient for their needs. And so after several years of futile effort, I grew wiser and learned to be quiet. I began to keep my inner life to myself and to accept church life for what it was, without asking for more.

It is frequently the case that when you stop trying to get the thing that you especially feel you need and reconcile yourself to living without it, it finally comes to you. One evening I was participating in a discussion group in which the question was asked of us: "What is it that you need from this church that you are not getting?" I seriously debated whether or not to answer truthfully, so much had I given up on the possibility of ever having what I really wanted. But I decided that here of all places I should be honest, and so I told the group that what I was not getting from church was an opportunity to talk about my spiritual life in the terms in which I experienced it.

Evidently my moment had come, for people were interested in this and wanted to know more about it. I tried to explain that the traditional language of the Church was not broad enough to take in my experience of the spirit of God flowing into me through my everyday life, through dreams, intuitions, and ordinary events, all of which take on a sacred quality when you really begin to pay attention to them. A number of people replied that they would like to broaden their spiritual framework in this way, but that I would have to teach them how to do it. Again, it is to the credit of the modern Church that at this point in the discussion the priest who was present said to me, "It sounds like you have a gift that is not being used."

It was with his encouragement that a few months later I put an announcement in the church newsletter offering to lead a seminar on "natural spirituality." I explained: "The focus of the seminar will be on learning to recognize the unfolding of our individual spiritual journeys in the ordinary events of our lives, including our dreams. We will explore basic Jungian concepts of consciousness and the unconscious; the phenomenon of synchronicity, or meaningful coincidence; and aspects of our masculine and feminine natures. The interconnection of natural spirituality and Christianity will be emphasized." The seminar would meet one night a week for twelve weeks. There would be required reading. Participants would have to buy their own books, but there would be no other charge. Enrollment would be limited to twelve.

I was not at all sure that there were twelve people who would be interested in taking the seminar, but I knew I wanted no more than that number, since I was uncertain how people would react to this material. I wanted a group small enough to allow me to stay personally connected to each participant in order to give a guiding hand where it was needed. I was surprised and pleased when there were more than twelve people who wanted to participate, and with the overflow I started a list for a repeat seminar the following spring.

The content of that first seminar was similar to what is contained in this book. In the first part I laid out the basic concepts of Jungian psychology as tools for recognizing and dealing with the natural spirituality that flows through all of life. In the second part I surveyed some of the issues that are raised when natural spirituality begins to be attended to in a person's life, especially the problem of reconciling the opposition between the masculine and feminine principles. And in the last part I examined the connection between natural spirituality and traditional Christianity.

The seminar was received differently, of course, by the different participants. About a third of the group had come out of curiosity and at the end of the seminar their curiosity was satisfied—natural spirituality was interesting, but it was not particularly for them. Another third connected more enthusiastically and yet did not feel ready at that time to embark on deep journeys of their own.

The remaining third were greatly stirred up. Their lives were at a point where they needed this deepening, and they came to this material like persons who were hungry. Most of these were strongly spiritual people with deep roots in the Church, faithful members for whom traditional religion still had meaning but who were no longer being completely fed by it. Essential nutrients were missing, and these they now recognized as being present in their own dreams and intuitions and in meaningful events of their lives. The problem now was how to appropriate this new food, since the symbolic language of the Spirit can be so difficult to understand. As we neared the end of the seminar, this group began to get anxious. "What will we do when the seminar is over?" they asked. "How can we go on from here? Now we know that our dreams are important, but we still don't know how to interpret them."

Thus began the Journey Group, which has become the heart of the natural spirituality program in our church. On almost every Wednesday night since that first seminar ended, the Journey Group has met to help its members puzzle out the meaning of their dreams and significant life events. The number of participants has grown steadily as the introductory seminar has been repeated, with the same pattern usually prevailing: about a third of the seminar graduates come into the Journey Group and begin the hard but rewarding task of connecting with the deeper levels of their souls. This task entails not months but *years* of commitment, and the personal change and growth that result are amazing to see.

We have found that this deeper experience of the Spirit does not diminish traditional church experience, but rather enhances it. As our journeys progress, the true meanings of traditional teachings emerge of their own accord from the depths of our individual souls. A truth arising from one's own soul in connection with one's personal life experience has a much stronger effect than the same truth read in a book or heard from the pulpit. When truth comes to us in this way, we can say with Carl Jung, "I don't need to believe. I know." [1]

Natural spirituality has become a rich room added to our church. It offers a new level of spiritual life for those who need it, and it provides for those same persons an experience of community life in the Spirit that

---

[1] References for all quotations can be found in the NOTES at the end of the volume.

is authentic and healthy in its balance of mutual support and letting be.
Each person in the group is on his or her own journey, each life unfolding
differently, each truth discovered independently. On Wednesday nights we
gather to help each other unravel new mysteries. On Sunday mornings we
join in communion with the greater Church to explore the Scriptures, sing
the beloved hymns, and participate in the time-enduring rituals. In our life
in the church community we do not clique together as a separate group.
Rather, we mix and mingle and participate actively in every aspect of parish life. Natural spirituality has turned us ever more toward service to God
and the work of the Church and has made us more effective in that service
than we were before.

Our natural spirituality program is now in its ninth year, and it continues to grow in strength and numbers. Now that we are confidant of its
value, we feel it is time to share with others our experience of this rich
room of the Spirit. This book is meant to help make it possible to build
similar rooms in other churches. At the same time, it is also meant to
illuminate the realm of natural spirituality for persons who are traveling
alone. It contains the material that I have found to be most useful in
preparing a person to look at his dreams and the meaningful events of his
life in a way that is both rationally informed and centered in God.

CHAPTER TWO

# Nature and Spirit
# in the Christian Tradition

ON THE NIGHT after I first conceived the idea of starting a natural spirituality program in my church community, I had this dream:

> I was in a church setting, which seemed mostly to be the Catholic Church [symbolizing the "Church Catholic," the universal Church]. There was a lot of activity, and there were people—women, mostly—sitting in what were school desks more than pews. There was a bishop there whom I knew and loved as a friend, although he was not particularly in touch with his wholeness. He was going among the women to lead them individually in prayer, which he would do in a rather severe manner. I saw it most clearly when he came to a childhood friend of mine, now a mature, independent, working woman. She wanted to pray for a friend, and so the bishop came to her and held her arms tightly against the desk in what was supposed to be a prayer position, forcing her to pray with him in this particular, rigid way. She would not have it. Pulling free of him, she got up and went off a little way and took another seat away from him.
>
> I went to the bishop, who was sitting now in an actual pew, and sat down in the pew behind him. Leaning forward, I put my hands lovingly on his shoulders and said quietly into his ear that if that had been me, I would have gotten up, too. He was hurt and sad and puzzled. The old way of the Church was not working anymore with modern women.
>
> Then I was somewhere else in this church setting and saw a group of clergy passing through the room. They were austere old men, lacking in wisdom and determined to hold their power. There was a colorless whiteness about them. The congregation was thinning out as people were giving up on the Church and turning away. There were almost none but old people left in the congregation, mostly old women.

*Somewhere in this last part of the dream was the understanding that my role is to help bring* color *into the Church.*

Whiteness and color. Masculine and feminine. This was the symbolism chosen by the dream. Whiteness for the spirit of the old men in the traditional Church. Color for my natural spirituality work. In earth's prism, the white light of heaven breaks into the rainbow colors of life. It is the same light—unified above, broken open below.

So too does the divine Spirit have more than one manifestation. The spirit of heaven is its masculine aspect, as powerful and dependable as the sun, as ordered and unchanging as the stars. We experience the heavenly spirit in the strength and courage that comes to us when we make the effort to rise above our daily problems, to take a higher perspective and act on nobler principles. It draws our attention upward and makes us aware of something higher than ourselves.

The spirit of earth, on the other hand, seems to flow into us from below as a part of the life of our bodies. This is the feminine aspect of God. As fertile and many-faceted as nature, it teems with life and moves and changes with time, its myriad forms ever evolving. We experience this natural spirit in dreams and waking visions, in emotions and instinctual energies, and in the actual events of life itself.

At the center of Christian doctrine is the idea that in the living Christ these two aspects, heaven and earth, masculine and feminine, are joined into one unified expression of Godhood. Partaking of his Father's heavenly nature and of his mother's earthly nature, the living Christ brings the two realms together into a single reality. Thus it should not boggle the minds of modern Christians to acknowledge the spirit of God alive and at work in the natural world. Saint Paul wrote in his letter to the Colossians: "There is only Christ. He is everything and he is in everything." But whether Christians or not, it does boggle the minds of almost all modern people whose roots are in the Western world to think that the material world of nature could have an underlying spiritual aspect.

The same is not true, however, for people in the religious traditions of the Eastern world. For them God has always resided at the heart of matter. They speak of the physical world as "the ten thousand things," the myriad manifestations of the many aspects of God. This is expressed beautifully and clearly in the Chinese notion of Tao, the underlying primal essence of life. Tao is what is there before anything is there, and from Tao everything flows. As the source of all, Tao precedes form and therefore is unknowable and undefinable. But Tao is also the life that flows out of the unknowable source. The flow of life comes from Tao and therefore is Tao, and from that flow we can become aware of Tao and learn something about its nature.

Although Tao is not noticed by those who are unaware of it, it is nevertheless continually unfolding itself before us, and not only before us but also in us, for we too are a part of the life flowing out of the primal source. This is true of our physical life—as we are born, mature, procreate, get sick, get well, age, die—we are experiencing manifestations of Tao. It is also true of our psychic life—our dreams, our fantasies and thoughts, our impulses and desires, our emotions and insights, our spontaneous body movements and artistic expressions, even our neuroses and psychoses—all flow out of Tao. Through Tao the life within us is meaningfully connected to the life around us. All things flow from a single, unknowable source, linked together by the mystery of Tao.

Central to Taoism is the understanding that if we pay attention, we can become aware of the flow of Tao and learn from it how to live. It will teach us how to move in harmony with it, how to be "in Tao," rather than struggle against it in ignorance of it, which is to be "out of Tao." When we are in Tao, we are supported by life, and we experience a harmonious oneness with the world. When we are out of Tao, our lives get out of kilter and things begin to go badly for us. The Chinese character for the word Tao is made of a combination of the characters for head and foot. The idea conveyed is of one who thinks as he steps, who is conscious of his path. Tao is often translated as "the Way." To be in Tao is to follow the Way of true life. The image is of a journey, of a path ever unfolding, of life that is ever changing and requires our constant awareness to change with it and remain at one with it.

It is not difficult to see the parallel between Tao and the kingdom of God in the Christian Scriptures. Like Tao, the kingdom of God is present in life as an unnoticed reality beneath the surface of things. Jesus said to a group of Pharisees, "The coming of the kingdom of God does not admit of observation and there will be no one to say, 'Look here! Look there!' For, you must know, the kingdom of God is among you." He expected men who were truly wise to understand that the coming of the kingdom of God is not an outer event, but an inner awakening to a reality that has been in the world all along.

In the teaching about the Lilies of the Field, Jesus pointed out that God is a supporting presence in all of life and that nature is at one with the kingdom of God, while people, with their self will, lose sight of the Kingdom and waste their energy trying to make their lives secure through purely human effort. This is fruitless, he said. Life cannot be secured in this way. Rather, a person should use his will first and foremost to seek the kingdom of God and its "righteousness"—the divine balance and rightness that belong to each moment. This will bring the person into oneness with the Kingdom (into Tao) and all the needs of everyday life will be met as they arise.

The notion of "the Way" is as explicit in Christian Scripture as it is in Taoist thought. "Follow me," Christ said again and again. "I am the Way." To those who would follow him, he added, "Foxes have holes and the birds of the air have nests, but the Son of Man has nowhere to lay his head." And, "Once the hand is laid on the plow, no one who looks back is fit for the kingdom of God." To be in the Kingdom is to be on a never-ending journey of constant change.

Jesus explained that the path along which this journey lies is a narrow one which few people recognize and take. Most stay on the broader, more obvious road of collectively perceived reality. The kingdom of God can only be perceived by individuals who separate themselves from the herd and pay attention to their inner lives and the private lessons that come from that realm.

Had there been Taoists in the crowds to whom Jesus spoke, they would have been nodding their heads, recognizing him as a spokesman for the Tao that flows through life. This is acknowledged in modern Chinese Bibles. The opening of John's Gospel—"In the beginning was the Word"—is translated into Chinese as, "In the beginning was the Tao."

Christ is to God the Father what Tao-the-manifesting-flow-of-life is to

Tao-the-unknowable-primal-source. Jesus said that no one "has seen the Father [the primal source] except the one who comes from God [the divine flow of life]." But, "If you know me [the divine flow], you know my Father [the primal source] too." He was careful to point out that "the Father [the primal source] is greater than I [the divine flow]." Yet, "The Father and I are one." And not only that, but oneness with the Father [the primal source] extends to all through oneness with the Son [the divine flow of life]. Thus Jesus said to the apostles, "I am in my Father and you in me and I in you."

He also told them that when the time came that he would no longer be on earth as Jesus of Nazareth, the Spirit of teaching and healing that he embodied would still be present in the world. It would be present in the psychic realm as the Spirit of truth, or the Counselor, and present also in the physical world, as symbolized by the bread and wine of the Eucharist, the common elements of everyday life.

The Apostle Paul understood the essential truth that the reality of the eternal Christ is greater than the historical figure of Jesus. Paul's own meetings with Christ were exclusively inner experiences, and from that he understood that the living Christ is present in the psychic depths of every person and in all created life. "The Spirit reaches the depths of everything," he said. Christ "fills the whole creation."

## Wisdom in Scripture and Tradition

THE BASIC NOTION of Tao is contained not only in the New Testament Christian Scriptures but also in the Old Testament Hebrew Scriptures, although here the emphasis is more on the unknowable primal source than on the manifest spirit flowing from it. The great truth of Judaism is that behind all lesser manifestations of the divine there is but one God, the author of all. Although God participates in the life of the earth, He is greater than all things and above all things. As with Tao-the-primal-source, it is impossible to name Him or portray Him in an image. God is the source of principles and laws that are higher than those possessed by human beings in their natural state. This law-giving factor gives Him a

fundamentally masculine essence, although He also has a feminine aspect—Wisdom—who has been with Him from the beginning, who in-
fuses created life with her presence, and through whose teachings God can
be known. Wisdom, in other words, is the manifest flow of Tao in life,
recognized here in its feminine aspect. Wisdom's presence in the Hebrew
Scriptures grows ever stronger as the Old Testament era draws to a close.
In the book of Proverbs she speaks of her origin: of how she belongs to
the very beginning of things; of how she is God's feminine side, His con-
sort, participating with Him in creation, infusing life with her vital spirit.

> Yahweh created me when his purpose first unfolded,
>     before the oldest of his works.
> From everlasting I was firmly set,
>     from the beginning, before the earth came into being.
> The deep was not, when I was born,
>     there were no springs to gush with water.
> Before the mountains were settled,
>     before the hills, I came to birth. . . .
> When he fixed the heavens firm, I was there, . . .
>     when he laid down the foundations of the earth,
> I was by his side, a master craftsman,
>     delighting him day after day,
>     ever at play in his presence,
> at play everywhere in his world,
>     delighting to be with the sons of men.
>
> PROVERBS 8 : 22 – 31

The book of Wisdom sings her praises as the teaching Spirit of life:

> All that is hidden, all that is plain, I have come to know,
> instructed by Wisdom who designed them all.
>
> For within her is a spirit intelligent, holy,
> unique, manifold, subtle,
> active, incisive, unsullied,
> lucid, invulnerable, benevolent, sharp,
> irresistible, beneficent, loving to man,
> steadfast, dependable, unperturbed,

almighty, all-surveying,
penetrating all intelligent, pure
and most subtle spirits;
for Wisdom is quicker to move than any motion;
she is so pure, she pervades and permeates all things.

She is a breath of the power of God,
pure emanation of the glory of the Almighty;
hence nothing impure can find a way into her.
She is a reflection of the eternal light,
untarnished mirror of God's active power,
image of his goodness.

Although alone, she can do all;
herself unchanging, she makes all things new.
In each generation she passes into holy souls,
she makes them friends of God and prophets;
for God loves only the man who lives with Wisdom.

WISDOM 7 : 21—28

The book of Wisdom, while known and quoted by Jewish writers of the New Testament, was not ultimately included in the Hebrew canon of Scripture, as it was in the Christian canon. This underscores the fact that the focus of the Judaic tradition is not on Wisdom, although she is acknowledged, but on recognition of the primal source itself and devoted relationship to it. This fundamental monotheistic teaching is as important today as it has ever been: "Hear, O Israel: The Lord our God is one Lord; and you shall love the Lord your God with all your heart, and with all your soul, and with all your might." When this basic truth about God is not heeded, when human attention is diverted by "the ten thousand things" and the one God behind all is not recognized, loved, and held firmly in heart, mind, and soul as the highest reality, life fails ultimately to thrive. Had this truth been outgrown through the ages, the Old Testament would also have been outgrown, but it has not—its words are still treasured today by Jews and Christians alike. The truth it contains is continually being discovered, lost, and rediscovered by individuals, families, and nations.

In both Judaism and Christianity it is the fundamental nature of this monotheistic teaching that has overshadowed the accompanying biblical teachings about the presence in the depths of created life of the manifest, teaching spirit of God, whether this be referred to in symbolic language as wisdom, Christ, the Counselor, the Way, the Spirit of truth, or the Holy Spirit. There is good reason for stressing awareness of the primal source over awareness of its manifest spirit in created life—good reason, we might say, for making a firm, committed connection to the white light at the initial expense of the colors of the rainbow. The fact is that by nature the "colors," or instinctual energies of life, always come into our awareness first, bedazzling us in our youth, sweeping us up in their irresistible power. These instinctual forces draw us into life and get us started, but they also scatter our lives hither and yon without regard to the final outcome, each "color" bent only on manifesting its own reality, on winning out against all the other "colors" without regard for any higher principle than its own survival and continuation.

Pure nature is intrinsically amoral. When, for example, the active, passionate, blooded life of "red" takes possession of us, it shuts out the dreamy, introspective, serene life of "blue" as naturally as a large tree shades out a small one struggling for life beneath its branches. If "blue" gets the upper hand, it closes out "red." And so on for all the "colors." Nature's many facets compete for the energy of life, and those which initially capture the devotion and commitment of our own energy prove ultimately to be too limiting. They lead us into conflicts and difficulties both within ourselves and in the world around us. Unless we move to a higher awareness, where the conflicting demands of nature are reconciled and unified by a greater reality, the colorful dance of life turns dark and goes nowhere.

It is a real advance, then, to become aware of the primal source of life, the one God above all from whom all powers flow, and to discover His qualities of justice, mercy, truth, and steadfast love. It is a victory for human life to learn how to relate to the one God, how to abide by His moral principles and experience the support, guidance, and loving-kindness that come from Him. "The Lord is my shepherd; I shall not want," wrote the psalmist. "Yea, though I walk through the valley of the shadow of death, I will fear no evil." Life lived in devotion to the one God is a better life than a purely natural one. From the point of view of a purely natural life, however, its principles are counterintuitive. Justice, mercy, truth, and love require one to act in ways that seem to go against one's natural self interest.

Knowledge about the one God, therefore, has to be *culturally* maintained, passed from person to person and generation to generation. It cannot be left up to nature. In this we can already see where the tendency arises for those who are conserving this knowledge to take a dim view of nature and to see it more as God's enemy than as God's manifestation.

The fact that the monotheistic truth must be maintained and passed on through cultural forms means that it must necessarily be put into collective terms to which everyone can relate. It must be consolidated into generally applicable rules and principles. These collective truths are immensely valuable when we are caught in the swirl of purely natural life and need to rise above it. But collective truths are adopted at the expense of individual knowledge. To know a truth because you have been told about it by a person of religious authority is not the same as discovering that truth for yourself. The natural wisdom of life—the teacher at the heart of life—also has something to say. It is not pure nature that holds this wisdom, but nature conjoined with the spirit of heaven. There can be no better teacher. Its lessons are individual and highly personal, leading each person in his own way to the fullest knowledge of himself and God of which he is capable.

## The Teacher at the Heart of Life

WE HAVE ALREADY SEEN that this understanding about the teaching Spirit of life is not absent from Judaism. It is beautifully stated many times in the Old Testament. But it took the gospel events to consolidate it, clarify it, and make it accessible to the greater world. Jesus tried to awaken his followers to an understanding of the natural wisdom of life. He modeled the kind of teaching and healing that flow from an individual connection to it, while at the same time he modeled the need to stay connected to the Temple, to the collective truth of the one God who never ceases to overarch the individual journey.

Jesus tried to head off a tendency to freeze his truth and make it static.

It was not his intention that his words be elevated to a new set of collective laws and principles that would again be taught from the outside instead of discovered individually in the context of life. He tried to explain that when he was gone, the teaching and healing that he embodied would still go on. The Counselor, or Spirit of truth, would be present in the heart of life and would teach his followers *more* than he had taught them, since he himself could only teach what they at that time were ready to learn.

The fact is that the region into which Christianity spread in its early centuries—the Greek and Roman world and pagan Europe—contained very few people outside of Judaism who were ready to take in Jesus' message about the teaching and healing Spirit at the heart of life. Non-Hebrew people were still worshiping at the many altars of polytheism and did not yet have the prerequisite understanding of and relationship to the supreme God. As Christianity spread into the Western world, taking with it both the Old and New Testaments of the Bible, it was the Hebrew teaching of the one God above all that was at the heart of its message, along with a Christianized emphasis on the ideal of brotherly love and a distinctly Christian value on the worth of the individual, who is mysteriously redeemed by the love of God through Christ. The Christian teaching of God's continually manifest presence in life on earth was carried intuitively and vaguely grasped, but its full implication was seldom understood or taught.

Despite Jesus' warning to the contrary, his truth was made static. God *once* manifested Himself on earth, back in Judea in 0–33 AD, in the person of Jesus, who afterward returned to heaven and now resides above with God the Father. Jesus still visits earth in the Eucharist, and he will also come in spirit to live in our hearts if we open ourselves to him by acknowledging the reality of his 33-year physical existence. His teaching about the Holy Spirit is understood to refer to the pervasive, unseen presence of God on earth, but the Holy Spirit's qualities are more heavenly than earthly, more aerial than chthonic. The Holy Spirit is seen not so much as a teacher in the midst of life but as a messenger from heaven, as symbolized by a white dove, and as inspiration from above, as symbolized by a burning flame that comes down from on high.

Somewhere between Saint Paul and the modern age, Christianity lost sight of the fact that the living Christ "fills the whole Creation." The domain of Christ, like that of the Holy Spirit, was narrowed. Christ was in heaven with God, he was in the bread and wine of the Eucharist, and he was in the hearts of men. But he was not *in* nature. Nature was hard, physical, material reality, separate and apart from spirit. As scientific rationalism took hold and grew in the Western world, it became increasingly unacceptable to recognize a spiritual dimension in the physical world or to say that there was any mystery there. In Christianity such an attitude came to be regarded almost as superstition or even pantheism.

At the dawn of the twentieth century, however, the solid, mechanistic world of scientific rationalism began to give way, undermined not by theology or philosophy but by science itself. With Einstein's theory of relativity and with the discovery of quantum mechanics, physical reality has turned out not to be so solid after all. It has been discovered, for example, that the smallest particles of matter actually consist only of waves of probability, *until they are observed*, at which point they become discrete and actual. No physicist claims to understand this. The concrete, fully explainable material world of scientific rationalism continues to exist at the everyday, practical level of life, but deeper reality is now known to be less straightforward.

While the world of physics has been discovering that the comprehensible physical world arises from an incomprehensible physical matrix, the world of psychology has been coming to a similar conclusion about the psychic world. At about the same time Einstein was introducing the theory of relativity, Sigmund Freud was ushering into general awareness the idea that beneath the known realm of human consciousness there exists in each of us an unknown realm of the *unconscious*, a dark, psychological arena where truths and realities that belong to us live outside our awareness and interact with our conscious lives in ways we do not realize. The "Freudian slip" is one way the unconscious shows itself, as when a man unintentionally refers to his wife as his mother, revealing an unconscious psychological truth. In searching for a more readily accessible door to that dark realm, Freud turned to dreams and raised them up from the dustbin of our awareness by pointing out their value as "the royal road to the unconscious."

Sigmund Freud was not a religious man. Born in 1856, he was steeped
in the scientific materialism of that century and did not believe there was
any mystery beyond the physical foundation of our being. He was dedicated to the idea that "God" is an illusion, an infantile wish for an eternal
parent. For him there was no such thing as spirit. The driving force of life
was sexual energy, or libido.

Freud believed the unconscious to be a repository of unfulfilled wishes
stemming from our experiences in the first three years of our lives, a time
of preconsciousness which is to the individual what prehistory is to humankind. The most troubling of these preconscious experiences, according to Freud, were sexual in nature—more specifically, they were infantile incestuous desires. Because of their unacceptability they remained
repressed in the unconscious, where they lived darkly, intruding back into
conscious life under cover of disguise. Anything that threatened to bring
them to light was also repressed.

Eventually, repressed wishes could create a neurosis, which could be
treated by analyzing the unconscious. Through psychoanalysis, the door
to the unconscious could be opened and its contents examined and integrated into consciousness. One of Freud's primary tools for this was the
analysis of dreams, which he viewed primarily as disguised statements of
sexually-based fears and desires.

It took courage to put forth these ideas in the first decade of the twentieth century. A young Swiss psychiatrist, Carl Gustav Jung, was one of
the first to embrace Freud's work, recognizing its value and welcoming the
boldness of its assertions. Since early childhood, Jung had struggled with
powerful personal experiences of the unconscious. He knew instinctively
that such experiences had meaning, but though he searched the literature
of philosophy and science, he could not find the concepts he needed to
construct an adequate intellectual framework for understanding them. In
Freud's concept of the unconscious, Jung found the key that he needed
for his own formulations. In 1906 he joined forces with Freud, accepting
the older man as his mentor and helping him spread the psychoanalytical
school of psychiatry from Vienna to the international community.

But there was an essential difference between these two psychiatrists.
Unlike Freud, Jung had a deep awareness of the spiritual dimension of

life. He came by this naturally—his father and nine of his uncles were clergymen. Religion was a core element of life for him, and Freud's insistence that the underlying energy of life was always sexual, whether disguised or apparent, ran counter to Jung's own experience and understanding. As Jung came into his professional maturity, this difference grew larger as an issue between them, until finally, in 1913, the two parted company over it. From that point on, Jung developed his own school of thought concerning the nature of the unconscious.

For Jung the energy of life flows to us in a broad spectrum that ranges from fundamental physical instinct to sublime spiritual awareness. It comes to us from the unconscious, which is not merely a dumping ground for repressed personal reality but is in fact the very source of consciousness and life: everything that is conscious in us was first unconscious. Like Tao, the unconscious is by nature unknowable. Yet contents from that unknowable realm arrive regularly in consciousness, and by observing this process we can gain some insight into the unconscious. Even more importantly, by paying close attention to the effects of the unconscious on our conscious lives, we can learn about ourselves and God. For as Jung discovered, first in his own life and then in the lives of his patients, when we relate to the unconscious in the right way, it becomes our teacher. It speaks to us in our dreams and waking visions, and it also speaks in the events of life itself, a phenomenon Jung named *synchronicity.*

From Jung we learn that what matters most is *how* we relate to the unconscious. Although the unconscious is a part of nature, right relationship to it does not come naturally. In the first place, its language is symbolic, and real effort is required to learn to understand it. But it is not enough simply to understand it. The unconscious requires a *moral* response to its teachings. If we are to have a fruitful relationship with it, we must take its truths seriously and integrate them into our lives in a real way.

This is no easier to do today than it was to lay down one's net two thousand years ago and follow the teacher from Galilee. But when we do make this moral response to the teachings of the unconscious, we find ourselves following the Way, coming into harmony with life and finding our unique place in it. All of life, waking and sleeping, becomes rich with the teaching and healing spirit of God. Then we can say with Saint Paul,

"The Spirit reaches the depths of everything." The living Christ "fills the whole creation."

The present age has given us the gift of Jungian psychology. By making use of its spiritual tools, we can heal the split between spirit and nature in our basic experience of God. If we were to try to do this by adopting ancient Chinese Taoism, or even first-century Christianity, we would not be true to ourselves and our time. We are modern people with modern minds, and if we are to relate to God fully, we must use all that we have in the effort. We must be Christians of our own day.

# PART TWO

# JUNGIAN
# SPIRITUAL TOOLS

CHAPTER THREE

# *Consciousness*

*Our consciousness does not create itself——it wells up from unknown depths. In childhood it awakens gradually, and all through life it wakes each morning out of the depths of sleep from an unconscious condition.*

CARL JUNG

THE FUNDAMENTAL CONCERN of Jungian psychology is the dialogue between consciousness and the unconscious. Before we can think about the nature of the unconscious and the dialogue it seeks with us, we must have a clear understanding of consciousness itself. Though all of us experience consciousness, few of us have ever stepped back and given it a hard look. Carl Jung spent years thinking about what consciousness is, and his work helps us to understand it more objectively.

According to Jung, consciousness is our awareness of ourselves and the world around us, our understanding of things, our conception of what life is. It is not synonymous with what truly is, but is merely our perception, our grasp, our construct of existence. It is, however, all that we know, all that we have. It is our terra firma, our grip on reality, developed little by little through the years of our life. It is the kingdom of our ego, and the finer and more varied the land of this kingdom and the stronger and healthier the ego that reigns over it, the better equipped we are to deal with the unknown, infinite, eternal sea of the unconscious which surrounds us.

Consciousness begins when we first connect one thing with another, when we first "know." Those first moments of consciousness, however, like so many afterward, fall back into the unconscious and do not remain a part of our long-term ego consciousness. Ego consciousness begins with our first *memories*, dim, wispy, and isolated. Those memories are important

just because they are remembered, because their energy was strong enough
to keep them with us and make them the first stones in the edifice of our
conscious life. When we examine our earliest memories for their symbolic
content, we find hints of what are to become the major themes around
which our individual lives will turn.

My own first memory, for example, is from a few weeks before my
third birthday. I had awakened from a dream about a giant mouse that
was dressed somewhat like Peter Rabbit in a blue jacket and red pants.
The dream mouse was not altogether unfriendly, but its large size was
disturbing, and I woke up to get away from it. When I opened my eyes, I
saw it standing in the darkness beside my bed. This was much more disturbing than the dream itself, and yet I kept my wits about me. I remember
thinking to myself that sometimes when you think you have awakened,
you actually have not, but if you do something intentional, then you really
will wake up. So I very deliberately turned my head and looked into the
darkness on the other side of my bed. There too was the giant mouse! I
was certain now that I was awake, and yet the mouse was still there! That
was too much for me, and I screamed with so much fright that both my
parents remembered it ever after. With my cry the dream mouse vanished,
and the veil between the inner world and the outer world fell back into
place.

Thirty-five years later that veil lifted again in the personal crisis that
awakened me to the reality of the unconscious. This time there were no
dream images crossing over into the outer world, but rather the outer
world itself began in a certain way to take on a quality similar to the inner
world. It could be read symbolically in the same way a dream could be,
and it produced meaning through noteworthy coincidences.

My reaction was similar to when I was three years old: I first tried to
shake off this disturbing perception, and then, when it would not go away,
I was overtaken by fear—anxiety attacks. This time, however, I did not
cry out for help. I stood and faced the new reality until I gradually became
accustomed to it. My ego consciousness—my sense of myself and my
grip on outer reality—had become strong enough to allow me to forge a
conscious bond with the inner world of the unconscious without being

overwhelmed by it. From that time forward the inner world and the outer world have co-existed for me without such a firm division between them, a development that has had central importance in my life and was prefigured by that earliest memory.

By the time we are four or five years old, our first isolated memories have usually given way to a steady stream of conscious contents. For me this transition to continuous memory was marked by a move my family made from the western suburbs of Chicago to a small town in southern Georgia around the time of my fifth birthday. I remember the long car trip—taking Dramamine pills crushed up in spoonfuls of honey—and the motel where we stayed while waiting for our furniture to arrive. I remember the house we moved into, the sidewalks and neighborhood and the nearby fields. I have a continuous, solid sense of my life from then on, whereas before that car trip I remember only isolated incidents that float freely in time and space.

Even after continuous memory begins, we retain in consciousness merely a fragment of our total experience. Consciousness is limited. It can only hold so much. In order to concentrate on one thing, we must let other things go, and even that upon which we concentrate eventually falls into the unconscious as future life supersedes it. Many contents that were once conscious return to consciousness through memory, but many others never do.

A good way to think about the limitation of consciousness is to stop, look up, and think about what your consciousness contains at that particular moment. You cannot do that and continue at the same time to read what I have to say about it, which in itself shows the limitation of consciousness and the kind of problem it continually presents to us.

When you do take a moment to look up, the demonstration will be more dramatic if you do not move your head. The only part of the physical world of which you will be conscious will be what you are able to see, hear, smell, taste, and feel. If there is a spider crawling up the back of your chair, you will be unconscious of it. If it crawls onto your neck, it will enter your consciousness. You will also have as a part of your consciousness whatever thoughts you are thinking, feelings you are feeling, and any fantasies or intuitive glimmers that might be arising in your inner world. You might want to bring back into consciousness something that happened yesterday, but to do that you will have to let your awareness of the present go dim—you may even need to close your eyes. And if you really want to know what is happening on the back of your chair, you will have to turn your conscious attention away from what is going on in front of you to get up and look around behind.

## The Four Functions of Consciousness

NOT ONLY ARE WE UNCONSCIOUS of most of what goes on beyond the range of our senses, but even much that goes on before our very eyes remains unconscious, or if it does enter consciousness, it falls right back out again. How many times have you laid something down and a moment later had no idea where you put it? You were so dimly conscious of what your hands were doing that your own act fell immediately into the unconscious.

Furthermore, there are whole *categories* of reality that might become conscious if we noticed them but that we do not notice, or only barely so, because of our particular makeup as individuals. When I reminisce with my two sisters about our childhood, it is a marvel to discover what they have carried with them all these years that I never picked up at all. One of them remembers physical details—how things looked, where things were, what different people's outward characteristics were. The other one remembers the feeling tone of our world, where there was warmth and relationship and where there was a chill. I myself remember what was going on beneath the surface of things, psychological subplots of which the others often had little or no awareness.

This difference in conscious orientation was described systematically by Carl Jung in terms that have been so widely accepted that they are almost commonplace today. He determined that there are four functions of human consciousness—*sensation, thinking, feeling,* and *intuition.* These are the gateways by which unconscious contents enter consciousness. Each of us has one of these as our primary function, with the other three following in descending order. Beyond the four functions there are two basic attitudes by which our consciousness is oriented—*extraversion* and *introversion*—and each of us is by nature aligned more with one than with the other. The relative strength in us of these six different factors determines our psychological type.

Jung devoted much of his early career to discovering and describing the four functions and two attitudes of consciousness, seeing in them a key to understanding the basic differences between human beings. The inner journey is both a journey of self-discovery and a journey toward reconciliation with those with whom we share our lives. To understand that there are basic, describable variables in the ways human beings experience conscious reality helps us come to know ourselves as individuals who are fundamentally different from those around us, while at the same time it helps us to be more tolerant of differences in others.

Many people are familiar with Jung's typology through having been tested with the Myers-Briggs Type Indicator or one of its several variants. These are diagnostic questionnaires which can reveal a person's psychological type through the answers to such questions as, "When you look at a landscape, do you tend to (a) notice details or (b) take in an overall impression?" As will become clearer from the discussion below, the choice of "a" suggests that a person has a strong sensation function, while "b" suggests strong intuition.

It is possible, however, to determine your own type without a formal testing tool by simply thinking about yourself in light of the four functions and two attitudes. Although this can be surprisingly difficult to do, it is worth the attempt in order to begin to grapple with the question of how you as an individual experience conscious life.

It was Jung who coined the terms *extravert* and *introvert*. Today almost everyone has some notion of these opposing personality types. We usually think of extraverts as convivial and outgoing and introverts as shy and withdrawn. While this is more or less true in the broadest sense, there can also be shy extraverts and convivial introverts. According to Jung, a more accurate way to think about the dichotomy is in terms of which way a person's energy flows—outward toward the objective world or inward toward the subjective world. An even simpler measure is to ask whether one tends to be energized by mingling with other people, as extraverts are, or drained of energy by it, as introverts are.

Generally speaking, extraverts, with their attention on the world outside, are the ones who do most to maintain the structure of outer life, while introverts, with their attention on what is going on inside themselves, are the ones who are most dedicated to the realms of creativity and spirituality. At the farthest extremes the extravert concentrates so much on the world outside himself that he loses his inner reality, while the introvert becomes estranged from outer reality through too much fascination with the inner world.

The principle of opposing tendencies is similarly present in the four functions, which, according to Jung, are actually two pairs of opposites. One pair, *sensation* and *intuition*, has to do with perception, and if a person is very strong at one end of this pole, he will be very weak at the other. Sensation is perception through our physical senses. It tells us that something in the outer world *is*. People who are strong in sensation have an affinity for concreteness and facts. They possess a powerful sense of the here and now and are finely tuned to the physical manifestation of life.

Intuitive perception, on the other hand, comes not through the physical senses but through the inner eye and ear. People with strong intuition sniff out things beneath the surface, sensing connections and patterns that are not manifestly apparent. They know in ways that seem impossible, or at least spooky, to a person with a strong sensation function. Intuition glimpses possibilities. Whereas sensate people tend to get stuck in present reality and have a hard time realizing that things could ever be different, intuitive people have difficulty living in the here and now. They are always running ahead with their intuition toward a more promising future, impatient with the slow development that reality requires.

The other pair of opposites, *thinking* and *feeling*, are described by Jung as judging functions. These provide a basis for decision-making, whereas the perceiving functions simply register what is there without regard to good or bad, logic or illogic. Thinking makes its judgements on the basis of logic, while feeling judges value. All of us tend to judge more with our heads or our hearts, and if we are strong at one end of this pole, we will be weak at the other. Intellectuals can be bloodless and cold in a way that is incomprehensible to a feeling person, whereas a feeling person can be so illogical and unreasonable that a thinking person can hardly bear it.

Thinking is the function that tells us *what* something is. It ponders, analyzes, solves problems rationally, and creates abstractions. It takes place in our heads and brings with it a degree of separation from the life of the body. The feeling function, on the other hand, has to do with evaluation, which should not be confused with emotion, or affect. People with feeling as their first function have a highly differentiated scale of value by which they continually assess the acceptability of things—to what degree something is good or bad, moral or immoral, beautiful or ugly, right for the moment or wrong for the moment, and so on.

Because we tend to think of feelings as emotions, it can be difficult to understand exactly what the feeling function is as Jung described it. When I was preparing to teach about the four functions for my first natural spirituality seminar, I was given a dream which helped me understand this function more clearly:

> *I dreamed that my husband and I were traveling in our car. We arrived at a town which we knew was a four hour drive from home. It was early evening.*
>
> *"Perhaps we should get a motel for the night and drive home tomorrow," I said.*
>
> *This angered my husband, who felt I was insisting that we do so. But I was not insisting. I explained to him that I make decisions by "trying on" each possibility and then noting what it feels like. It is with my feelings that I am able to choose the right course. I can only do that, however, if I seriously try on each alternative. Then I go with the one that feels best.*
>
> *I had some difficulty explaining this to him, since he is a thinking type and feeling is his weakest function. But eventually I succeeded.*

Not only does this dream illuminate the feeling function in its introverted form (I being an introvert), but it also shows the value of Jung's typology for helping us understand the difficulties we all have in relating to each other. Ever since I dreamed it, I have been more mindful of the way in which I make such alternative-testing statements to my husband. If I remind him at the outset that I am not yet committed to whatever suggestion I am trying out, things go more smoothly between us.

## Ranking the Four Functions

THE FOUR FUNCTIONS, then, are a combination of two pairs of opposites. Sensation and intuition are the poles of the perceiving axis; thinking and feeling are the poles of the judging axis. All four functions are available to each of us, although they do not operate in us with equal degrees of consciousness. They are ranked in a hierarchy of awareness that is based not on choice but on natural endowment. Individual ranking can be diagramed in the form of an equal-armed cross, with one axis representing the perceiving functions and the other one the judging functions.

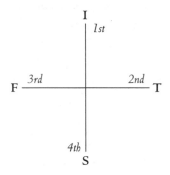

*I = Intuition; T = Thinking; F = Feeling; S = Sensation*

Figure 1. The Four Functions

The first function, which can be any of the four, is placed at the top of the cross, highest in consciousness; the second strongest function is placed on the right, which is also a position symbolically associated with consciousness; the third is on the left, which is symbolically associated with the unconscious; and the fourth is at the bottom, symbolizing its place in the depths of the unconscious. Because the functions are pairs of opposites, the strongest function (the one at the top of the diagram) determines which one will be the weakest (the one at the bottom). And in the same way, the second function determines which function will be in the third position. If intuition, for example, is a person's first function, sensation, at the other end of the perceiving axis, will be his fourth and weakest function; and if thinking is second, feeling will be third.

When we try to think about ourselves to determine how our functions are ranked, we often run into difficulty. Complications in our particular situation can obscure things. It is sometimes easier to determine our first function by considering which function is weakest, since another function might seem so near in strength to our first that it is difficult to decide between them. This is especially true for introverts, who tend to meet the world with their second function rather than their first, which is reserved more for their inner life.

To use myself as an example, it was only by looking for my weakest function that I was able to identify intuition as my first function. Thinking is my second strongest function. But as sometimes happens with lesser functions, second-ranked thinking received more development in my early years than did first-ranked intuition. Thinking, therefore, masqueraded as my first function.

Ordinarily it is our first function that undergoes the most development in childhood, since it is the mode of functioning at which we are best, and thus it is usually the one with the most payoff for us. But there can be a family bias, or even a cultural one, against a person's primary function, so that he is pushed to develop one of his lesser functions in its place. No matter how well he does with this substitute function, however, so long as he has not developed his actual first function, he will always operate at a disadvantage and be a little off his true mark, never rising to the fullness of his own strength.

In my own case, as with most intuitives, especially introverted ones, I had the problem of our society's strong cultural bias against intuition. This bias was even stronger in the 1950s, when I was a child, than it is today. There was no model in the greater culture for introverted intuitive functioning and very little comprehension of it. Nor was there much correction for this in my family. However, thinking was a strong function in my family, and since thinking was my second function, I followed the family pattern and developed that as my primary mode of consciousness. Intuition, my natural strength, remained undeveloped and semiconscious, although it still had a great deal of power and manifested itself in an active fantasy life. I have more memories of being alone on the playground lost in my fantasies than I have of playing with other children. In the sensate world I was miserable. I was slow to learn to ride a bicycle, clumsy at jumping rope, and got nauseated on swings and merry-go-rounds.

In compensation I became good at thinking. I did well in school and had interesting conversations with other thinkers, graduated with honors from college, and married a college professor. Despite all this, however, I never found an official place for myself in the thinking world. I lacked the drive to dedicate myself to a thinking path such as teaching or graduate school. Instead I hooked up my college degree in anthropology with my orphaned intuition and wrote novels for young people that were set in the traditional culture of the Indians of the American South. Although I was successful at writing fiction, I never considered it to be an intuitive enterprise. I was only conscious of myself as a thinking person, and thinking dominated my work. My intuition was there in my ability to imagine a story, but it was still operating in semi-darkness.

This lack of recognition of my natural strength in life contributed in large part to the midlife crisis I have already described. At the heart of that crisis was intuitive functioning forcing its way into my conscious awareness and demanding to be recognized and integrated. Thinking had usurped the throne long enough. In an inner struggle that lasted several years, intuitive functioning pushed thinking back to its rightful second place.

So strongly developed had thinking become, however, that I still stop now and then and ask myself whether thinking or intuition is actually my first function. I can never decide this with certainty until I look at my third and fourth functions and ask: Which is weakest in me, feeling or sensation? While I know I am not particularly strong in the feeling realm, I am at least competent there. I have learned to be aware of feeling and I often decide things on the basis of it. Sensation, on the other hand, has always been dim and probably ever will be dim. It is difficult for me to pay attention to the physical world around me and experience it in a vivid way. Every now and then, in a moment of grace, my senses come fully awake and I see, hear, smell, taste, and feel everything, or at least it seems to me that I do. But this only lasts a few moments before the normal vagueness sets in again. There is no doubt that sensation is the weakest function for me, the one deepest in the unconscious. That means that intuition is indeed my first function, thinking is my second, and feeling is third.

## Integrating the Four Functions

IN A LIFE FULLY LIVED, one open to inner guidance, growth, and change, each of the four functions is eventually integrated into the total personality. Their hierarchy of relative strength, however, remains unchanged. The first two functions will always be the most differentiated and powerful in a worldly sense. They are the ones we use for competition against others. The third and fourth functions, on the other hand, with their deeper connection to the unconscious, will always be more primitive, slow, and simple—but also potentially more profound and God-centered.

Our first function comes to us most naturally and is usually the one that dominates our personality from our earliest years. However, it takes the inclusion of the second function to give us both a perceiving and a judging function, and we need both kinds if we are to get very far in the world. The second function, therefore, usually also undergoes at least some development in the first half of life.

There is little initial impetus, however, for developing the third function. It does not give us an obvious competitive advantage in a worldly sense, since we are not very good at it by nature. An even greater stumbling block is that it brings with it the problem of reconciling opposite modes of consciousness. This is because the third function is the polar opposite of the second function. In order to use both the second and the third functions, we must resolve within ourselves the conflict between either thinking and feeling, or sensation and intuition. The use of two opposite functions creates such an inner conflict that it can only be resolved by moving to a higher level of consciousness that includes both ways of judging or perceiving. Growing to a higher level of consciousness, however, is always painful and difficult. Therefore, the third function is not usually integrated before midlife, if at all.

Although Jung did not put it this way, I find it useful to think of the first two functions as "power" functions and the third one as the "salvation" function, which only comes into play when we have become exhausted from trying to use our power functions to win the world for ourselves. When that approach to life has played itself out, our salvation is to turn to our third function, which in turn brings with it our fourth function. In turning to these neglected parts of ourselves, however, we have to accept new ways of perceiving and judging life. This is always a defeat for our power functions, which are required to step back and give up some of their energy and truth.

A feeling of defeat also comes from the fact that our third and fourth functions are more primitive—less differentiated and sophisticated— than our first two functions. But it is precisely because of this quality of greater unconsciousness that when we turn to our third function, we are led down to our earthier, simpler self and toward our deeper truth.

It is through our third function that we gain access to our fourth function, which is so deep in the unconscious that we cannot bring it directly to the surface and put it under our conscious control. Because of its place in the depths, the fourth function, which is the least valued and the most overlooked, is the one that is closest to God. It is like the insignificant baby born in the lowly stable behind the inn in the darkest time of the year. When we turn to our third function and consciously make room for it in our life, it brings with it, clinging to it from the depths, that fourth, "divine" function, which comes as grace and completes our life, not in an ideally perfect way, but in a way that is just right for the individual that we are.

In my own case, for example, my power functions are intuition and thinking. With these I can have deep glimmerings and "knowings" about the unconscious and easily spend all my time and energy spinning them into theoretical frameworks, with little regard for what is truly important and valuable for life and even less regard for the physical reality around me. Who cares what my house looks like, or what I wear, or what I eat, or whether the garden has been weeded? Who cares whether real people in real life can understand my complicated insights and make use of them or whether they even need them?

It is a constant struggle for me not to go out too far in this direction. What brings me back when I lose my center is a growing difficulty in functioning. Something in me rebels. A mood sets in—vague discontent at first, or if that is ignored, a more notable stress. If I still fail to realize the problem, a physical symptom will arise to slow me down or stop me. When I finally halt and turn my attention to what is wrong, it is feeling that can give me the answer.

I must stop intuiting, stop thinking, and feel where I need to be and what I need to be doing. What *feels* like the most important thing? To rest. To sit with the cat. To go somewhere. To do something or see someone. To wear this sweater with this skirt, and these earrings—they feel just right. To go into the kitchen and cook something, a particular something with particular ingredients that *feel* like the one and only right thing for this day.

My feeling brings the sensate world to me in a way that is ordinary and yet touched with beauty and meaning that reverberate in my soul. Feeling puts me on God's path, brings me into Tao. With that my intuitive thinking comes down to earth and simplifies. Because it is now sharing its energy with my weaker functions, it has to slow down and operate at a lower level. This brings it into accord with the reality of the world in which I live and makes it more effective than it was before.

This process would look quite different in persons of different types and even in others of my own type. Each person must find his individual way, but the basic principle of going to the third function for centering and salvation will be the same.

## Stages of Life

IT IS ONE THING to talk about integrating a new function, or making any other change in consciousness, but it is quite another thing actually to do it. Consciousness undergoes constant revision on our journey through life, or at least it wants to be revised. There is an inner pressure for revision and change, for growth toward complete realization of individual potential. But at the same time there is an inner conservative force that resists change. Present consciousness always feels threatened by whatever future consciousness is trying to break through, no matter how beneficial the new reality promises to be. This resistance serves the positive purpose of making sure that the hard won consciousness of the past is not completely swept away by whatever new consciousness is trying to arise. The tension between the pressure for change and the resistance to change is what makes the transition from one stage of life to the next so difficult.

In order for each new stage of life to be truly realized, there must be a change in *consciousness*. Outward, physical change is not enough. The two most fundamental changes required of us come, first, at adolescence, when we must move from childhood to young adulthood, and, second, at midlife, when we are supposed to move from young adulthood to mature adulthood. Not everyone makes a successful transition at adolescence, and even fewer meet fully the challenge of midlife. Carl Jung considered the time of childhood and young adulthood to be the "first half of life," and mature adulthood and the transition to it to be the real business of the "second half of life."

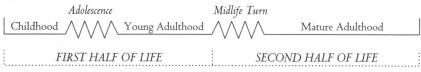

Figure 2. Stages of Life

Each of the three stages of life—childhood, young adulthood, and mature adulthood—has its own primary source of consciousness. In childhood that source is the family. A child's reality is defined by his family's reality. Whatever consciousness rules the house also rules the child. Whether he embraces it positively or sets himself up in opposition to it, it is still the family's consciousness that has the most influence on how he sees the world. The family, however, is not his only source of consciousness. School, television, other children, adults outside the family, and striking life experiences all make their contributions. So, too, does the unconscious itself.

Children are naturally open to the unconscious, especially when they are very young. That is where spontaneity, imagination, and the amazing "wisdom of a child" come from. In imagination and play, in dreams and fantasy life, and in a child's thoughtfulness and reflection, important truths come to light regarding the child's development and destiny as well as the general situation of the family. These contents from the unconscious are usually couched in symbolic language and are not often recognized as particularly meaningful by the child or his parents. Very powerful experiences of unconscious contents, however, may stay with a child and have a lifelong effect on his understanding of the world. Big dreams, God experiences, and deeply fascinating play activities often become foundation stones of consciousness and are referred back to time and again in later life.

As a child gets older and his ego consciousness grows stronger, he gradually loses his openness to the unconscious. This is bemoaned by that part of us that would resist the adolescent transition to young adulthood, but this loss of natural connection to the unconscious is necessary for the consolidation and focusing of the child's emerging personality. The same ego strength which helps an adolescent consolidate consciousness at the expense of the unconscious also helps him move away from the family toward the greater world. In order to make a place for himself in life, the young adult must get in step with the world and assimilate its ways. He must learn to construct reality as the world constructs it, with sharp, rational thinking, and he must familiarize himself as much as possible with the shared knowledge of his time. The high school and college years are meant to help a young person prepare himself in this way.

The layer of consciousness added in young adulthood is primarily a collective one. A young adult lives as a member of the herd, whether it is the mainstream herd or a countercultural one. The contents of consciousness come primarily from peer groups, from television, books, and newspapers, from work and its focus, from relationship experiences, and from significant life events.

The dual engines driving this stage of life are instincts and ideals. Young adulthood is a time when nature demands that her needs be met, and she supplies the sexual drive, the power drive, the parenting instinct, and other forms of the earthly spirit that flow into the young adult from the depths of his being and help him perform the tasks necessary to reproduce and sustain life. From the realm of the upper spirit come the high ideals of youth, some of them inherited from the young person's family, some breathed in with the air of his time. They inspire him and spur him on.

Young adulthood is the time of the hero. Its success depends upon the strength and development of the ego.

If a young adult is fortunate enough to have a parent or mentor who has made a connection to the wisdom of the unconscious, he can begin at this stage of life to become aware of the unconscious in a new way that takes the place of his lost childish connection to it. With rare exception, this more mature awareness of the unconscious is something that can only be taught, for it requires a conscious framework of understanding. When a young adult is able to begin to be aware of the guidance that comes from his inner processes, he will be able to make his way through the first half of life in a more balanced way. It is important, however, that he does not go overboard in this direction and try to substitute inner knowledge for outer effort. The balance of attention in young adulthood should be on the outer world.

The more usual time to awaken to the deeper wisdom of the unconscious is at the midlife turn, which typically begins sending out its first signals between the ages of thirty-five and forty-five, although this sometimes happens earlier or later. The strength of the signals varies greatly, bringing some people to a grinding halt and fazing others not at all. The midlife call to a change in consciousness may elicit an immediate positive response, or it may be put off for years by various dodging maneuvers, even until death.

Whether it arises from within as a vague dissatisfaction and unease or from without as the traumatic events of a full-blown midlife crisis, the aim of the midlife turn is to make the person break his identity with collective reality and begin to know life from the Spirit of truth within himself. This is the process Carl Jung refers to as *individuation*. It requires a new kind of thinking and reasoning that allows a dialogue with one's inner processes and the discovery of one's individual truth. In this stage of life, new contents of consciousness begin to come in large part from the unconscious, which brings a return of the spontaneity and wonder of childhood. Unlike childhood, however, there is now a strong ego consciousness to reflect upon the natural flow of unconscious contents and draw meaning from them.

When a constructive dialogue with inner processes begins before midlife, it is either because there is an individuated adult already present in the young person's life or because there has been a developmental crisis which has forced the young person to go out and find a mentor, usually a professional counselor. In either case the young person is led by his inner processes toward the goals of the first half of life, whereas a person at midlife or beyond is led toward the goals of the second half of life. Many people do not open up to their inner processes until they are well into the second half of life, even into old age. Many others never open up to them at all.

The process of individuation, once consciously engaged, is never-ending. It goes on for the rest of our lives. But the tumultuous intensity which initiates individuation, and which is similar to the tumult of adolescence, lasts about as long as adolescence does. This is a difficult time, but also a joyful one. There is suffering as one is led to sacrifice the instincts and ideals of young adulthood, and with that the primacy of the ego, but there is deep joy and satisfaction in realizing the richer existence of life lived under the primacy of the guiding God-center within. As the individuation process evens out into mature adulthood, it leads us to our most particular and most effective contribution to the human community, ushers us into a meaningful old age, and gradually prepares us for death by shifting our focus from things temporal to things eternal.

Consciousness is the business of our life on earth. Our challenge is to allow it to arise continually from the darkness of the unconscious, to nurture and protect it when it is new, and to let it die and give way to new reality when it has seen its time. The ever developing consciousness that we gain through this process is what makes us solid and real, and most importantly, it is what makes us *human*.

As a conscious being you must remember this as you begin to learn about the unconscious. The unconscious is vast and full of mystery, but it is not human. It is good to open yourself to the unconscious if you have the strength to do so. It is good to listen to it and take promptings from it. But it is also right that you contend with it, that, like Job, you state your position over against it. Our relationship with the unconscious is meant to be a *dialogue*. As carriers of consciousness we have the responsibility, small as we are, to stand up to the great unconscious and say to it, when we need to, that what it is asking of us is too painful or too blissful for the human life that is ours, that it must take account of our humanity and help us find a way that we can bear.

God is not the unconscious itself. God is all that is, conscious and unconscious. In order to most fully reflect God's reality in our lives, we must stand firmly in our human consciousness and from that vantage point open ourselves to dialogue with the unconscious.

CHAPTER FOUR

# The Unconscious

*Just as conscious contents can vanish into the unconscious, other contents can also arise*
*from it. Besides a majority of mere recollections, really new thoughts and*
*creative ideas can appear which have never been conscious before.*
*They grow up from the dark depths like a lotus.*

CARL JUNG

JUNG'S OBSERVATIONS of the effects of the unconscious on conscious life convinced him that the dark realm of the unconscious is not a mere absence of consciousness. Rather, the unconscious has an autonomous reality of its own, and whether we are aware of it or not, it is engaged in a dynamic relationship with consciousness.

Jung also knew, however, that by its very nature the unconscious cannot be known. All that we claim to know about it is but inference drawn from its effects on consciousness. Just as no physical model can be constructed to illustrate Einstein's four dimensional universe and no words can adequately describe the quantum reality of subatomic particles, so no picture or words can adequately portray the true nature of the unconscious. Yet we must make an attempt to get some grasp of it, no matter how inadequate that may be, for it is only by trying to understand the unconscious that we can become more conscious of its dialogue with us.

The unconscious portrays itself symbolically in dreams, visions, art forms, and in life itself using many different images. Some of the most common of these images are water in all its forms, underground realms, wild places like forests and jungles, and great beasts like whales and dragons. Noah's flood, Orpheus' journey into the underworld, Joseph Conrad's African journey into "the heart of darkness," Jonah's ordeal in the whale,

49

and St. George's fight with the dragon are all symbolic images of encounters with the unconscious.

Although the unconscious is not located in space—it is beyond space and time—it often seems to us, as we struggle to put into words our experience of it, that it is somehow *underneath* our physical reality, or *within* that reality, or that it somehow *surrounds* us. Concrete models can be made of it for explanatory purposes, but none can capture it. In putting forth such a model one must always say, "It is as if . . ."

I find it helpful to think of the unconscious as if it were an infinite realm beneath the surface of consciousness. While the unconscious in this model is all one undifferentiated, continuous reality, consciousness rises from it in discrete units.

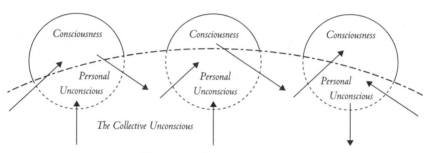

Figure 3. The Unconscious

According to Jung, each individual person carrying his own bit of consciousness experiences the unconscious on two levels. The first, most accessible of these levels Jung called the *personal unconscious,* because its contents are personal to us, part and parcel of our individual, temporal lives. In our personal unconscious is everything that *could* be in our consciousness but is not. It is like a basement or a closet in our house where things accumulate in a dusty clutter and from which we avert our eyes.

In the personal unconscious are all those contents that once were conscious but have fallen away due to a lack of energy. If we make an effort to remember them, we can bring many of those contents up from the unconscious into the light again. Some of the contents in the personal unconscious, however, can never be retrieved through memory because they entered that realm subliminally. These are events and details of our life that our senses registered at such a low level of energy that we never consciously noticed them. We often encounter them as if for the first time as elements in our dreams, fantasies, and artistic expressions.

The personal unconscious also contains those aspects of our life that we have repressed—truths that we have not wanted to know or have not been strong enough to handle. All of us relegate some of our truths to the darkness of our being by refusing to be conscious of them. They are a large part of the reason that there is something in all of us that would rather not open the door to the unconscious, even when we believe in theory that it would be beneficial to do so. We all have aspects of our lives that we do not want to see. Each of us has a *shadow*, a part of ourselves that is inconsistent with the light side we consciously cultivate and try to present to the world.

Your shadow parts are not so much the unsavory things that you know about and consciously keep hidden from others, but rather they are truths about yourself that your own psychological processes keep hidden from yourself. *You* are the one who is most in the dark about your shadow. Some parts of your shadow are obvious to everyone except yourself, while other parts are so well-disguised that almost no one can discern them. Your shadow includes both inferior aspects of your personality that you are unwilling to see because they are unacceptable to you and superior aspects that you have not yet discovered and claimed.

Among the inferior aspects that everyone finds it hard to own are unconscious instinctual drives such as power seeking, sexuality, and parenting. Instincts are an integral part of us and only belong to the shadow when they operate unconsciously. It is when you think you are being generous and noble in a situation but are operating instead from an unacknowledged power motive that your shadow is present; or when you believe you are behaving innocently with another but in fact have an unrecognized sexual agenda; or when you think you are relating equally to a peer but instead are playing mother or father; or when you take the other side and play the child.

Every individuation journey includes the revelation of unconscious instinctual behaviors. They are always present, but because they are unconscious you cannot discover them by sitting down to think about them.

Usually it does not even help very much to have them pointed out to you by others. It is through life that you learn about them. The teachings of life that lead to the fullest realization of them come when a person turns a positive face toward the unconscious and opens himself to its contents by taking note of his dreams and looking for meaning and lessons about himself in his outer life experiences.

Other inferior aspects in the shadow that none of us wish to see are those that belong to the weaker departments of our personality—the un-starred, unpracticed parts of ourselves, those opposite our gifted selves. They often have to do with our third and fourth functions. These inferior parts of ourselves threaten our self-confidence, and so we try to live as if they do not exist. But if through a person's dreams and the events of his life he is led to acknowledge his weaker parts and bring them forward into conscious life, he will find that these dark aspects of himself contain a sparkle of gold.

Creativity comes from the unconscious, from the same realm as the shadow. When a person faces his shadow, he makes contact with God's creative spirit. As the Spirit does its work in him and moves him to new expressions of life, he finds that his inferior aspects are bound to superior aspects that are also hidden in his darkness. In accepting his own rejected truth, a part of himself that was gray and dead-seeming is transformed into colorful vitality. The shadow, when claimed, paradoxically brings gifts, authentic qualities like strength, beauty, leadership ability, tenderness, incisiveness—qualities that hitherto a person only pretended to have or else never believed could be his at all.

Until we are able to claim our shadow qualities as our own, we project them onto others. Whenever you have strong, obsessive feelings—positive or negative—about another person, something unconscious is present and is being projected. A quality of your own is being seen not in yourself, where you cannot see it, but in the other person, who may or may not actually possess it.

Thus there may be certain people—in your family, at work, at church, in the news—who strongly affect you by drawing your irritation, anger, and outrage, or else your praise, admiration, and devotion. Often the other person possesses the despised or admired characteristic in an exaggerated form, which makes it easy for you to see it "out there" and hard for you to see its more subtle version in yourself. If it were not a quality that in some way belonged to you, you would not be so strongly affected by it. You could look at it with clear eyes, see it for what it is, and turn away and go about your business. But when projection is involved, you get caught by what you see "out there," and until you stop to reflect upon it, you cannot disentangle your feelings from it nor recognize that the cause of your agitation is in yourself and not in the other.

## The Collective Unconscious

STRONG AFFECT in general is an indication that an unconscious content is present. When you are angry, frightened, moved to tears, filled with love, or otherwise overtaken by emotion, a truth hitherto unknown has come toward the surface and is available for recognition. If you are aware of this, you can follow the emotion down into its depths and bring to consciousness what you find there, thus strengthening your individual reality and becoming more whole and fully human. Otherwise your emotions simply possess you. They play themselves out in eternal patterns that lead you blindly into situations which unfold like Greek or Shakespearean dramas, and when all has passed you are none the wiser—no growth in consciousness has occurred.

Those eternal patterns that arise in us, either to be consciously integrated or to take possession of our lives, come not from the personal unconscious but from the second, deeper level of the unconscious, the *collective unconscious.* Here are unconscious contents within us that have not come from our life experience. The collective unconscious is the eternal realm beyond time and space. In it is everything that has ever been or seeks to be in human consciousness, past, present, and future. It is the source of our being. We emerge from it when our life on earth begins, draw our energy and vitality from it while we are here, and return to it when our time is over. All life is connected to it, and through it all life is interconnected. Because of our link to it, we sometimes receive intimations of the future or know, without being told, about events that are occurring elsewhere, as sometimes happens at the moment when someone of special significance to us dies.

The patterned effects that come from the collective unconscious are called *archetypes* in Jungian terminology. They are the themes and motifs that drive and shape our human lives. We can see them depicted most clearly in myths and fairytales, where they have been crystallized into some of their purer forms. The Greek gods and goddesses, for example, are images of archetypal aspects of life that belong to each of us. So are fairytale kings and princesses, youngest sons and only daughters of millers and woodcutters, and non-human motifs like lost rings, wise frogs, and golden slippers. Archetypal contents arise from the collective unconscious in universal symbolic patterns that appear in our dreams, thoughts, fantasies, and art forms, as well as in the elements of our outer lives, whether or not we have ever seen or heard of them before.

Archetypal effects come to us along a continuum that ranges from the physical and instinctual to the psychological and spiritual. The "mother" archetype, for example, is physically manifest in the person of our actual mother. Because of the archetypal effect behind it, our relationship with our mother is highly patterned and predictable, although each mother-child relationship also has a unique and individual manifestation. It is the archetype that produces the eternal aspect and the circumstances of temporal life that produce the individual aspect. The mother archetype is present in an instinctual form when we mother our own children. It begins to move toward the spiritual end of the continuum when we extend mother love to the children of others, and it is present in psychological form when we mother ourselves, especially when we gain wisdom about the unconscious and allow ourselves to be nurtured and led by it.

Besides the direct and obvious manifestations of the mother archetype, there are myriad other forms in life that carry the mother's archetypal attributes of nourishing and protecting, enclosing and containing, fostering growth, and inspiring awe and devotion—as well as the dark attributes of smothering, seducing, poisoning, and devouring. Thus, for example, we encounter "the mother" in the Church, the university, and the community hall, in the Virgin Mary, Mother Nature, and the Holy Grail, in the plowed field and the enclosed garden, in the Holy City, and in the shaded grotto. In her dark form, "the mother" is present in the conjuring witch, the ensnaring spider, the devouring beast, and the yawning grave.

Although archetypal effects may be present in any and all forms of life, the forms themselves are not the actual archetypes. The archetypes precede existence, having themselves no form, but only a tendency to form. They remain forever in the collective unconscious from whence their effects come, imbuing life with the images and actions expressive of their particular qualities. The degree to which an archetypal effect is experienced as fascinating or gripping is based not on the thing that seems to carry that quality but on the experiencing individual and his relationship to the underlying archetype in the collective unconscious.

The archetypes in the collective unconscious are the divine energies of life. They belong to the living reality of the unconscious, which is autonomous and beyond our control. Because the archetypes in the unconscious are larger than we are—more sublime and more terrible in their eternal aspects than human life can carry—they can distort a person's life or even destroy him if they get too strong a grip on his personality. And yet we cannot live authentically without them, nor do we have the power to keep them away. They arise unbidden within us. Our task is to stand up to their turbulent effect on our lives, to recognize that they and we are not the same, and to become consciously related to them rather than unconsciously possessed by them.

One of the archetypes, for example, is that instinct that makes us want to be on the top of the heap. I call it the Zeus archetype, after the Greek god who ruled from Mount Olympus, although it could also be called the king archetype or any other name that carries a comparable image. Regardless of what name it is given, this archetype activates that part of human nature that makes each of us think that we know exactly how things in the world should be and that it is our role to direct the world around us to that end. All of us experience times when this archetype takes possession of our personality, making us unpleasantly all-knowing and domineering.

The answer to this it to recognize that it is happening. We can learn that when things go badly in a certain way, it is because this godlike pattern of behavior has arisen in us without our awareness, and our limited, mortal self has become unconsciously identified with it. At moments like this we must remind ourselves that we are not Zeus. We are not the King. Even an actual king in a worldly sense is not the King in this archetypal sense, for, king or not, he is just a man. If we can cease to identify with the archetypal pattern, we will then be able to form a *conscious* relationship with it and integrate it little by little into the totality of our being, bringing it down to human size as we adjust its demands to the ordinary reality of our life. The Zeus archetype, when we relate to it in a positive way, is a crucial ingredient in our ability to exercise effective leadership.

# The Self

THE FACTOR that makes it possible for us to integrate the archetypes with all their conflicting demands is the God-center within us, a coordinating "center point" which is itself an archetype in the collective unconscious. This is the archetype that unites all archetypes into its own comprehensive totality. When a person makes a positive connection to the God-center, the chaos of the unconscious is brought into order, its overwhelming power is subdued, and its images and energies are channeled into that person's life in an individual, just-right way that teaches, heals, protects, and leads.

Jung named this unifying archetype the *Self* to emphasize its quality of God within, although he did not mean by this to refer to one's limited human self. His German term *das selbst* is more accurately translated, "the Itself." Jung understood the Self to be the greater reality to which our human lives belong, the Lord of lords that our egos must learn to recognize and serve. It is the screen or gate through which God is manifested in human consciousness. When we experience an image or understanding that arises from the Self, it is as close as we can come to knowing God, who is by nature unknowable in His fullness. Thus all images and experiences of God arise from the archetype of the Self, including many we might not ordinarily think of as divine.

In my own dreams the terms "God," "the Self," "the center," and "the Christ" have appeared interchangeably. I take this to mean that God, from whom I feel such understandings come, regards them as interchangeable. One dream, for example, which came in words, not images, said, *"To inte-grate the Self is to integrate God."* I took this to mean that God is to some extent incarnated in human life when a person awakens to the reality of the unconscious, makes a positive connection to the Self, and takes into himself or herself the teachings, understandings, and life experiences that this connection brings.

Another dream I had about the Self also came as directly conveyed meaning, although this time it was illustrated by an image.

> *I saw a line running from my viewing point to what I understood to be "the center." The line extended forward along a horizontal plane to a point on the horizon that I knew was only there because it was as far as I could see into the distance, while the actual center point lay beyond at infinity. "Jung gave you your first line to the center," the dream voice said. I knew that this referred to the understandings I had gained from Jung's work.*
>
> *Then the dream showed a second line starting at some distance to the right of the first and also running to the center, making a triangular area between the two lines. In the dream I understood that this second line was the Church in its present, institutional reality and that this, too, was now in place for me. I knew that although this second line pertained more to the outer world, and was therefore less profound than the first line, it was essential for providing me a playing field. I understood that the triangular area between Jung and the Church was the area of human reality in which it was possible for me to live my life "from the center."*

Because of yet another dream about the Self that I had had earlier, I was aware even as I was dreaming this dream that it is important that one's life be lived "from the center." That earlier dream also had at the heart of it meaning directly conveyed through words which were accompanied by a simple, visual illustration.

> *I dreamed of an elderly, old-fashioned woman who was a school librarian. I knew that she had no children of her own. She was explaining to us that you have to tell children exactly what to do because, being children, they do not otherwise know.*
>
> *Then the dream shifted and became an illustration, as if on paper, of a framework that I knew to be an equal-armed cross, although the focus was on only one quadrant*

*and the center point. A line from the center radiated out through the quadrant at about a 50° angle from one of the arms of the cross. On that arm and on the radiating line were two dots, one on each line, at equal distance from the center. Then the dream showed a line connecting the two dots:*

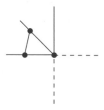

*A dream voice said, "That is going across," conveying the understanding that it was not good. "God wants everything from the center," the dream voice said.*

As I understand the dream, the radiating lines with the dots on them have reference to individual lives, and the point being made by the dream is that God does not want us ultimately to receive our understanding of life from other people. We may need this when we are in an early phase of learning, but in the end God's way is not the school librarian's way. We must be taught and led by our own inner guide, the God-center within us—the Self.

This dream also makes it clear that God and the Self are not entirely synonymous. *"God wants everything from the center."* God is greater than the center, or the Self, and presides over our relationship to it, although it is only through that relationship that we can know God as He wants to be known. Jesus incarnated the eternal, or archetypal, Christ, which is a living image and truth that arises from the Self. The Christ is the Self in potential human form, seeking to be known and integrated into human life. Speaking as the Christ, or the Self, Jesus said to his followers, "The Father is greater than I." But he also said, "If you know me, you know my Father too."

Like the center point on the horizon in my dream, the Self is as close as we can come to an actual experience of God, whose total reality is infinite and thus beyond our powers of perception. Jesus was speaking for the Self when he said: "I am the Way;" "I am the gate;" "come . . . through me;" "believe in me." All of his teachings were about what it is like, and what is required, to have a positive relationship with God through the Self.

The very fact that we can have a positive relationship with the Self means that we can also have a negative one. All the archetypes in the unconscious have a dark side as well as a light side. I once had a dream that spoke explicitly about the dark side of the Self:

> *I dreamed deeply of "the negative or dark Christ, also called Self," of what it is. The dream was mostly a mood or perception of a kind of dark energy with this label on it. I was aware of a brooding, turbulent sky. Then I saw two doves flying up into the dark heavens, bound to earth by long tethers around their necks. They had flown to the end of their tethers and were straining against them. I understood the dark Christ or dark Self to be the resentment or protest of the Self against those bonds.*

For me the dove is first and foremost a symbol of the Holy Spirit, and that is how I understand the image of the doves in this dream. The dream, therefore, seems to equate the Christ, the Self, and the Holy Spirit and to show as their dark side the resentment of the divine Spirit against the limitations of earthly life. We see this side of Jesus when he asks in exasperation, "How long must I put up with this generation?" We also see it when he gives way to anger and overturns the tables of the moneychangers, certainly to no lasting avail.

Just as we have the light side of the Self within us, so also do we have the dark side. Something within all of us that is greater than we are resents the fact that the Kingdom has not yet come, that we must live in a world with so much imperfection, that our material life is not as we would like it, that our jobs and marriages cause such difficulty and disappointment, that our children give us as much trouble as they do, that our government at all levels is as corrupt as it is, that the ministers and leaders of our churches have no more awareness of the Spirit than they do, that nothing is as it should be and would be if the compelling sense of divine perfection that resides in us were realized. This dark resentment, unless balanced by the light, gives rise to evil.

The light side of the Self accepts the limitations of life and willingly sacrifices its own greatness and unfathomable potential for what is realizable in a specific place and time. In doing so, it redeems life on earth bit by bit and step by step. But this does not happen without the accompanying presence of the dark Self. The dream suggests that the dark Self is especially present when a new experience of the Self first comes into awareness. A duality in dreams, such as the two doves, usually indicates an unconscious content that has just entered consciousness, at which point it divides into two, a set of opposites that had been whole and undifferentiated in the unconscious, where all exists in primal unity.

In consciousness there is always a light and a dark side to everything, a good and a bad, a positive and a negative, just as in subatomic physics a particle is always paired with an antiparticle. When a baby is born, for example, it is a blessed and joyful event. And yet even the most welcoming parents have also to face the dark side of increased responsibility, curtailed freedom, and the renewal, in this new life, of the cycles of human imperfection of which they are already a part. Post-partum depression registers in a dramatic way the inevitable presence of the dark Self as new life enters the world. Every further development in that new life will bring with it dark moments as the Self continually seeks incarnation and confronts the limitations of reality.

## The Compensatory Nature of the Unconscious

CONSCIOUSLY OR UNCONSCIOUSLY, all the archetypes, including the archetype of the Self, are universally present in every person. An archetype may be experienced one-sidedly with only its light aspect admitted to consciousness and its dark aspect denied, or, conversely, with only the dark side admitted and the light side denied. In either case life will be imbalanced, and the excluded quality will continually seek to make itself known.

The longer the rejected aspect is kept knocking at the door of consciousness, the greater and more threatening its power will become. But however dark and ugly one may fear it to be, it is one's own truth that seeks admittance through the door of the unconscious. So long as a person has a strong ego structure and a conscious connection to the God of heaven and light, that person's rejected truth will bring redemption when it is faced and integrated. In the end he or she will come to realize that the unconscious is not an enemy but is in fact a valuable source of ongoing, personal truth.

The unconscious always seeks to *compensate* our conscious attitude. If we do not find new understanding in its messages, we have not interpreted them correctly. The unconscious tries to bring to our awareness what is missing and needed for our proper functioning and for the greatest possible realization of our human wholeness. It tries to help us balance the light side and the dark side of life by bringing opposing realities together into a single new reality that is less light than the unbalanced light and less dark than the unbalanced darkness and yet greater than either of these in its unity and completeness.

Carl Jung once said, "We know that the mask of the unconscious is not rigid—it reflects the face we turn toward it. Hostility lends it a threatening aspect, friendliness softens its features." Some people have turned a hostile face to the unconscious for so long, and have become so separated from it, that its contents have become too dark and overpowering to be faced. Such persons live under the threat of a psychosis and for them the unconscious is a real danger. Their best course usually is to leave it alone and to hang on to whatever adaptation to life they have managed to make for themselves.

Many others have not consolidated enough ego strength and moral will to stand up to a direct, unmediated relationship with the unconscious. Their connection to the Self is sufficiently maintained by collective religious experience. They are like the Hebrews at the foot of Mount Sinai: "'Speak to us yourself,' the people said to Moses, 'and we will listen; but do not let God speak to us, or we shall die.'"

Those persons who would be overwhelmed by the unconscious usually have a strong resistance to it—often to the point that they can hardly bear to hear it discussed. Such resistances should always be honored. No one should ever try to harass or cajole another person into opening the door to the unconscious. Those who need a direct relationship with the unconscious will be led from within to seek it. For the rest there are other valid paths.

A person who is ready to meet the unconscious directly is one who has a strong ego, a well-developed moral sensibility, and the ability to be detached and analytical about his or her own inner processes. He or she must also have a compelling need for inner growth and healing. There is a zone of anxiety through which everyone must pass in establishing a direct relationship with the unconscious. Persons in whom the above qualities and conditions are present are more likely than others to stay the course with courage and not turn back. For those who are called to this path, the light of the Self waits in the darkness of the unconscious to be their guide. In the language of Christianity, this is the light of the eternal Christ, that same light which the darkness cannot overpower.

CHAPTER FIVE

# The Language of the Unconscious

*The unconscious is the only available source of religious experience. This is certainly not to say that what we call the unconscious is identical with God or is set up in his place. It is simply the medium from which religious experience seems to flow.*

CARL JUNG

THROUGHOUT TIME AND HISTORY there have been many methods devised for making contact with the unconscious, usually, but not always, for religious purposes. Among these are disciplines of meditation and prayer; vision quests and shamanistic journeys; spontaneous artistic expressions; active imagination, or waking fantasy; and various oracular devices such as the Urim and Thummim of the Old Testament, the Tarot cards of Europe, and the *I Ching* of China. There are, however, two *natural* ways by which the unconscious continually expresses itself in our lives, day and night, without requiring from us any method or device.

The most noticeable of these natural ways is through our *dreams,* which come to us every night, whether we remember them or not. The second natural way is through experiences of *synchronicity,* or meaningful coincidence, which occur every day of our waking life, whether or not we are aware of them. This ongoing dialogue with the "Other" is always present. The only question is whether it is noticed, understood to some degree, and consciously integrated into life. It is a process that is so natural that it can always be discovered anew without instruction by thoughtful persons everywhere.

Abraham Lincoln was one such person who, without encouragement from the culture around him, was alert to the natural inflowing expressions of the divine. Many instances were recorded in which he let it be known that dreams and synchronicity were important to him. Of course, he did not know the word "synchronicity." This is the term Jung has given us for the events of life that have deeper meaning than their mere surface-of-life, physical reality. But Lincoln did not need a special word for this. He understood it when he saw it, as he did on the day of his second inauguration in an event recorded by Noah Brooks, a reporter who was a particularly close friend of his.

That 4th day of March, 1865, had dawned cold and gray with drizzling rain. At midday, just before Lincoln made his entrance onto the inaugural platform, the rain stopped. In the company of the nation's leading public officials, Lincoln emerged from the Capitol Building and took his seat on the crowded platform above the mass of spectators. In solemn ceremony the sergeant-at-arms of the Senate invited him to step forward to give his inaugural address.

"As he advanced from his seat," wrote Brooks, "a roar of applause shook the air, and, again and again repeated, finally died far away on the outer fringe of the throng, like a sweeping wave upon the shore. Just at that moment the sun, obscured all day, burst forth in its unclouded meridian splendor and flooded the spectacle with glory and light."

The synchronicity of the moment was not lost on Noah Brooks, nor on Lincoln himself. As they were returning to the White House after the ceremony, Lincoln said to Brooks, "Did you notice that sunburst? It made my heart jump."

Lincoln also paid attention to the messages of the night, a trait regarded as peculiar by most people around him in that highly rational age. On the day he died, Good Friday, 1865, he told some colleagues about a dream he had had the night before. This conversation took place in a Cabinet meeting in which the topic of discussion had turned to news of the army. The Civil War at this point was essentially, but not quite, over.

Lincoln told his Cabinet secretaries that he had no news, but that he had had a dream the night before which he felt signified that good news would be forthcoming. He had had this same dream several times before, he explained, and it was always followed by a great moment in the war, usually a victory. In this recurring dream he would be in some sort of indescribable vessel, moving swiftly across a body of water toward an unknown shore. "I had this strange dream again last night," he said, "and we shall, judging from the past, have great news very soon, I think."

The Cabinet members stepped politely around this contribution to the discussion, avoiding an abrupt dismissal of it, but suggesting that the dream's conjunction with major events was probably coincidental or else could be explained by Lincoln's agitated state of mind in times of crisis, when such major events would likely be forthcoming. Lincoln put up no argument. "Perhaps that is the explanation," he said and let the matter drop.

But the incomprehension of his Cabinet did not dampen the high spirits with which the dream had infused him. As he rode with Mrs. Lincoln to Ford's Theater that night, she noted a mood of happiness in him that was so strange and unusual that it troubled her. Because of Lincoln's firm belief in his own inner experience, his dream had been able to do its work in preparing him for the moment of his death—for the completion of his journey to the "other shore." This is not to suggest that he had such a specific understanding of the dream, but rather that his general grasp of it was enough to move him to the place inside himself where it seems God wanted him to be for these last hours of his life.

What little Lincoln knew about dreams and synchronicity he had to discover for himself in a world in which such things were not taken seriously except by "old women and by young men and maidens in love," as he himself once put it. He lived just at the end of the rational, mechanistic age, embodying what was best in it and anticipating the new age to come. Sigmund Freud was a nine-year-old boy in Vienna when Lincoln died. Carl Jung would be born ten years later and Albert Einstein four years after that. Had Lincoln lived a little more than a century later, he could have filled several shelves of his library with easily accessible books that describe systematically the nature of the unconscious and the rudiments of its fascinating but difficult language.

## God's Feminine Voice

THE NATURAL LANGUAGE of the unconscious is the language of symbol and metaphor. There are occasional instances when it states a truth forthrightly, but these seem to come only when a person is ready to grasp a particular truth, which implies that the cooperation of consciousness is required for the unconscious to be able to make a straightforward statement. Since the purpose of the unconscious is to compensate our consciousness by revealing to us aspects of our truth that we do not already understand, much symbolic and metaphorical expression of an unfolding truth precedes and prepares those rare moments of clarity.

The unconscious speaks to us symbolically because that is the language of life itself. Unfolding creation reveals the reality of God in picture story. The symbolic language of nature is God's feminine voice, and it requires union with consciousness, which is the masculine principle, in order to be perceived and understood. Human beings are the vehicles through which this process takes place, since we are the ones who carry together in our beings both unconscious nature and consciousness. Because consciousness rises out of the unconsciousness of nature and stands above it, somewhat separate and apart from it, consciousness is able to perceive nature with a degree of objectivity and thus is able to *know* it. Without consciousness, life can be lived, but it cannot be known.

It is in our capacity for consciousness that we experience God's masculine spirit, while in the natural reality of our lives we experience God's feminine aspect. In the feminine part of ourselves we partake of nature, reality, and specificity, while in our masculine part we stand above nature at the level of objectivity, abstraction, and ideal.

The abstract quality of the masculine principle is, in fact, the great problem we have with consciousness. It has the tendency to prefer abstraction and idea to reality. The masculine part of us does not want to be bothered with natural reality. It would rather dream about an ideal world or talk about general principles. It resists limiting itself to the here and now. Although it is able from its objective vantage point to perceive unfolding nature, it does not easily take the next step of valuing natural reality in all its fullness and entering into true relationship with it.

One-sided consciousness—the pure masculine principle—is such a straightforward, linear process that it has difficulty recognizing that the symbolic expression of life is even a language at all. It dismisses the feminine voice of God as nonsensical and irrational. The tendency to this attitude seems to be a condition of consciousness in all human beings, whether men or women, although in general men carry it more strongly than women do.

In its love of abstraction and idea, one-sided consciousness has little patience for the daily unfolding of particular life processes, but this is precisely where the symbolic language of God is found. Wherever this language of life is ignored, the feminine principle is closed out. Unless a person gains understanding of the symbolic language of the unconscious, a full relationship between the masculine and feminine elements of life cannot take place. It is only when there is a true union of the masculine and feminine principles that human wholeness can be achieved and the wisdom of life attained.

## Collective Symbols

THE SYMBOLIC LANGUAGE of the unconscious has both an individual and a general aspect, depending on whether the material is coming from the personal or the collective unconscious. In seeking the meaning of an image that comes from the unconscious, we must always begin by asking about one's personal associations with that image. If I dream, for example, about a place by the sea, the first question to ask, before looking at the collective meaning of "by the sea," is whether I have any personal associations with that particular locale.

In my life I have experienced the sea in different places and contexts. Why was this location chosen by the unconscious? Sometimes I dream, for example, of a place on the South Carolina coast where my husband and I have vacationed with my relatives. I particularly associate it with my mother, who liked to gather our family there. Other times I dream of the blue Gulf waters at Bradenton, Florida, where there is a national park commemorating the landing of the Hernando de Soto expedition in 1539. That expedition has long been my husband's major research project. Each of these dream locations are "by the sea," but they address very different aspects of my being. Not totally different, however. "By the sea" also has a collective meaning, and these two locales are but variants, albeit important ones, of an underlying, universal human reality symbolized by this general image.

Water is an archetypal motif that almost always refers to the unconscious, the nature of which is symbolized by the nature of water in its every aspect. In the form of the sea, water symbolizes the unconscious as the source of our being, the primal mother, vast and overwhelming, chaotic and beautiful, life-giving, eternal, mysterious, soul-restoring. To be "by the sea" is to be in a place in myself that is close to the unconscious in its primal aspect and thus close to the creative source of my own being.

There are many basic images that almost always carry the same general meanings in everyone's dreams. The collective meanings of the most commonly occurring symbols can be picked up by reading widely in Jungian literature, although no two persons who work with dreams will agree completely on the meanings of even the most basic symbols. The unconscious is too creatively expressive to be caught and nailed down. Individual nuances are always present to forestall the possibility of a pat answer in any interpretation of a dream symbol.

However, the collective meaning of a symbol usually has some light to shed on the interpretation process once the personal associations elicited by that symbol have been reviewed. Over the years I have arrived at my own understanding of the collective meanings of commonly occurring symbols. I offer some of these as examples of the metaphorical nature of the language of the unconscious.

In the image of water, for example, many different attributes of the unconscious can be seen. The unconscious flows like a stream or a river in a winding path through the midst of our lives. Like groundwater, it stores itself in the ground of our being, beneath the surface of visible reality. Like a spring, the unconscious emerges clear and pure from an unseen "Source." Like rain, it periodically pours down on us from above, surrounding us with its presence, merging the heaven and earth of our being and bringing forth new life. Like water piped into our individual houses, the unconscious washes clean the contaminations of our being that we inevitably pick up as we live our daily lives. Like a cool, clean drink of water from a well, it assuages the thirst of our souls. And like the danger of deep water, it can obliterate our individual reality if we do not know how to "swim" in it or if it floods over us with too great a force. We can dip into the watery realm of the unconscious, but we cannot live in it. It is not a human environment.

Light is another symbol that brings a collective, archetypal meaning into our dreams and into the synchronistic events of our waking lives. Light symbolizes consciousness. To "see the light" is to awaken to a new level of consciousness, to realize a truth we have previously been unable or unwilling to grasp. If you dream of being in a dimly lit room or of groping about in total darkness, you are probably being told about a part of yourself of which you have little consciousness or even, in the second instance, no consciousness at all. The sun is symbolic of the divine source of consciousness in its emanating, masculine aspect, while the moon symbolizes the reflective feminine consciousness of divine wisdom. Electric lights, on the other hand, usually refer to ego consciousness.

The surface of earth is the normal physical realm of human life. In dreams it can symbolize our earthly reality. The region beneath the earth usually symbolizes the unconscious and the roots of things in the past. People often dream of being in a basement or of finding a place in the ground with stairs going down. The world underground sometimes symbolizes death, or the world of the dead, which is itself a reference to the unconscious, where everything from the past still lives. It can also indicate depression, an inner state in which a person sinks deeply into his earthly energies, growing heavy and inert as he loses contact with his higher spirit. Although a depression is a difficult and sometimes dangerous time in a person's life, it brings with it the possibility of making a needed reconnection with the fundamental root of one's being.

The realm of the upper spirit is symbolized by the air and sky above the earth. This is the world of thought, abstraction, and ideal, of faith and soaring hope, and of heaven. Birds are at home at this level, but humans are not. If you dream of flying like a bird you are probably being shown that in some aspect of your life you do not have your feet on the ground, that your upper spirit is overbalanced and is carrying you away from human physical reality. A dream of being in an airplane, however, would show an aspect of your life in which you are being carried along by a system of thought or ideals that may not be grounded but at least is a viable human way of going.

Vehicles of all kinds symbolize culturally-based ways of getting around in outer life. In this context a car symbolizes an independent way of going, while buses, planes, and trains are collective ways. A dream of driving a pickup truck, for instance, might be a picture of being in one's working mode, while riding in a bus might symbolize being carried along by a collective process, such as taking a class. To go on foot is to move through life naturally and individually, without the drawbacks, but also without the benefits, of a cultural system.

Animals in our dreams symbolize instinct, with different species representing different parts of our instinctual life. Cats, for example, usually symbolize a natural aspect of our feminine being. They show us an instinctive part of ourselves that has a strong sense of self-worth, that values being over doing, that is oriented toward inwardness, and that has a streak of wildness that can never be fully tamed. Dogs, on the other hand, represent a masculine instinct for doing, proving, and earning. Dogs portray a life energy within us that is extraverted and that imparts to us a natural social instinct and a preoccupation with competition and hierarchy. This energy helps us delineate and guard our personal boundaries, sets off a warning within us when our space is being violated, and gives us the snarling teeth and fighting spirit we need to defend what is ours.

When we dream of wild animals we are dreaming of the primeval nature that lives in the depths of us. A dream of jungle animals, for example, might be a compensation for an overly cultural adaptation to life, reminding the dreamer that he is not only a cultural being but also a magnificent creature of earth meant to live in close connection with the natural rhythm of life. Birds are generally symbolic of our higher, spiritual nature. Cold-blooded animals symbolize our deepest, most primal, and least conscious energies. Fish symbolize the living, autonomous contents of the unconscious, which can be fished up and "eaten," or integrated. This makes the fish an apt symbol of the living Christ. The snake symbolizes the energy of life at its most fundamental level, unconscious and instinctual, inhuman but strangely intelligent and purposeful, a source of danger but also of healing and transformation. The snake sometimes symbolizes the unconscious itself.

Another common symbol in our dreaming and waking lives is "the child." We often dream of our own children, or of a child who belongs to us but is not one of our actual, outer-world children, or of a baby we are supposed to be taking care of but have forgotten about and neglected, or of a child who is wise beyond his years and knows what to do when we do not know, and so on. "The child" represents something new that is growing in us, something that will come to maturity in the future, something crucial and central to our lives. It might, for example, refer to a significant new relationship, or to an important development in one's working life or in one's spiritual life. There are times, however, when a child in a dream refers not to something new but to something from the past, to an aspect of our own childhood about which we need to become conscious.

At the heart of the symbolism of "the child" is an image of the newly emerging Self. This is what is being emphasized if we dream of a child who is unusually wise and knowing. "The child" in this aspect would be the Divine Child, God within, incarnated in one's individual life both by grace and by one's own effort to attend to one's inner processes and to follow the narrow and dimly lit path of one's own true being.

There are many other symbols of the Self, including all the many images with which the Christ has been identified throughout the centuries of Christianity. Jesus himself is our most elaborate symbol of the Self, being its human incarnation. But the simplest and most fundamental symbol of the Self is the circle, or *mandala*. Images of roundness that appear in dreams—balls, plates, rings, people arranged in circles, and so on—usually indicate the presence of the archetypal wholeness of the Self. When the center is emphasized, as when a circle is quartered by a cross, it symbolizes the Self as both a unifying and an ordering principle. The flower, with its center and radiating petals, is a natural mandala and a profound symbol of the Self. Christ is often symbolized by a flower, as is the Virgin Mary, and to dream of a flower almost always has a healing effect on one's soul.

The circle symbolizes the Self as it arises spontaneously from nature, within our psyches as well as in the outer world. The sun and the moon are round. So are many fruits, nuts, seeds, and flowers. The eyes of animals are round. All of these symbolize the natural presence of a tendency to wholeness that is carried by life itself. The square, however, which is a constructed form, is also a symbol of the Self, one that points to a cultural aspect of the divine and indicates a human factor that enters into the process of wholeness. Rare natural occurrences of formal line and angle— as in crystals and honeycombs—symbolize the fact that even this tendency to culture has its seeds in the depths of nature itself.

There is a sacred quality to four-squareness. This symbol is found in the Christian cross and in the image of the square-walled City of God in the book of Revelation. There is a human spiritual instinct for squaring off a sacred space within which one can stand in safety to face the power of the divine. It is very common for a person who is coming into conscious relationship with the unconscious to dream of walking in a square or rectangular pattern—perhaps, for instance, around a city block—sometimes repeatedly. This shows that inside himself this person is shoring up his boundaries, drawing to himself human consciousness, tradition, and structure in order to make a safe place in which to stand to receive the potentially disintegrating contents of the unconscious.

One must face the chaos of the unconscious with tools for integrating it, with some sort of guidebook from those who have gone before. We need a positive connection to the defining boundaries of human society in order to balance the limitlessness of the unconscious. Jung used the Greek word *temenos* to refer to this archetypal, squared-off, sacred space where a person can meet the unconscious without being overwhelmed by it. A temenos is a well-ordered place of healthy consciousness. Churches carry this deep, archetypal symbol, as do ball fields, courthouses, city parks, and even tables around which we gather for meals or meetings.

A temenos serves the function of bringing chaotic elements into order through a human system of customs, rules, insights, and understandings. When a person who is trying to connect with his or her dream life takes care to use Jungian tools and a religious attitude, he or she stands in the safety of a temenos. Or to give another example, sometimes when I am suffering one of life's overwhelming and disintegrating pains, I will hear the line of a hymn arise within me. If I get out my hymnbook and sing that hymn, I will find that it has just the right words, feelings, and understandings for building a temenos for myself. To sing each verse is to walk around my boundaries, squaring my corners, making a sacred space in which my pain can be integrated and transformed.

As in the archetypal dream image of making a square, much of the symbolic language that arises from the unconscious has to do with the *process* of becoming conscious. It is fairly common, for example, to dream of an intruder who is trying to get into one's house. This usually symbolizes something yet unknown that is trying to come into consciousness from the unconscious. It tells the dreamer that he or she is being so resistant to a new understanding, to new life of some kind, that it has taken on a dark and threatening aspect. It feels threatening because it is unknown.

If you have a dream like this, you should not be frightened, but rather you should stand bravely and face it, acknowledging that there is something arising in you that you cannot yet see and affirming that you are willing to come to grips with it. After all, it is nothing more than your own truth trying to get in. It may turn out to be a pleasant truth or an unpleasant truth, but either way you will be better off when you have found out about it and dealt with it. If you do stand and face it, you may then have another dream that shows it in a less threatening form, perhaps as a stranger whom you meet, a part of yourself that no longer frightens you but that you still do not know very well. As life continues to bring you to new consciousness about this unfolding aspect of yourself, you might dream of being with a new friend.

Another theme having to do with the process of becoming conscious is that of toilets and bathrooms. These are very common symbols, especially in the dreams of people who are consciously engaged in the individuation process. There are, for example, dreams of not being able to find a bathroom, of finding one that offers no privacy, of a clogged toilet filled with excrement, or of a toilet that is like a throne. The variations are endless. This theme has to do with shadow work, with the need to periodically deal with the darkness, or unconsciousness, that accumulates naturally as a result of living. The regular cleansing of the soul requires solitude and privacy, times of withdrawal from active outer life. Shadow work requires inner work.

Defecation symbolizes a natural process by which we eliminate the residue of life gone by. This speaks of our need to periodically rid ourselves of old attitudes, old relationships, old activities, old passions, old answers to life's questions, and so on. When our dreams show problems with defecation, it is usually an indication that we are having trouble doing our shadow work.

Urination has to do with the natural flow of the unconscious through our individual beings. We are channels for the symbolic images that flow into us from the unconscious and seek to flow out into consciousness through our dreams, fantasies, spontaneous artistic expressions, and deeply felt emotions. The release of these images is private inner work, not meant for public display but for our own personal growth toward human wholeness. On another level, urination has to do with the flow of life itself, the river of time, the demands of the hour which are constantly changing throughout each day and throughout our lives. Life is a flow of images and experiences in which one must participate in a timely way. It cannot be held back.

These are only a few of the most common symbols through which the unconscious speaks to us. No symbol can be completely or rigidly defined. The fact that it is a symbol means that it refers to a mystery of life that is always just a little beyond our grasp. We can never quite lay hold of the full meaning of our dreams or of life itself as it unfolds before us. But we must do the best we can, always holding our constructs lightly, letting further insights rearrange them in our hands, going forward with a conscious balance of understanding and not understanding.

## Regular Features of the Language of the Unconscious

BESIDES ITS USE OF SYMBOLS there are other definable characteristics of the language of the unconscious. One of these is the frequent use of *analogy*. The unconscious often says to us in effect, "It is as if——." I had a dream like this one night, for example, after I had been tossing and turning, sleeping fitfully, vaguely aware that something was trying to come into my dreams that could not get in. Finally I awakened a little and said to God, "What is this? What do you want me to understand?" Then I slept again and dreamed:

> *My husband had a groundskeeper working for him to whom he gave a mail-order item that had just arrived, some kind of gardening equipment. My husband asked*

*him not to open the package yet, for there was a similar item coming later and the man would need to choose which one of these he wanted to keep.*

*As my husband was telling him this, the groundskeeper proceeded to open the package. My husband again asked him to wait, explaining that the item coming later would have with it neither packaging material nor an invoice and that if this present one were chosen over that later one, this packaging material and invoice would be needed to send the other one back.*

*The man kept on as if nothing were being said to him. My husband got angry and raised his voice and then angrier still as the man continued to ignore him. The growing intensity of anger awakened me, and I felt shaken.*

As I collected myself and felt around for the place in my life where this dream fit, I realized it had nothing to do with my actual husband. I knew it was pointing out that I had failed to listen to a dream that had come to me the night before. I had not allowed that dream to change my conscious attitude. This current dream was saying: *It is as if* you are this groundskeeper and God is your employer trying to give you directions to which you are not listening. The dream took the form of a parable and even used the imagery of biblical parables in which God is shown as the master of an estate and we as His workers. Upon seeing this picture of my stubbornness, I submitted to the message of the previous night and let go of some feelings I had been holding close concerning something in my outer life. After that I slept peacefully for the rest of the night.

The unconscious also frequently uses *plays on words* to get its messages across. A dream of someone named Hightower, for example, might have more to do with a haughty attitude or with being too much up in one's head than with any particular characteristics of the person in the dream. We can never be sure where the meaning will be found. In each case we have to try out all possibilities—personal associations, symbol and metaphor, analogy, plays on words—until something "clicks."

The unconscious uses *repetition* to signal importance and to construct themes. If a dream is repeated, we know it is of special significance. Sometimes a particular dream is repeated from time to time throughout a person's life until he or she finally understands the issues that lie at the heart of it. Once a dream has been truly understood, it will not come back again, unless there has been a regression.

Life events will also repeat themselves until we get their message. A person might, for example, find himself involved in repeated minor auto accidents for which he is not at fault. When the first event happens he might not think to look beneath the surface of events. But if a second one occurs soon after, he should know that something serious is going on and that he should look around in his life for someone who is "not in control of his vehicle." There might, for instance, be someone in his current life from whom he needs to distance himself. Or he might look at where he was going when these mishaps occurred. Was he straying unwittingly from the safety of his true path? The repetition means that it is important for him to wake up to a danger that is threatening the integrity of his life.

The unconscious relates to us over time by constructing *themes* through repeated motifs. This happens regularly in dreams, but it also happens in outer life through synchronicity. I might be driving along a country road, for example, and see a cow that has gotten out of its pasture. That would be interesting but not necessarily thought-provoking. If later in the day, however, I ask for directions and am told to go to the Brown Cow Dairy and turn left, my antennae would begin to go up. And if that night I find myself drawn into a conversation about the sacredness of the cow in Hindu religion, I would know I have a theme going. I would at least give some thought to the symbolic meaning of "the cow" and wonder what part of my life this theme might be addressing. Then I would stay tuned for further developments both in my dreams and in outer life. The theme might last only a day or it might go on for weeks. And if I did not draw from it everything that pertained to me, it would eventually come around again.

At any one time we have several related themes threading their way through our sleeping and waking lives. Every theme common to humankind comes to us at one time or another, although some are more central to our individual lives than others. Some of the many possible themes a person might be dealing with at any particular time are: balancing the high and the low; finding one's vocation; relating in a conscious and balanced way to mother energy or father energy; accepting old age; realizing the spiritual value of being at home without working; accepting the authority of the unconscious; letting go of power; coming down to earth to accept responsible adulthood; healing relationship wounds; accepting the true nature of the masculine or feminine principle; letting go of hands-on parenthood; and so on.

Most themes stay with us for a few weeks or months. As they go out, new ones come in, and all eventually come around again. If we are learning the lessons they offer, their continual cycling through our lives will be a spiral toward the God-center within us, each return bringing a new and deeper level of integration and understanding. Each time a theme comes around, we will feel ourselves in better balance than before, more conscious of what it is all about, and more accepting of the shape of our individual lives. When a person is not learning his lessons, his themes will repeat themselves, unchanged, in an endless circle, and each episode of life will only be more of the same old story, going nowhere.

Because the unconscious is a part of nature, *cycles* are intrinsic to its expression. We each have personal yearly cycles, whether we are aware of them or not. Dramatic events bring this to consciousness, as in the inevitable psychic disturbances a person experiences on the anniversary of an important death or a divorce. But you can also see a less obvious personal cycle if at some random time you look back in your journal, if you keep one, to see what themes you were working on at the same time the year before. Usually you will find that at least some of those themes have come around again a year later. Another personal cycle that can often be seen is the nine-month gestation period. If you look back at what happened nine months before an important new development, you often find a noteworthy event in which, through some sort of word, action, or realization of truth, you committed yourself to new life.

The unconscious also resonates with the great impersonal cycles under which we live, both natural and cultural. Thus we will find our themes tied to the natural seasons of the year, to national holidays, and to the Church calendar. It is good to keep an eye on the many strands of your unfolding story as special days and seasons come around. There is often more being taught to you than you might imagine about the deep meaning in your individual life of springtime, Independence Day, Halloween, or Christmas. Sometimes a person dreams that it is Christmas in July or Lent in November, telling him that regardless of what is going on for everyone else, the Christ has just been born in him anew or a season of sober introspection is upon him.

The language of the unconscious is the language of mythology and fairytales, of religious rituals and of music, of color and of number, of kinship, friendship, and enmity, of food, of body and sexuality, of plants and animals, of heaven and earth. It is a universal language, common to all mankind. And yet, while our souls always know it by nature, our minds do not, and the more highly developed one's mind, the more estranged a person tends to become from his or her soul and its natural language.

Primitive people had the advantage of a more direct knowledge of the language and wisdom of the unconscious, not because they were more conscious than we are but because they were less conscious and therefore more at one with the unconscious. Despite the romantic yearning we sometimes have to be like them, we can never go back to a less conscious state without bringing harm to ourselves, just as we cannot return to childhood or adolescence or young adulthood once we have grown past those stages of life.

Embracing the outer trappings of primitive life and religion, therefore, will not remedy a person's estrangement from the language of his or her soul. The only viable remedy in our time is to make a conscious effort to learn to understand the language of the unconscious in its modern context of dreams and synchronicity, or meaningful coincidence. In this way a person can open himself or herself to the vitality, healthy wholeness, and natural wisdom of primeval humanity while at the same time remaining true to his or her own reality as a modern person rooted in a several-thousand-year development of religious and scientific understanding.

# CHAPTER SIX

# *Dreams*

*The dream is often occupied with apparently very silly details, thus producing an impression of absurdity, or else it is on the surface so unintelligible as to leave us thoroughly bewildered. Hence we always have to overcome a certain resistance before we can seriously set about disentangling the intricate web through patient work. But when at last we penetrate to its real meaning, we find ourselves deep in the dreamer's secrets and discover with astonishment that an apparently quite senseless dream is in the highest degree significant, and that in reality it speaks only of important and serious matters.*

CARL JUNG

THE FULLEST EXPRESSION of the unconscious comes to us through our dreams, and for this reason the interpretation of dreams is a central element of natural spirituality. Unless a person learns to interpret his own dreams, he cannot receive the full benefit of the individuation process. Put another way, unless he learns to interpret his own dreams, he cannot listen with a fully open ear to what God is trying to tell him in his life.

The idea that full attention to God includes the interpretation of dreams is strongly supported by many scriptural passages throughout the Bible. One of the most dramatic examples is found at the beginning of the Gospel of Matthew. In the first forty-eight verses of this first book of the New Testament, five different dreams are recounted, each one crucial to the survival and protection of the Christ child. Four of these dreams came to Joseph and one to the Wise Men.

The first chapter opens with a lengthy recital of the ancestry of Jesus, after which we are taken straight to Joseph's plight in learning that Mary, his betrothed, was with child. Joseph was an upright man and did not want to disgrace Mary publicly through the legal procedure of nullifying the betrothal, and so he decided to end their relationship informally. "He had made up his mind to do this," Matthew tells us,

> when the angel of the Lord appeared to him in a dream and said, "Joseph son of David, do not be afraid to take Mary home as your wife, because she has conceived what is in her by the Holy Spirit. She will give birth to a son and you must name him Jesus ['Yahweh Saves']. . . ." When Joseph woke up he did what the angel of the Lord had told him to do: he took his wife to his home and, though he had not had intercourse with her, she gave birth to a son; and he named him Jesus.

Matthew then moves directly to the story of the Wise Men who came to Jerusalem looking for the new "king of the Jews," having seen his star rise in the sky. Pretending a religious interest, King Herod directed the Wise Men to Bethlehem, the prophesied birthplace, and asked them to revisit him on their way home and let him know exactly where the child could be found. The Wise Men went to Bethlehem, found the Christ child, and offered him their gifts.

> But they were warned in a dream not to go back to Herod, and returned to their country by a different way. After they had left, the angel of the Lord appeared to Joseph in a dream and said, "Get up, take the child and his mother with you, and escape into Egypt, and stay there until I tell you, because Herod intends to search for the child and do away with him." So Joseph got up and, taking the child and his mother with him, left that night for Egypt, where he stayed until Herod was dead.

Matthew goes on to tell about the Slaughter of the Innocents. And then:

> After Herod's death, the angel of the Lord appeared in a dream to Joseph in Egypt and said, "Get up, take the child and his mother with you and go back to the land of Israel, for those who wanted to kill the child are dead." So Joseph got up and, taking the child and his mother with him, went back to the land of Israel. But when he learned that Archelaus had succeeded his father Herod as ruler of

Judea he was afraid to go there, and being warned in a dream he left for the region of Galilee. There he settled in a town called Nazareth.

Matthew's nativity story turns almost entirely upon dreams. It shows Joseph as a man who had deep trust in the divine nature of his dreams and a remarkable willingness to respond to them. For persons today who have not learned to work with their dreams, this story might seem incredible or fanciful, a quaint way the ancients had of talking about the discernment of God's will. But for those of us who pay close attention to our dreams, Joseph's experience is entirely credible. We, too, are taught and closely led by our dreams. We, too, change our attitudes and alter our paths and take unexpected actions because of the guidance that comes to us in the night. We know what the writer of the Sixteenth Psalm was saying when he wrote, "I bless Yahweh, who is my counselor, and in the night my inmost self instructs me." And we know what Carl Jung meant when he said, "Every night a Eucharist."

Dreams offer us daily instruction, guidance, and illumination for the unique individuals that we are. They address our particular circumstances and help us understand ourselves and God through the metaphors of our own life experience. Dreams show us our truth as it really is—not as our minds think it should be nor as our hearts would like it to be, but *as it truly is.* To walk hand in hand with our dreams is to walk with the Spirit of truth, with an understanding that comes to us directly from the realm of the living God.

With this in mind you may say with all good intention that you do wish to pay attention to your dreams. And yet there is a powerful force in you—always in everyone—that is highly resistant to discovering the real truth of your life. Your mind will not want to give up its own ideas of how things are. Your heart will not want to give up its own insistence on what is good. This force of unconsciousness will often keep you from being able to remember your dreams; or if you remember them, it will make you feel too busy to write them down; or if you write them down, it may keep you from putting your mind to analyzing them; or if you analyze them, it might make you see them in the wrong terms and miss their meaning. No one is ever free of this resistance to truth, but as a person grows in consciousness, its power weakens and its tricks are more easily recognized.

## Remembering and Recording Dreams

IT IS EASY TO DREAM, but it is not so easy to know what to do with your dreams. I myself have been following my dreams day by day for more than fifteen years, having learned on my own how to interpret them. Besides relying on the natural gift for interpretation that comes with my strong intuitive function, I gathered insight and understanding about the language of dreams by reading deeply and widely in the writings of Carl Jung and of Jungian analysts. For the past eight years I have helped others analyze their dreams in the context of our church's Natural Spirituality Program. From this wider experience I have learned much about what is required for a person to awaken to his or her dream life and to begin to deal with dreams in a constructive way.

The first challenge in working with your dreams is to remember them. For some people this is no problem, but for others it is, especially for individuals who are strongly extraverted. One has only so much energy available for life, and if most of it is going into outer activities, there will not be much left to activate and illuminate the inner world. Usually, however, when you consciously turn your attention toward the dream world, you will begin to remember your dreams. Talking about dreams, reading about them, writing them down, and, if possible, participating regularly in a dream group, will almost always bring dreams to consciousness, although the amount of dream material recalled will vary from person to person.

Some people do well to remember one dream a week, while others regularly remember several dreams from each night. Most of us also experience variation in dream recall in different periods in our lives. A time of trauma and transition can bring heavy dream activity, while a dramatic swing toward outer life involvement can cause the dream world to recede into darkness.

Assuming that you do remember at least some of your dreams, the next question is, what to do with them? The first thing you must do is gather them up as you awaken, and for this there must be time allowed between waking up and getting out of bed. Most dream material slips away very quickly. Outer life activity, even simple tasks like making coffee, will usually dispel it. To counter this, you must lie quietly in bed and gather up what threads and fragments you can catch and go over any story lines you can recall. Conscious thought helps solidify the material and hold it, although much of this will soon be lost if you do not then write it down.

It is very good, therefore, to allow further time in the morning for recording your dreams. This can be done after you have made your coffee or even later in the day, although the more time that goes by, the more details will be lost and the more the mood of the dream will fade.

Setting aside time in the morning for dream work has the same value as taking time for prayer and meditation. I once dreamed about Dame Julian of Norwich, the fourteenth-century anchoress who left us her beautiful mystical writings. I dreamed that if she were alive today, she would not live out her spirituality in the same way she did in her day but would live closely with her dreams in a modern way.

Most people keep a separate dream journal, although others record dreams along with other journal material. While it is useful to note down associations you have with the motifs and moods of a dream, it is generally not a good idea to record your interpretations, at least not at length. Initial interpretations are almost always inadequate, and writing them down tends to freeze them, whereas if you carry them along in your mind, you can continue to work with them and readjust them to new insights. Furthermore, while it is very useful to go back from time to time and read through old dreams, it is not very rewarding to wade through the tedious windings and twistings of old interpretations. Old dreams are like old gems, sparkling and valuable, carrying an abiding truth that you can often see more clearly as time goes on. But if they are buried in outdated musings from the past, you will be less likely to want to return to them.

It is essential to index your dreams so that you can later go back and look up specific ones. Sometimes in outer life you will encounter elements that you have dreamed about earlier, sometimes years earlier, and you will want to go back and read that dream again. Often you will have a dream that reminds you of one from the past and you will want to compare the two. Or you might want to refresh your memory about an insight that once came to you in a dream. It is very hard to find a particular dream without an index. I myself use the last few pages of my journal for this. After recording a dream, I turn to the back and list the date under which I have written and note the key motifs of the dream. It is easy at a later time to scan the index and find the dream I am looking for. Some people give titles to their dreams and use these in their index.

In writing down your dreams, you will encounter the problem of how much to write. You may, for example, get more dream material than you can deal with in a practical way. A night of dreaming is like a net full of fish: you must take what you can use and throw back the rest. Even material you do not consciously process does a certain amount of work in you unconsciously. And anything you miss that you really need will come around again, usually in a different form.

If it has been a night of hazy, jumbled dreaming, you should gather up the fragments that you remember most clearly—the most vivid images, the strongest emotions, the most troubling scenes, or the most impressive ones. Often a small fragment yields great meaning all by itself, even when you know it was surrounded by an entire night of dreaming that can no longer be recalled. I always assume that I remember what the unconscious wants me to remember, and if it is only a fragment, it is because that was the most important message of the night.

Sometimes, on the other hand, a person can recall endless details that would keep him or her writing for hours, none of it adding up to much of anything except a picture of confusion and lack of focus. If this is your problem, you can help bring focus to such chaotic dreaming by foregoing the many details and looking instead for what the overall theme might be. You should try to feel what part of your life the whole night of dreaming pertains to. You might also select a few of the more vivid details and look closely at those, while ignoring the rest. If you can pull out a thread from an overloaded dream, the next dream might respond to your increase in focus by being more focused itself.

Some dreams feel like big dreams. They come to us with vividness and energy and powerful emotion, sometimes with archetypal material strongly present. These dreams should be reviewed in every detail and thoroughly pondered, although their full meaning may not become entirely clear for weeks, months, or even years to come. If possible they should be written down with all details included. Their energy means that they are important. The biggest of our big dreams are those I call "flag-ship" dreams. They project the progress of our lives forward for the next year or so, sometimes for the next several years, and in some cases for an even longer span. You are especially likely to get far-reaching flagship dreams when you first begin to pay attention to the unconscious.

There is a discernable difference between these big dreams, on the one hand, and the smaller dreams that lead us day by day through the personal developments the big dreams have projected. Smaller dreams feel less im-portant. Their energy is weaker and they seem to have to do with ordinary daily activity. These you can think through quickly when you awaken, focusing on their stronger points and taking what bits of meaning you find in them. They will add to your understanding of what is currently going on in your life and give hints and guidance for the immediate future. Generally, if you feel unsettled by a dream, it needs more thought, but if you feel at peace about your understanding of it, you can let it go.

Whether or not you record all of your smaller dreams depends on your inclination and on how much time you have. You can always see more in a dream when you write it down, and ideally you should record every dream you can remember. But on the other hand, you must balance your dream work with the legitimate demands of outer life. There is not always time to wring out the last drop of meaning. One can get just as much off balance toward too much inner life as toward too much outer life. There are even times when you may need to restore the balance toward outer life by foregoing your dream journal altogether for a while. At two different points in my own journey I have found it necessary to stop writing down my dreams for rather long periods of time. But even then, I never ceased to think about them every morning and to take what guidance I could from them, and I can still remember many of the dreams that I never recorded.

## Interpreting Dreams

THE NEXT STEP in dream work is interpretation. Because our dreams are always just a little bit ahead of our consciousness, interpretation is never easy. Many people throw up their hands and assume they lack the knowledge and expertise to do it, but dreaming is a natural process that belongs to every human life. No stethoscope or x-ray equipment is needed to perceive its activity. It is an integral part of us, and that means there is something in us that knows how to respond to it at some level. Just as a person with even the most minimal musical ability can listen to music and derive some enrichment from it, so can even the least gifted dream interpreter gain something from his or her dreams. Therefore you should approach your dreams with confidence. The fact is that no other person, however highly trained, can ever understand a dream as well as it can potentially be understood by the one who dreamed it. Your dreams use your own language to talk about your own life in terms best suited to your own particular consciousness.

What gets in the way of the dreamer's understanding is the resistance that comes from that very state of consciousness that is being addressed. Dreams are always seeking to make an adjustment in the way you understand things, and this requires from you a constant sacrifice of some aspect or another of your personal sense of reality. It is here that a religious attitude can be of more value than an advanced degree in psychology. The more willing you are to enter into the real give-and-take of a dialogue with God, the more successful you will be in interpreting your dreams. The more dedicated you are to the triumph of your own ego's point of view, the more likely you are to misinterpret your dreams or to see nothing in them at all.

This is not, however, an either/or situation. There are times when your ego needs to win at the expense of the view from the unconscious. The strength and health of ego consciousness is the most important factor of all in the total balance of your psyche, for without the ego you cannot function in the world. The ego needs to try to understand and accommodate the unconscious, and it needs to have a willingness to sacrifice its cherished illusions, desires, and outworn truths when it sees that it must do so. But it must proceed with this at its own pace if it is not to crumple and be overrun by the potentially overwhelming power of the unconscious.

This is why it is not important that you understand everything a dream is offering. Sometimes you can handle a lot from the unconscious and other times you can handle only a little. What is important is that you start trying to understand your dreams *as best you can.* When you make this effort, your dreams respond to it by addressing themselves to your developing understanding.

The first rule of thumb in dream interpretation is that the dream is almost always a picture of your own personal truth. You look at the setting of the dream and ask, "What part of myself does this dream address?" If the setting is at the place where you work, the dream may be about your working self. As with all the examples given here, it may be about something else, the situation at work perhaps being an analogy for a problem in some other realm of your life. You will always have to feel around for the arena of life to which the dream belongs. It makes sense, however, to start with the most obvious possibility.

With that caveat, it can be said that if a dream is set in a city, it may be about your higher, cultural self. A natural setting suggests your earthier, instinctual self. A setting in a church is likely to be about an aspect of your spiritual self. A member of our church's dream group was dreaming of being in a hotel when, in the midst of the dream, she was explicitly instructed by the dream itself that a hotel symbolizes a situation in life that is temporary, a condition in which we live for a short time and then move on.

I myself often dream of being in a vacation house by a body of water. The houses and the bodies of water vary and are seldom the same as any I have known in outer life. For a long time I had only a vague sense of the part of my life to which this setting referred, but then one night, while dreaming, the meaning clarified itself:

> *I dreamed again about a waterside vacation house. While I was dreaming, I understood more than I ever have before that this is the theme of the family side of myself, that when you are on vacation you are in your family side, and when you are in your family side, you are on vacation. I also dreamed about my hometown and my childhood, and I understood that this, too, refers to my family side. I sensed the distinctive reality of the family side, as opposed to the work and achievement side.*

The question you must always ask about the setting, and about every aspect of the dream, is: "What do I associate with this?" And then you must listen carefully to your answer. The process of dream interpretation is very much like solving a mystery. Clues are given that must be sorted out, and some of the best clues come from your associations. You might say, "The setting reminds me of a scene from a show I just saw on television about a mother whose teenage daughter ran away." Or, "It was the town we lived in when we first married." Or, "This place makes me think of the underground house where Peter Pan and the Lost Boys lived."

These associations are clues for you to follow. With the first example you would go on to ask what part of your life is like that mother whose daughter ran away? Are you having actual, outer-life difficulty with a teenage daughter? Or is there an inner problem with your youthful feminine energy? What does the dream say about this problem? It is important always to come back to the dream rather than move away from it through a chain of associations.

In the second example your attention would be drawn to the person you were when you first married. Is the dream saying that in some way you are still that person, that a part of yourself has not adapted to new times and circumstances? Or perhaps it is saying that some present situation is like a new marriage for you.

In the third example you would look to see what the dream might be saying about a part of yourself that, like Peter Pan, does not want to grow up. And you would ponder what it means to make your home beneath the earth.

Sometimes it is the association we make with the mood of the dream rather than with the setting that tells us what the dream is about. When you feel that the mood of the dream somehow fits a situation in outer life, then that may be the part of your life that the dream is addressing.

In always coming back to the dream from your associations, you are asking what the dream images themselves have to say to you about that arena of your life that is being addressed. Is the vacation house shabby and rundown? This would suggest that your family side does not have much "money," which symbolizes psychic energy. Are you lost in the hotel? This would indicate that your temporary situation is so unfamiliar that it has put you into a state of confusion. A dream I once had suggested I was in danger because the church I was attending lacked a basement. I took that to refer to a collective spiritual situation that could be harmful to my spiritual self because it lacked roots in tradition and openness to the unconscious.

This same process of discovery must also be applied to the characters, both human and animal, who appear in your dreams. If you dream of a dog, for instance, what kind of dog is it, and what does that kind of dog suggest to you? Is it a dog you know, and if so, what do you associate with that particular dog? If you dream of a bear, what do you personally associate with bears? What do dogs or bears symbolize in a general way? And then, coming back to the dream, what does the dream tell you about this dog or this bear? With a dream animal you can always say at least that you are being told something about your instincts.

With human characters the situation is more complex. When you dream about someone you know but with whom you are not in day-to-day relationship, you can almost always be certain that you are dreaming about some part of yourself that this person represents. This is true even when the person is your sibling, parent, or child. To find out what part of yourself this is, you ask, "What do I associate with this person? What are his or her defining characteristics? What does he or she represent to me?" Then look for similar qualities in yourself.

It is more confusing when you dream about someone with whom you are in active, daily relationship. Is it a part of yourself you are dreaming about, or is it rather that you are being told something about this actual person that you need to understand? Often our dreams do help us see the people in our lives more clearly, but even more often a dream is primarily about ourselves—our own mothering part, our own son aspect, our own intellectual self, our overbearing self, whatever that person represents. When a person you dream about is very close to you in outer life, it is especially difficult to see what he or she represents symbolically and to see that the dream is about a quality in yourself and not about that other person.

This question of inner meaning or outer meaning is one of the greatest areas of ambiguity in dream interpretation. Jung suggests that when the dream is about the people and places of our everyday life, we should try first to interpret it as if it had objective, or outer, meaning. If this fits and seems to click, then we can accept the likelihood of objective meaning, although we should reflect further on the dream to see if it also applies to an aspect of ourselves. But if the interpretation does not fit the outer situation, if the objective meaning does not square with reality, then we should look for a primarily subjective, or inner, meaning.

Sometimes we dream we are with "another person" without knowing who that person is. An unknown person in a dream refers to a part of ourselves of which we are not yet fully conscious. Usually we know whether the unknown person is male or female, and that in itself makes an important distinction about the part of ourselves to which the dream refers. Any person in a dream, whether known or unknown, who is of our same sex can be seen as a part of our shadow, which is to say it is an aspect of our outer personality of which we are not entirely conscious. A person of the opposite sex, on the other hand, refers to a contrasexual aspect of our inner selves that completes us as whole human beings.

## Anima and Animus

CARL JUNG understood that every man has a feminine component in his psyche and every woman has a masculine component in hers, just as in the physiological realm each sex carries a minority component of the opposite sex. He called the feminine part of a man's psyche his *anima*, or soul. The realm of the anima is the life of body and soul rather than the life of mind and spirit. A man's feminine component is present when he relates to other people, when he experiences his emotions and feelings, when he tends the limited, everyday reality of physical life, and when he is receptive to the wisdom of nature, including the unconscious.

If he relates poorly to people, if resentment, rage, and sentimentality are his predominant emotions, if he neglects the real in his pursuit of the ideal, if he tramples what is natural and ignores the unconscious, then he will have feminine figures in his dreams—anima images—who have unpleasant characteristics. They may, for example, be dangerously seductive, or blatantly hostile, or perhaps sickly or abused. The parts of a man's feminine self that are more conscious and well-developed will appear in his dreams as positive feminine figures. When an anima figure is an unknown woman, she symbolizes a part of a man's inner, feminine self that he does not yet know. When the dream figure is someone he knows, she represents an aspect of his feminine side of which he already has some consciousness.

Jung called a woman's masculine side her *animus,* or spirit. The animus presides over the life of mind and spirit rather than the life of body and soul. When a woman is speaking her mind or is inspired to action, her animus is present. When she organizes and focuses, when she appeals to high principles, when she reads, writes, and masters objective information, and when she is creatively or religiously inspired, she is experiencing her masculine side. Her animus is also present when she breaks relationship or keeps others at a distance.

If a woman misses the point when she speaks her mind or digresses interminably, if she is generally disorganized and unfocused, if she is rigidly devoted to political, intellectual, or spiritual principles, if she is seduced away from genuine, grounded life by the lure of an intellectual, spiritual, or creative activity that arises from the collective spirit and thus is not truly her own, or if she breaks relationship destructively or alienates other people unconsciously, there will be unpleasant masculine figures in her dreams who reflect these dark aspects of her animus. The healthy and positive manifestations of her masculine spirit will be portrayed in her dreams by friendly, helpful, and sometimes loving animus figures. Unknown masculine figures will symbolize parts of her animus of which she is unconscious, while those parts with which she has some familiarity will appear in her dreams as male persons whom she knows.

It is important to keep in mind that our experience of the opposite sex is an experience of "the other," which at a deep level symbolizes our relationship with the unconscious, and through that our connection to God. Sexuality, therefore, with all its fascination and power, is linked to our experience of God. This is a difficult fact that wreaks havoc with human life when it is not properly understood. When we are young, the pull of sexuality and romantic love serves the positive purpose of entangling us in life. For the sake of the warmth and comfort of intimate human love, we risk ourselves and make decisions and commitments that establish us, however tenuously, as adult participants in the real world. Even more importantly, a close connection with the opposite sex gives us a preliminary version of a completeness and fulfillment that we are not yet ready to find wholly within ourselves.

Later in life, however, this same sexual energy can have a destructive effect when we take it to mean exactly the same thing that it meant when it came to us in our youth. The pull toward a person of the opposite sex is not always a pull toward sexual and romantic union in the outer world. It is often a pull toward a deeper level of relationship with God.

The image of woman is the image of soul for a man, and when he feels powerfully attracted to a woman, it is at some level a projection of his own soul that draws him. That woman has qualities that reflect the qualities of his soul and that need to be realized within himself. He can come closer to them by relating to her in a positive way, but he cannot make them his own by physically possessing her. Those projected qualities can only come to life within him when he accepts the painful fact that he cannot have them in the form of another person. This sacrifice of outer, physical fulfillment opens the door to a deeper, more spiritual level of relationship to the feminine within, which leads toward human wholeness and oneness with God. The same is true for a woman, who unconsciously projects her own spirit onto the man to whom she is romantically and sexually attracted. He has attributes that ultimately need to be realized in the depths of her own being.

This basic understanding of the underlying spiritual reality of our experience of the opposite sex is necessary if we are to handle wisely the images and feelings of sexuality and love that sometimes come in dreams as well as in waking life. Is it the real person to whom you are being drawn, or is it a part of yourself? If human warmth and companionship are lacking in your life and if the person to whom you are attracted is available and suitable, the feelings and images arising from the unconscious may have as their true goal an outer-life relationship, possibly a romantic one. But it is just as likely that you are simply being invited to know and love a part of your inner being that wants to become a part of your consciousness.

Everything that belongs in us is first projected out onto the world around us—we always have to see it there before we can see it in ourselves.

This means that every new aspect of your anima or animus has to be met initially in a projection onto a person of the opposite sex. It is important to keep this in mind when you awaken from a dream of a sexual or loving encounter with someone you know but with whom you do not have an actual intimate relationship. As you lie there in the warm glow of feeling that has been stirred by the dream, you must remember to ask yourself, "What does this person represent?"

## The Structure of Dream Life

ALL THE IMAGES in a dream are important, not just the setting and the characters. The unconscious is very careful with its language. Each image is specially chosen for the nuance of meaning that it carries. It is important, therefore, to pay attention to the inanimate objects in a dream, especially the ones that remain vivid in your memory. Just as with the other components, these should be pondered for your personal associations with them and also for their general symbolic significance. You must ask: What does that bracelet remind me of? Whose car was that we were in? Where have I seen a table like that? What do bracelets, cars, or tables represent in a general way? Sometimes the key to a dream is in a seemingly insignificant object or detail that you might be tempted to let go unexamined.

Dreams are not individual and unrelated. All the dreams of one night usually belong together as different views of the same subject. Dreams on successive nights form a sequence, one dream leading to the next. When you are baffled by a dream and have done all you can with it, you can let it go knowing that clarification will be coming to you in the dreams ahead, as well as in the developments of waking life.

Dream sequences form cycles that vary in duration, usually lasting for several months. You will become aware of these cycles once you have learned to work with your dreams. In the beginning of a cycle your dreams will be murky, dim, and somewhat chaotic, their settings and the people in them will tend to be unfamiliar, and you will not be able to remember much about them when you awaken. In waking life you might feel vaguely out of sorts, a bit unfocused and unsure of what you are about.

Then gradually life will begin to sort itself out. Your dreams will become a little clearer and you will begin to recognize their themes. There will be interaction between dream life and waking life—they will work together to develop your themes and to bring to you the new understandings of this present chapter of your life. As your dreams grow in clarity, life will develop in decisive ways. Often the new understandings will culminate in a dream that lays out a relatively explicit picture of what you have come through and what you have learned. I call these "summary" dreams. There will also be events in outer life that add to the feeling that you have come through to something new.

Then for a few days, at most, you will feel at peace. Life will be in balance. These little respites that come between cycles remind me of how the hobbit heros in Tolkein's *Lord of the Rings* were always given brief interludes of rest, feasting, and singing in the mystical safety of elven glens after each stage of their harrowing adventure. Like the hobbits, we are never allowed to linger in this restful place for very long. Before we know it, another cycle has started. Once more our dreams are dark and murky and our life feels somewhat out of joint as the next phase in our journey begins to take shape.

## Giving Dreams Their Proper Weight

As you take up the task of paying attention to your dreams, you must go through a process of learning just how much weight to give them. It usually requires several years to work this out. Those persons who identify very strongly with consciousness and outer life will at first give their dreams too little weight. They will use "nothing but" statements in regard to them: "This dream was nothing but me dreaming about some things that happened the day before." Or, "It was nothing but me worrying about my situation at work." Or, "That dream of someone knocking was nothing but the shade bumping against the window." This is a very common attitude in the beginning.

When you do this, you are interpreting your dreams as if they can only complement or support what you already know. Having not yet truly accepted the fact that it is possible for dreams to bring you new information, let alone that this is their main function, you fail to ask, "What is the compensatory purpose of this dream? What does it tell me that I do not already know?"

It is also symptomatic of undervaluing dreams when people go to the trouble of recording their dreams and yet can never make heads or tails of them, or when they pay attention to their dreams for a while, but then turn away for a long period and reimmerse themselves completely in outer life. They have not yet had enough experience with their inner life to realize that it is worth the effort to learn its language and to keep up with it every day.

Other people begin dream work off balance in the other direction. They identify especially strongly with the unconscious and give too much weight to their dreams. Often they try to use their dreams as power tools to know the future or to engineer outer events. On the basis of a dream, for instance, a person might call up an acquaintance and say, "I dreamed about you last night. I think that means we need to get together." In fact the dream probably had nothing to do with that other person but was all about the dreamer himself. This arranged meeting, therefore, will likely be empty of any real meaning and purpose and will probably strike the other person as somewhat weird.

People who give too much weight to their dreams have to learn that life proceeds from life, not from dreams. Life has it own reality, with one real moment leading to the next. Dreams do their work on the inside, beneath the surface, helping us understand things more clearly, giving us hints and helpful leads. It is wonderful that we have these marvelous communications from the unconscious, but when it comes to integrating them into life, they are merely factors to be considered, additional aspects to be weighed in and measured against our actual experience of life.

If life opens to what you think a dream is saying, then you can go with it, cautiously. But if life is resistant, it may be because you are not seeing the dream clearly. Or it may be that you do see a truth clearly but that the world around you is not ready to accept that truth. There is nothing you can do about this. You cannot use your dreams as weapons to badger other people into seeing what you see. That never works and will only bring you trouble. Life proceeds from life and no other way. A person in touch with his dreams has to learn to walk silently at times as the only one who sees certain realities beneath the surface of his shared life with others.

As for the value of dreams in foretelling the future, it is true that dreams are oriented primarily toward life that is unfolding. What they tell us, however, is the *essence* of what is coming, not how that essence will be made manifest. Dreams of death and of weddings, for example, are usually about inner, psychological developments, although occasionally they are about actual outer-life realities. The problem is that much the same symbolism is used in either case. It is tempting to say, "I know from my dreams that so and so is going to happen." But after a while we learn that we can never be sure what is actually going to happen in outer life, even though we can get some sense from our dreams about the spirit or underlying truth of what is coming.

Some dreams about the future are warning dreams. The essence they show is not what necessarily *will* be but what *could* be if we fail to grasp the reality of our situation. Many dreams are not about the future at all but about what is happening now. Others are about what has already taken place, sometimes in the recent past, sometimes in the distant past. Still others give us a picture of what we fear to be true in order to help us see that it is not true. We awaken from these with our hearts pounding, thinking, "There! It is just as I feared!" But as we try to line ourselves up with the picture the dream has given us, we begin to realize it does not fit the reality of our situation. The picture in the dream is *not true.* Our fears are *not true.* The dream has objectified them for us so that we can see them clearly and measure them against reality.

## A Supporting Context for Dream Work

THERE IS NO EASY FORMULA for understanding dreams. Some people have a greater gift for it than others. Anyone who is serious about his dreamlife, however, whether he is especially gifted or not, needs to do extensive reading in Jungian psychology, a field in which much has been written for laypeople. The source list in Appendix A is offered as a starting place for this.

It is also important to have an interested person with whom to talk about your dreams, even if that person does not understand very much. Telling a dream to someone else does something to illuminate it, whether the other person has anything helpful to say about it or not. It is as if in the presence of another consciousness, your own consciousness can more easily expand and open itself to intuitive insight.

Where it is feasible, a weekly dream group can be of great value in keeping you focused on your dreamlife and in giving you help in interpreting your dreams. Others in the group can often show you your blind spots. And by listening to the dreams of others, you will learn more than you otherwise would about dream interpretation and the universal themes of human growth.

The value of other people when working on our dreams has in it something of what Christ meant when he said that wherever two or three are gathered together in his name, he will be there. The Holy Spirit plays a large role in dream interpretation, provided we go about it with a religious attitude, aware that dreams come from God and have to do with the fulfillment of the life God intends for us, which is not necessarily the same life we initially have in mind for ourselves. When that is the spirit in which we are discussing a dream, insights almost always come to the surface once we begin to make our associations with its images. It is for this reason that the best context for a weekly dream group is in a church rather than a private home or some other secular setting.

I am continually amazed at the process through which clarity arises from even the most puzzling of dreams. Often when a person tells me a dream, he or she has no idea of what it means, and when I hear it, I also have no idea. I wonder to myself how we will ever find anything in it. But then we begin to talk about it. We start at the beginning and look at the setting or the opening situation. What are the dreamer's associations? What does the dream situation say symbolically? Then we look at the characters and the other striking images. We talk about these, and before we know it an element of the dreamer's life has come to the fore and we are beginning to grasp something of what the dream might be saying about it.

We keep talking, looking at the dream this way and that, always paying attention to what the dreamer himself is saying. The elements of the dream lead the dreamer to talk about his life in words that are significant. The way the dream unfolds suggests connections and underlying realities that begin to coalesce for us. Then finally comes the "Aha!" moment when the dreamer feels we have found the key. An important insight "clicks," and he feels satisfied that yes, this is what this dream is saying, now he has seen something that helps. It does not matter whether he has gotten from the dream all that someone else might have gotten. He has gotten from it what he was able to get, and the unconscious can work with that and build on it in future dreams.

This is typically how it goes when we work with our dreams, whether we ponder them alone or talk them over with others. Our penetration into the meaning does not depend solely on human skill and knowledge. The message of the dream comes from the realm of God, and the Holy Spirit participates in our understanding of it. It is necessary that we apply ourselves and do our part in working with our dreams, but in the end it is grace working in us that makes the difference and helps us arrive at those insights that we are ready to receive.

CHAPTER SEVEN

# *Synchronicity*

*Since psyche and matter are contained in one and the same world and moreover are in continuous contact with one another and ultimately rest on irrepresentable, transcendental factors, it is not only possible but fairly probable, even, that psyche and matter are two different aspects of one and the same thing. The synchronicity phenomena point, it seems to me, in this direction, for they show that the nonpsychic can behave like the psychic, and vice versa, without there being any causal connection between them.*

CARL JUNG

I DID NOT LEARN about synchronicity from Carl Jung. I learned the *term* from him, but the natural reality to which it refers is something I first discovered for myself. This was not an intentional discovery. It never would have occurred to me to look for a manifestation of meaning in the natural world. Rather, the realization of synchronicity forced itself upon me, causing me much anxiety and dread, an anxiety which arose in part from my lack of knowledge that any other modern person understood the world in this way.

My awakening to synchronicity happened gradually over a period of a little more than a year, the first year of my midlife crisis. While I struggled to adjust to the disorienting events in my life during that time, I noticed that little things happening in the outer world seemed strangely meaningful. Birds made dramatic appearances in significant times and places. There were startlingly coincidental meetings with persons about whom I had just been thinking or speaking. Even more disturbing were the objects, places, and circumstances I sometimes encountered for the first time in outer life *after* I had dreamed about them. I did not know how to think about any of this except with the idea that God had something to do with it.

After about a year of these sorts of observations, I found the work

99

of Carl Jung. I did not, however, immediately come across a discussion of synchronicity, for Jung elaborated upon this phenomenon in very few places in all his written works. For most of his life he felt that if he made too much of synchronicity he would be misunderstood and dismissed as a mystic even more than he already was. So at first I found only hints of it. What I did find explicitly laid out in Jung's writings was the notion of the unconscious and the symbolic reality of dreams. Putting this with my experience of strangely meaningful events in outer life, I began to formulate the idea that in a certain sense life itself is like a dream, that it can be read and interpreted symbolically just as a dream can be.

This was still an idea and not true knowledge, but it was leading me close to the breakthrough realization toward which this stormy period in my life was leading. With this my anxiety intensified, an inner state that my reading of Jung helped me understand. I understood that a new truth was trying to come through from the unconscious and that my ego consciousness felt threatened and was trying to bar the door, thus raising this great anxiety. My old consciousness feared its imminent death, for it was about to be superseded by a new level of consciousness. Although understanding the anxiety did not make it go away, it helped me bear the process. Part of myself could stand aside and watch and analyze while the other part suffered through a psychological death and rebirth, a harrowing baptism in the symbolic waters of the unconscious.

It was at this time that I sought help from the priest at my church. In him I found someone who could listen while I talked about all that was happening to me. Even though he had not been through a similar experience, he was able to comprehend my journey with his intellect and feel it with his soul, and thus he provided crucial support for me in an hour of great need.

This intensified period of anxiety began on the exact day of Ash Wednesday and lasted through the forty days of Lent without resolution, although some progress was made during this time. I was watching my dreams very carefully, and even though I was still a novice at interpreting them, I was able to gain the important realization that I identified more strongly with my father than with my mother and that my feminine being was therefore neglected and underdeveloped. This knowledge was crucial to the process, but it was not the great breakthrough toward which the anxiety was pitched. Another important development during this time was the discovery that my inner processes—my thoughts and emerging understandings and the themes arising from my dreams—were running in tandem with the Sunday scripture readings and sermons. The parallel was uncanny. This heightened my sense of the significance of my journey.

Then on Good Friday the real breakthrough began. Late that afternoon I met my husband at a movie theater to see *Amadeus*, the story of the life of Mozart. This was a troubling time in our marriage. For sixteen years we had been close companions, sharing our thoughts, feelings, and understandings. But now that I was going through this deep water, my husband could no longer understand my experience. I had to keep most of it to myself, which I found to be very difficult. I worried that the change through which I was passing would separate us so much that it would bring an end to our marriage. As it happened, *Amadeus*, with its depth of spirit, was a good film for us to see at this time. We both were deeply moved by it, and it helped us feel connected again, giving us a little respite from our trials.

When we came out of the theater, darkness had fallen. We were in separate vehicles, he in our pickup truck, I in our car, and so we parted for the thirty-minute drive to our home in the country. As I drove out of town onto the rural roads, a spring storm began to blow in, the wind growing stronger and stronger, whipping the trees under a darkened night sky. When the rain finally came, it was a tremendous downpour, a deluge. Though I could barely see in front of me, the shoulder of the road was not wide enough to let me safely pull over and stop. Creeping along, I finally came to a place where the shoulder widened around someone's driveway. There I stopped and waited. I had never been out in such a storm. Branches of trees were blowing across the road before me. Knowing that tornados came in storms like this, I felt grimly that I could die there.

Another vehicle pulled up behind me on what was left of that little wide spot beside the road. I thought how comforting it would be if that were my husband. I imagined running back and jumping in the truck with him and the two of us waiting out the storm together. But I knew how unlikely it was that it would be he, since we had not stayed together in the traffic after we left the theater. And anyway, I would get drenched the second I stepped out of the car, and whoever was back there would think

I was out of my mind coming up to peer in their window at them. So I sat alone and waited, my headlights and those behind me illuminating the storm.

After a little while the rain began to let up and the wind dropped. As I pulled back onto the road, the vehicle behind me followed. When I got far enough ahead of it to be able to see it without being blinded by its lights, I saw to my joy that it was indeed my husband. He had been with me all along, following behind in his sturdy truck, weathering the storm with me, even though we each had to experience it separately and alone. Now as the storm passed, he was still with me, following me home.

That event spoke powerfully to me about our marriage in this stormy time. But how did one think about something like that? Was it all just happenstance? Or did God make that storm just to bring that message to me? That idea seemed absurd, much too egocentric to be seriously considered. And yet I knew that the incident had real meaning for me, that the images through which it spoke were just right, and that its message felt like a gift from God. *But how to think about it?* That was the great question for me now.

Although Easter Sunday passed without a resurrection experience, the new truth that began emerging on Good Friday continued to unfold. On the Monday after Easter I realized that a particular dream about an important personal matter had been repeated in various forms on all the major religious holidays since Christmas. These were the only times I had dreamed this particular theme. I had had one of these dreams on Christmas night, another on the eve of Epiphany, another on the eve of Ash Wednesday, and yet another on Easter Eve. This particular realization hit me especially hard and raised my anxiety to new heights.

I was learning from this experience that the oft repeated phrase in the Old Testament that the fear of God is the beginning of wisdom means what it says. It means fear, not awe. The realization that God is not an abstract principle "out there" somewhere in a vaguely removed spiritual realm but is actually present in the natural events of one's life, orchestrating those events toward an end one has not chosen and cannot fathom, is truly frightening. It means the end of the ego's illusion of control. It means one's life is not in one's own hands. Someone else is calling the shots.

I wrote in my journal that day: "That business of the dreams and the Church holy days is certainly the finger of God on me. That is what has thrown me so. Now I *know* I'm not in control. My intellect doesn't see how I can go on like this, but some other part of me knows that I can."

The next day I went to my appointment with my priest friend. I told him about the dreams lining up with the holy days and about the storm on Good Friday. He did not know how to think about these things either. Having the answers, however, is not the only way to help another person. I also told him of a dream I had had recently about being in a clear, natural pool of water and of dropping something I had been holding in my hand. I dove down deep to the bottom to retrieve it.

"What was it?" he asked.

"I'm not sure," I said. "I think it was a hair comb, the kind a woman uses to hold back her hair."

He looked at me for a moment without speaking. There was love in his eyes and a kind of amazement. Then he ran his hand over his arm. "That gives me chills," he said. We both understood that the dream was a picture of me retrieving my feminine being from the depths of the unconscious.

That moment of human connection, of love, empathy, and understanding, registered deeply in my soul and gave me the courage I needed to stand firm and claim the new reality that was coming through. On the morning after that conversation I was standing on my back porch when I suddenly saw clearly the new truth.

I knew in that moment that everything around me was in some sense an image of what was within me. Those birds were my thoughts flying by. Those trees were my rootedness. This house was a manifestation of my personality. All was Being. All was God. Within and without, it was all the same. And I knew that everything out there, all of Being, was working to bring me into my own true being. I knew that when I failed to understand things on the inside, the world outside would speak the meaning. I knew what Jesus meant when he said on Palm Sunday that if his supporters were silenced in their celebration of his entry into Jerusalem, the very stones would cry out. I understood that stones *do* cry out, that in its symbolic language the physical world *does* speak. I also understood in that moment that God did not send that storm on Good Friday just for me. That storm was there for *all* the people who experienced it in *all* the different ways it was experienced.

I wrote in my journal that day: "Today I know that all of Being wants me to be. We are all one with all Being. The very stones cry out. They always have. I just didn't hear them."

What followed was two or three weeks of intense synchronistic experiences, a constant flow of messages constellating in the ordinary events of the world around me, a flood that gradually decreased to a manageable level. It was as if the flow of life, which had been closed off, was suddenly open again, rushing out under the pressure of its impoundment and stabilizing only gradually into a moderate, steady stream. It was a challenge for me to take in this heightened experience, but it no longer felt so threatening, and my anxiety gradually dissipated.

Once I said yes to synchronicity, the worst of my crisis was over. My old consciousness was dead and in its place a new consciousness had arisen that allowed for meaningful connection between my inner psychic processes and the physical world around me. I still had to learn how to live with this new ingredient of life, how to balance it with all the other ingredients that were already there, but through experience of it I gradually learned how much weight to give it and became accustomed to it.

Synchronistic experiences are now an ordinary aspect of my daily life. I am guided by them in the same way I am guided by the weather or by a hunger pain or by the look in another person's face. To live with synchronicity is to maintain a waking relationship with the unconscious, to be always alert to God's will and meaning and to be guided by that with unusual precision. Synchronicity, once admitted into consciousness, reinforces itself, for one quickly learns that life goes better with it than without it.

## The Wisdom of Nature: Divine Mother

CARL JUNG understood synchronicity to be an acausal connecting principle that is present in nature. Through it, events in life are linked not by physical cause and effect but by meaning arising from the unconscious. Synchronicity does not deny or negate causality, but exists alongside it.

My experience with the storm on Good Friday, for example, can be thoroughly explained by cause and effect. A warm front met a cold front, and a storm resulted. My husband and I were in separate vehicles because there was not time before the movie started for him to come home from work and ride back into town with me. He pulled into that spot behind me during the storm because he saw my car there and because he, too, needed to get off the road. All of this, perfectly obvious to my rational mind, has never been in doubt. But there was more to that event than these mechanical details. There was also a nonrational element involved. My soul recognized a display of meaning, and my mind joined with my soul to process that meaning. My deepest being reverberated with it, and I was changed by it. Causality and acausality, rationality and nonrationality, meaninglessness and meaningfulness existed together in those events, a balance of opposites, neither pole negating the other.

It is significant that my awakening to synchronicity came in conjunction with my awakening to the more personal issue of my own lost feminine being. In a way, my individual problem was a reflection of the larger, collective problem of our time. Since the rise of modern scientific rationalism in the seventeenth century, the Western world as a whole has come to identify more with the "father" than with the "mother." With the seeming triumph of rationality over nonrationality, of mechanistic science over spirituality, of the outer world over the inner world, feminine reality, which has to do with inner life and the connectedness of all things, has dropped from our hands and sunk down into the depths of the collective unconscious, denigrated and denied. One end of the pole of opposites on which the world is balanced has almost overturned the other, and an out-of-balance, neurotic world has been the result.

This seems to have been an inevitable stage of our human development. Rational, scientific thought had to come into our consciousness and establish itself as a necessary counterbalance to the naive medieval worldview, which was one-sidedly nonrational and spiritual. In the usual way of new developments, scientific rationalism seemed at first to be the ultimate achievement and final answer to life. But inevitably this has proved not to be so. Now we must retrieve the lost value, bring up the denied nonrational element, the feminine reality of the connectedness of all things, and integrate this with the masculine reality of rationality and scientific thought. If we are to be healthy and whole, it cannot be one or the other. It has to be both.

The principles of modern science are not in conflict with synchronicity. Twentieth-century physics has shown the universe to be a single fabric, a unified field of energy. Solid objects are not ultimately separate and distinct but are concentrations of energy in the unified field. Time and space are relative. Until they are observed—until they enter consciousness—subatomic particles are only waves of probability, which means that nothing is absolutely predictable but only statistically probable. In such a world there is room for synchronicity, regardless of whether we fully understand it or not. The physicists themselves do not fully understand the phenomena *they* are observing. Despite the best efforts of scientific rationalism, mystery has not been eradicated from life after all.

Although there is a spiritual element in synchronicity, it is no more a supernatural phenomenon than dreams are. Both are natural. Just as most people begin to remember their dreams when they turn their attention to them, so do most people begin to notice synchronicity when they turn their attention to it. Even more than dreams do, synchronicity makes us aware of the divine wisdom at the heart of natural life. This is the Wisdom of which the Old Testament speaks: "She is so pure, she pervades and permeates all things. She is a breath of the power of God."

In the wisdom of nature we rediscover the aspect of God that is "Mother." The words "matter" and "material" are derived from *mater*, the Latin word for "mother." In synchronicity we experience the material world as a vibrant expression of divine motherhood, an aspect of God that is present in created life and provides us with nourishment and support both physically and spiritually.

My experience in the storm on Good Friday was like the comforting words of a wise mother: "Don't worry. Go forward with courage through this storm of growth and change. He will stay by you. He will come along in his own way." In times of tumult and change, times when we need a greater wisdom than we actually possess, synchronicity is especially active. Most people have noticed it around the events of a death or at the beginning of a significant new relationship.

There are also times when a synchronistic display of meaning breaks into our complacency, times when we are not aware of any particular issues. At times like this synchronicity tries to wake us up to a mistaken path or to alert us to an unrecognized truth beneath our outward journey. One clear example of the latter occurred in our church one Easter morning. The church was full. Spirits were high. The choir was larger than usual and augmented by trumpets. As we were singing a hymn in the middle of the service, a vase of Easter lilies fell from the altar to the floor. I immediately looked to see what words we were singing at the moment the vase fell. "The Spirit's power shakes the church of God." Seeing those words underlined by God on that Easter morning was a moving, grace-filled moment that few others in the church shared with me, though the event was there for all to see. Most people saw nothing but a mishap—water on the carpet, a glitch in the service.

So much that happens to us is experienced as annoyance when it is actually meant to get our attention in order to alter our course or to teach us something. The key is often to be found in the coincidence between the startling or annoying event and what we are doing or saying or thinking at that same moment. Such manifestations of the spirit of God arise out of nature itself and are fully in keeping with physical laws. The vase of lilies fell because of the vibrations of the music—the pipe organ, trumpets, and voices—and because someone had placed it too near the edge of the altar. The mystery was in the timing. That was where the unconscious revealed itself. In living with synchronicity one learns to accept this nonrational but undeniable aspect of reality. One gets used to the idea that through the Self, the unifying principle that is both within us and around us, God coordinates the life of the world in something of the same way a composer coordinates the many parts of a symphony or a writer ties together the many threads of a book. At the bottom of physical life, somewhere below the subatomic particles, there is this mystery.

## Artists of Life

THROUGH SYNCHRONICITY the physical world not only manifests meaning but it also provides for our physical needs, just as a mother takes care of her children. As Jesus pointed out in his Lilies-of-the-Field teaching, every day brings its own difficulties and its own solutions. The answer to an immediate problem is always at hand, even though that answer might be that we must submit to misfortune. The question is whether we are open to the answer, whether our conscious attitude is flexible enough for us to recognize and follow the true path of the moment. There is in the midst of the chaos and tumult of everyday life a vital flow that is the true "river of life, rising from the throne of God," and our challenge through the moments of our lives is to recognize it and join with it.

There is, for example, an answer to the demands on our time, a way through the hours of the day. Synchronicity gives us hints. The phone call that will not go through may not need to be made. The elevator that is too full directs us to the stairwell where we meet just the person we need to see. The jammed aisle at the grocery store gives us the hint that the meal we had planned, from whose main ingredient we are being blocked, is too elaborate, that the simpler solution that now comes to mind would be better.

Through synchronicity the unexpected check comes in the mail just in time to cover the unexpected dental expenses. The car breaks down near a gas station that has a mechanic on duty. We find the shoes our daughter needs at a bargain price we can afford. A friend happens to call just at the time we are beginning to sink into an emotional quagmire. We uncharacteristically forget our car keys and go grumbling back into the house where we discover we had turned a stove burner to "High" instead of "Off."

Through synchronicity we learn that life has its own wisdom, much greater than our own, and that to avail ourselves of it, we must be constantly aware and alert. Attunement to synchronicity makes us artists of life, conscious participants in God's creative spirit. With its help our efforts become more effective, more graceful, more meaningful, more helpful to others, and more satisfying to ourselves. And although synchronicity does not shield us from difficulty and pain, it brings mercy into our dark times in the way events unfold.

There is no method that can be taught for how to live with synchronicity. Each person must begin to notice it for himself and work out his own relationship with it. The vital stream that flows through life is different for each individual, so that what glows with meaning for one person in the unfolding of a moment may not mean anything to the person next to him. It is the connection to our inner processes that gives meaning to what would otherwise be meaningless.

In working with synchronicity, we must learn how to balance it with ordinary consciousness. Because synchronicity is an expression of the unconscious, it functions as a compensation to consciousness, just as dreams do. Our proper relationship to it is a dialogue, our own consciousness neither overrunning it nor being overrun by it. It is very much like a relationship with a spouse. We supply conscious intent and direction, while synchronicity supplies encouragement, hints, or corrections. We weigh its suggestions and decide for ourselves what to think or how to proceed. If we look to it too much for guidance, we fall into a muddle, for consciousness as a rule needs to be strong and to keep charge of itself. But if we fail to take account of it and push on stubbornly against the flow of life, we wear ourselves out and experience difficulties or even tragedies that might have been avoided.

Synchronicity calls us to an attitude toward life that is unceasingly religious in the truest sense of the word. Without it, religious life is reduced to a one-sided affair that depends primarily upon our intentional engagement in prayer, reflection, and good works. While these are important, they are not enough. The natural spirit, with all its dynamic expression, is left out. But when we are open to synchronicity, life itself teems with the presence of God. Synchronicity calls from us careful and constant watching and following, and it can fill us at any moment with amazement and thanksgiving. It is all we can do to keep up with its dialogue and to play our part as servants of God in the lively drama of creation.

# CHAPTER EIGHT

# Carl Jung and Christianity

*If Christian doctrine is able to assimilate the fateful impact of psychology, that is a sign of vitality, for life is assimilation. Anything that ceases to assimilate dies.*

CARL JUNG

THE ELEMENTS of the basic Jungian framework—the concepts of consciousness and the unconscious, the symbolic language of the unconscious, and the natural spiritual vehicles of dreams and synchronicity—are tools with which the natural spirit can be comprehended and received into a deepening Christian life. But when Christians are offered the Jungian tools, the question naturally arises: What kind of Christian was Carl Jung? Is he a person the Church can trust?

Midway through the writing of this book I had the following dream, which came in words with no images:

*"The reason Christians have disdained Jung is because of his assassination on religion. But they should get from him what he has to offer before they leave him behind."*

I realize "assassination on religion" is not grammatically correct, but these are the words of the dream as best I could recall them when I awoke. If I were to change them, it would change the meaning I sensed as I dreamed. "Assassination *of* religion" would imply that in some sense Jung had actually done away with religion, but this was not what the dream was saying. "Assassination *attempt* on religion" was not the dream's words nor quite the meaning that I understood as I dreamed. What I understood in "assassination on religion" was the hostile attitude Jung sometimes showed toward organized Christianity, which he felt ignored the gospel message that Christ is the teaching and healing Spirit that seeks us through the unconscious.

This is a good example of the compensatory nature of dreams, for I myself would never have characterized Jung's quarrelsome attitude as that of an assassin. I have always considered him to be a deeply religious man. It was not until I had this dream that I was able to look at him through the eyes of organized Christianity and see the hostility that it has with some justification perceived in him.

Although the dream led me to take a clearer view of the darker side of Jung, it has not swung me into a reversal of my previous estimation of him. Rather it has made me acknowledge and accept the paradox of Carl Jung, as the dream indicated all Christians should do. The fact is that despite his hostility to the keepers of traditional religion, Jung was at the same time a deeply religious man. Even in *Answer to Job*, the work in which his impatient attitude showed itself most clearly, Jung's concluding words were:

> Even the enlightened person remains what he is, and is never more than his own limited ego before the One who dwells within him, whose form has no knowable boundaries, who encompasses him on all sides, fathomless as the abysms of the earth and vast as the sky.

Jung's hostility toward organized Christianity was not that of an avowed enemy. It was more like that of a creative son toward the traditional family from which he sprang, a genius of a son so filled with the vision of his creative contribution that he was unable at the same time to hold in full value the time-honored structure for which God intended his creativity. There is no doubt that Jung loved God and lived closely with Him all his life, nor is there any doubt that he valued the core content of the Christian tradition in which he was deeply rooted. This is obvious in his letters as well as in his autobiography, *Memories, Dreams, Reflections*. In that he wrote:

> I falter before the task of finding the language which might adequately express the incalculable paradox of love. . . . I sometimes feel that Paul's words—'Though I speak with the tongues of men and angels, and have not love'—might well be the first condition of all cognition and the quintessence of divinity itself. . . . I have again and again been faced with the mystery of love, and have never been able

to explain what it is. Like Job, I had to 'lay my hand on my mouth. I have spoken once, and I will not answer.' (Job 40:4f.) Here is the greatest and the smallest, the remotest and the nearest, the highest and the lowest. . . . Man can try to name love, showering upon it all the names at his command, and still he will involve himself in endless self-deceptions. If he possesses a grain of wisdom, he will lay down his arms and name the unknown by the more unknown, *ignotum per ignotius*—that is, by the name of God.

Of Christ, Jung said in a letter written in 1953, "The Christ image as we know it certainly did not appear as the result of human intervention, it was the transcendental ('total') Christ who created for himself a new and more specific body." To Upton Sinclair, whose book *A Personal Jesus* Jung criticized for stripping Jesus of his divinity, he wrote:

> *I have a certain picture of a personal Jesus.* It has been dimly suggested to me through certain New Testament data. Yet the strongest impression came to me from the [Shroud of] Turin. . . . Its stern and august countenance has confirmed my formerly vague expectations. I am, as a matter of fact, so profoundly impressed by the superiority of this extraordinary personality that I would not dare to reconstruct its psychology.

According to tradition, the image of Jesus was somehow imprinted on his burial shroud, which was left behind in the tomb after the Resurrection. Jung had a copy of the face of Christ as it appeared on the Shroud of Turin and kept it in his study, behind a curtain.

Jung also had in his study, hanging in a window, a stained glass image of the Crucifixion. Once when Pastor Walther Uhsadel, a theologian at the University of Hamburg, was visiting him, Jung pointed to that image and said, "You see, this is the crux for us." When Uhsadel asked what he meant, Jung replied,

> I've just got back from India, and it has struck me with renewed force. Man has to cope with the problem of suffering. The Oriental wants to get rid of suffering by casting it off. Western man tries

to suppress suffering with drugs. But suffering has be to overcome, and the only way to overcome it is to endure it. We learn that only from him.

And here he pointed to the crucified Christ.

Jung's near-death experience when he suffered a heart attack at age 69 gave him certainty about the reality and desirability of the afterlife. He had experienced himself moving into the next world and then, to his dismay, being pulled back into this one through his doctor's intervention. To a friend with terminal cancer he wrote concerning what he had learned:

> On the whole my illness proved to be a most valuable experience, which gave me the inestimable opportunity of a glimpse behind the veil. The only difficulty is to get rid of the body, to get naked and void of the world and the ego-will. When you can give up the crazy will to live and when you seemingly fall into a bottomless mist, then the truly *real* life begins with everything which you were meant to be and never reached. It is something ineffably grand. . . . Death is the hardest thing from the outside and as long as we are outside of it. But once inside you taste of such completeness and peace and fulfillment that you don't want to return.

Because I came to Carl Jung through his autobiography, in which he speaks freely of his spiritual nature and his life-long experience of God, I have never doubted that he was in God's camp, so to speak. His difficulties with organized Christianity have not seemed problematic to me, especially considering the fact that the time during which he lived (1875–1961) was a time when the Church was especially stiff and self-satisfied. It was only in the 1960s that the Church began to open up to the winds of change—to greater lay leadership and to the ministry of women—signaling an opening to the feminine side of spirituality, which has led increasingly toward a recognition of the unconscious and natural spirituality. My experience of the Church in my own time has not been of a closed and unreceptive institution. Because of this difference in climate, I have been more willing than some Christians to grant Jung his gruff opinions about the Church. I have never felt that I had to share all those opinions with him.

# Problems with Jung

WHILE I VERY MUCH TRUST Carl Jung as a spiritual leader and admire him as a human being, I have always had my own problems with him—two problems, which seem on the surface to be very different but which I feel to be somewhat related. The first problem is that Jung seems to me to have been too much in love with the unconscious. The world of the unconscious is not a human realm, just as the bottom of the sea is not a human realm. I personally would not like to live in a submarine, nor would I want to live as deeply immersed in the unconscious as Jung seems to have lived. In his investigation of the unconscious he became so familiar with its archetypal language, so fascinated by it, and so much its champion, that he almost seems to have lost his full citizenship in ordinary life. At times his ideas and understandings were of such depth and couched in so arcane a language that hardly any other human being could sustain a creative dialogue with him, though he wanted dialogue and continually searched for it in both the worlds of psychology and theology.

In my own studies I have found that although Jung's writings are immensely valuable to me, if I follow him too far in his thinking, I begin to take on a conceptual framework that is more complex than my needs require. This has the effect of leading me away from the heart of my own life. The world of symbol and image that comes to me through my dreams certainly does contain recognizable mythological and archetypal themes, but on the whole it seems closer to the world of everyday life than Jung's inner world seemed to be. This is partly due to the fact that Jung was more introverted than most of us and therefore more open to the depths of the unconscious. But I think it is also because his experience of the unconscious came to him not only through dreams and synchronicity but also in large part through a technique he named *active imagination.*

Active imagination is a process in which inner images from the unconscious enter into waking consciousness—as if one were dreaming without being asleep. There are techniques for bringing on this state, though it can also occur spontaneously. It is very close to daydreaming, the main difference being that consciousness usually manipulates daydreams to bring about scenes and images which are wish-fulfilling. In active imagination images are allowed to arise without interference and are respected as autonomous manifestations of inner reality. One then consciously enters the fantasy material and *relates* to it in an honest way, creating a dialogue between the needs and viewpoint of consciousness on the one hand and of the unconscious on the other.

This can be as simple as a spontaneous dialogue with an unseen inner figure, or it can go much further and lead one deeply into impressive imaginative scenes, full of mythological symbolism that arises from the depths and unfolds like pages of a modern fantasy novel or a medieval alchemical treatise or a Gnostic gospel from the early Christian era. Jung felt that active imagination was an especially effective way to resolve the tensions between the competing demands of consciousness and the unconscious. It was, in a way, the central religious sacrament he offered to his patients.

It seems clear that active imagination when practiced faithfully within a grounded, moral framework has real value for some people. The spiritual exercises of Ignatius Loyola are based on a particular version of it. I myself, however, have found it to be of limited usefulness in my own journey. Nor have I observed it to be of long term, regular usefulness to most of the people with whom I am journeying in the Church, where dreams and synchronicity seem to be the staple foods of the natural spirit. It is as if active imagination were too rich a food for most of us.

There is a myth that warns of the dangers of eating lavish food offered up by the unconscious. In the Greek tale of Psyche and Eros, one of Psyche's tasks is to go to the underworld to fetch a box of beauty ointment from Persephone, the queen of the underworld. Among the many admonitions Psyche is given for surviving such a venture is that once she has entered Persephone's hall, she must decline the soft chair and rich food she is offered and instead sit on the ground and ask for common bread. Otherwise she will not be able to return to the human world.

Psyche is told to stay grounded and eat simply. This is something that introverts especially need to hear, for they are tempted by inner riches in the same way extraverts are tempted by outer ones. The lure away from authentic human life is the same in either case. All we need from the unconscious are the teachings and understandings that help us resolve the specific problems of our own lives and some of those of our own communities.

There is, however, much more than that floating around in the unconscious depths. When we tap into the unconscious, we sometimes get tantalizing glimpses of what seem to be answers to huge questions. There is a decided tendency in the unconscious for intricate systems of knowledge to try to form up into something which the human mind can comprehend, but which often in fact cannot be fully comprehended, at least not in our present state of being, except perhaps at a prohibitively high cost in mental energy. It is these sorts of foods from the unconscious that are so tempting and yet are too rich for human digestion. As I was struggling with this problem in my own journey, I had the following dream:

> From the deep part of the night, no images, just this understanding: Meaning should not be sought or reached for in a big way, separate and apart from life. It should be taken in a little at a time within life itself, as life is being lived. Meaning and life should go along together, neither getting ahead of the other.

For the most part Carl Jung brought up from the unconscious meaning and understanding that we can use. His depth of wisdom and clarity of insight were immense, and his writings will be a valuable source for the human community for a long time to come. But in some of his writings we do find a feast too rich in meaning to be absorbed into everyday life. In a book like *Aion*, which is about the development of the symbol of the Christ through the Christian era, the many nuggets of gold which are there to be mined are buried in a difficult and not particularly useful framework of Gnostic and alchemical discourse. The point Jung seeks to make in this, and in some of his other works, is that these early, arcane systems of knowledge—Gnosticism and alchemy—refer to the basic principles of the psychology of the unconscious, which was yet undeveloped and for which these ancient authors had no other language than these raw, symbolic utterances.

I am sure he is right about this, and we should be grateful to him for having the curiosity and intellectual capacity to delve into the ancient manuscripts and make sense of them for us. But I disagree with his implied suggestion that we should retrieve the languages of alchemy and Gnostism in order to revive the true spirit of Christianity. We can get a little help from these sources to elucidate the symbols in our dreams, but for the most part, Jung's own psychology has replaced these premature constructions. He has given us a more straightforward, more *conscious* framework, one that is hard enough to mesh with the collective discourse of our time without cluttering it with these archaic symbolic systems.

The second problem I have had with Carl Jung is that he broke a basic tenet of the Christian moral code by trying, in effect, to have two wives. This is an unsettling picture from the standpoint of feminine feeling, as well as from the Christian viewpoint that monogamy is a symbol of faithfulness to one's own true path with God. Early in Jung's marriage, when he already had several children, he fell in love with Toni Wolff, a gifted patient who herself soon became an analyst. Evidently she was a true soul mate, a manifestation of Jung's anima, someone with whom he was meant to journey spiritually.

It is my feeling that in the same way he ate too lavishly from the banquet table of the unconscious, he partook too deeply of this relationship. Toni Wolff became his mistress in a completely public way. His wife Emma, who was a friend of Toni's, had to adjust to this or give up her marriage. Evidently she did eventually make peace with it in large part, feeling that Toni was able to help Jung with his difficult inner journey in a way Emma herself could not. Jung's own feeling seems to have been that because he loved both women, he was justified in redefining marriage in such a way that both could be included. He considered himself to be like an African chief with two wives. Reportedly, he spent every Wednesday evening at Toni Wolff's house, and Toni came to the Jung house every Sunday for dinner. The community that formed around Jung accepted this, and the threesome often attended professional and social events together.

This experiment in a new morality was not entirely successful, however. Besides the initial emotional toll on Emma, some of the Jung children were understandably and unremittingly resistant. Even Toni Wolff herself came to resent her fate as the other woman, always the lover, never wife or mother, although the relationship endured. As for Jung, I feel he painted himself into a corner with this arrangement. Convinced he was following a higher moral path, he publicly pitted himself against the established morality of the greater community. This must surely have hardened his already defiant outsider's attitude toward the Church and made it that much more difficult to find a bridge back to the tradition that he deeply cared for and to which he had so much to offer.

## Jung and the Problem of Evil

MY OWN PROBLEMS WITH CARL JUNG, then, are his tendency to extreme interiority and his questionable attempt at redefining marriage in his own life, although neither of these negate the overall positive value I place on his life and work. Many other Christian writers find that their greatest problem with Jung is his contention that evil is not merely the absence of God, as Christianity has sometimes defined it, but is in fact a spiritual reality that is as much a part of God as goodness is.

Satan, Jung often pointed out, was, in the Old Testament, a member of God's court, one of God's own sons. He was thrown from heaven in a celestial event that Jung understood to have occurred alongside the incarnation of Christ. For Jung it was self-evident that good and evil are two parts of a whole, necessary opposites in God as well as in man.

Space and time break wholeness apart into its separate, conflicting components, which human consciousness is then able to perceive and reflect upon. Therefore it is only in this world of space and time that the problem of the opposites, including good and evil, is constellated and can be worked out. Jung felt that just as humankind needs God, God needs humankind in order to resolve the problem of the opposites: of good and evil, light and dark, masculine and feminine, spirit and nature, consciousness and unconsciousness—all the many paradoxical aspects of the unknowable, transcendent God.

This means that evil is not something *caused* by man but rather is something that *happens* to him, just as grace happens to him. It is a problem put upon him by God, not because man is bad and needs to be punished but because he is alive and must answer the challenge of a world where good and evil, light and dark, order and chaos, certainty and fear, joy and sadness, are the alternating currents of life, the inhalation and exhalation of the very breath of being.

Man does not cause evil in Jung's way of thinking, but he must deal with it when it arises in him and around him, and for this he needs all the strength and moral courage at his command. Man must realize the necessity of choosing the good and of trying to align himself with it. But he must not delude himself by thinking that he can banish evil, which is a part of God, a part of life itself, and is not in man's power to eradicate.

The idea that man causes evil, and therefore can eliminate it, inflates man to God-like status and underestimates the reality and power of evil. When man thus fails to look at evil with clear eyes, evil gains an advantage and can catch him unaware. Jung felt that Nazi Germany was a terrible, large-scale example of this.

When man knows, on the other hand, that evil is an eternal aspect of life, that it is a part of God and will always reappear as surely as night follows day, then he is ready for it. As he sees it arise, whether within himself or without, he accepts the challenge, looks to the unconscious for guidance and teaching, appeals to God for mercy and divine help, learns the lessons that proceed from the struggle, and finally transcends to a more integrated state of being. And then he waits for the next round, just as Jesus did after the Temptations in the Wilderness: "The devil left him, to return at the appointed time."

Many Christians have trouble thinking about evil in this way. They are unable to reconcile this presumed dark side of God with their knowledge that God is the ultimate in goodness and love. They cannot accept such a paradox. The important thing to realize, however, is that it does not matter what Carl Jung has said about this. With the spiritual tools he has given us, we no longer have to depend on him or anyone else for answers to these kinds of questions.

So long as we stand within the protective framework of Scripture and tradition, our dreams and the synchronistic events of our lives can bring us whatever further understanding we need to have about the nature of evil and other such difficult matters. Each of us can be met in the place where we are and led to the understanding that is right for us. An ultimate answer to the question of evil can probably never be given, because an ultimate single viewpoint can never be reached from which to ask the question. What is important, therefore, is that each of us learn enough about evil to handle the challenge of it in our own lives.

In my own journey, for example, I have had a hard time reconciling myself to the fact that most people are not interested in learning to relate individually to the unconscious, that for them the challenges of ordinary conscious life, supported by its collective opinions and viewpoints, are quite enough. For some time I made a pest of myself trying to force upon family and friends an awareness of the lessons I saw coming to them from the unconscious, whether they wanted to hear about these things or not. After several years and many difficult experiences, I began to get the message that this was not the way God wanted me to proceed.

At that point, when I was ready to receive it, a deeper understanding about this was given to me in a dream. In the evening preceding the dream I had watched a movie about betrayal and dark intrigue. The film portrayed an atmosphere of evil that was overwhelming, a powerful, inescapable force that relentlessly entangled the hero in its web. When I went to bed that night, my dreams continued in the same vein:

> I was with a friend and was trying to extricate him from the clutches of evil, from a kind of Mafia force that was making him work too hard. It was night and we were walking along a road, the shoulders of which had just been widened. I was taking up the new strips of asphalt, removing them. But I was not using gloves, and so my fingerprints were left behind.
>
> The next day the Mob's hitmen came and got me. They knew from my fingerprints that I was the guilty one. One of them, a grizzled, hardened old man, took me to a sofa to sexually assault me. Instead of being terrified, I accepted the situation, aware that I was overpowered. While I did not exactly embrace this man as a lover, I acknowledged the pleasure of sexuality, and as a result he did not carry through with the rape nor even molest me very much. In my acceptance of him I had humanized him a little bit.
>
> Then a higher-ranking thug joined him. They were now going to do what they had come to do, which was to beat me up, maybe kill me. Again I was not terrified. As they began to rough me up, I understood that I could not fight against them, that they and their organization were much stronger than I, and that they were never going to let someone like me bring them down or even persist in the effort.
>
> I expected them to accuse me of taking up the asphalt strips, but they never did say what it was I had done. They were completely silent on the subject. They simply set about to punish me for it. Noticing that, I suddenly realized what I must do.
>
> I said, "I promise I will never again say anything about you-know-what." I

*meant that I would never again try to expose their nefarious doings, not even to them. I would never again try to close them down. And with that, they let me go.*

*As I was waking, but perhaps still dreaming, I understood that these mobsters represented consciousness that would not be opened to enlightenment and understanding.*

About a year later I had another dream that carried this theme a little further. Again I had seen something on television about the problem of evil. This time it was a documentary implicating the Mafia in the assassination of President John Kennedy. If the Mob-connected informant interviewed for the film was speaking truthfully, Kennedy was assassinated in order to remove his brother Robert from the post of Attorney General. Robert Kennedy, as head of the Justice Department, had declared all out, total war on organized crime. The Mafia reasoned that if they killed Robert Kennedy, the President would intensify the war against them. But if they killed President Kennedy himself, Lyndon Johnson would come to power, and because of Johnson's personal antipathy toward Robert Kennedy, he would remove him from the Justice Department. "Kill the head, and the tail dies," the Mob bosses said.

After watching this, I went to bed and had this dream:

*A lot of dreaming about the Mob. I understood it to symbolize human evil. I understood that one must not throw in with it, nor must one declare total war against it. One must live between those extremes, or somehow above them.*

A member of our natural spirituality Journey Group had a dream with a similar message but with an important additional component. Hers was more archetypal than my two dreams. It portrayed evil as but one aspect of a fundamental life force in the unconscious that is symbolized by the serpent. In general the serpent represents not only evil, as in the Garden of Eden, but also healing, as in the medical emblem of entwined serpents on a staff. In the conversation with Nicodemus in the Gospel of John, Christ compares himself to the healing serpent that Moses held aloft on a staff to save the lives of those who had been bitten by serpents. The same unconscious life force that brings destruction, then, brings healing when it is lifted up, which is to say, when it is joined with the spirit of heaven. Interestingly, my friend's dream on this subject also came after the problem of evil had been constellated in her consciousness by something she had seen on television. After watching a documentary about Anne Frank, the young Jewish diarist who died in a Nazi concentration camp, she went to bed and dreamed:

> *I was swimming underwater. Very clear water. Plenty of light. There were snakes on the sandy bottom. They were harmless, coiled in circles. But near a fence I saw a viperish-looking one with a triangular head. It was not coiled but was swimming toward me, coming from the opposite direction. I was not frightened. I simply veered wide and avoided it. It looked at me as I swam past.*

The dream assures the dreamer, who was born just before World War II, that she has met the problem of evil that has arisen so horrifyingly in her time. Having developed a conscious relationship with the unconscious, she can swim confidently in its waters and discern the difference between its healing (circular) forces and its destructive ones. When evil comes toward her, she recognizes it and knows what to do. She simply steers clear of it, and it passes by without harming her.

Although such dreams leave many questions unanswered, they nonetheless shine light on the subject of evil and bring helpful understanding to those who dream them. Carl Jung had his own revelations about evil and came to his own conclusions about it. It would violate the spirit of his work, however, if we were to accept his answers for ourselves. It is to the teaching Spirit of the unconscious that we each should look for answers, for it is here that we find the true Teacher who gives us understanding by degrees as we are ready to receive it. Jesus said in his farewell discourses: "I still have many things to say to you but they would be too much for you now. But when the Spirit of truth comes he will lead you to the complete truth."

## Jung's Problems with Modern Christianity

CARL JUNG knew that he had found the spiritual tools that modern Christianity needs in order for its members to open themselves to the

Spirit of truth in a new and deeper way. The religious problem facing Western man, Jung felt, was the need for mature individuals to break their identity with collective consciousness and set out on the more difficult road of individuation. This, he would say, is the deepest meaning of that admonition in the Gospel of Matthew, "Enter by the narrow gate, since the road that leads to perdition is wide and spacious, and many take it; but it is a narrow gate and a hard road that leads to life, and only a few find it."

In *Aion* Jung wrote that the Christian tradition describes the individuation process "with an exactness and impressiveness far surpassing our feeble attempts." Jung could see that the elements of Christianity symbolize at every point what life is like when, in the context of a strong moral relationship with God, one opens to the reality of the unconscious and begins to take it into account. As Jung grew older, he turned his attention more and more to the task of explicating the connection between the symbolic language of Christianity and the natural process of individuation, which seeks realization at some level in every human life.

Even though Carl Jung dedicated himself to the problem of Christianity in the modern age and hoped to see his insights picked up by theologians, he had no use in his own life for the Christian Church as an institution. He saw its value for others, but he felt that he himself had moved beyond it. It was while still an adolescent that Jung turned away from organized Christianity, disillusioned by its reliance on faith and dogma without any accompanying emphasis on individual inner experience. Even at that early age he had already had quite a bit of inner experience of his own. Because of what he had learned from that experience, he felt he had a better understanding of what God is really like than did the upright people of his father's congregation or even his father himself or any of his many clergyman uncles. Feeling that he had outgrown the Church, Jung left it behind and never returned. From that point on, he judged organized Christianity from an outside position.

Jung was especially troubled by the fact that most Christian leaders do not have a conscious relationship with the unconscious and are resistant to developing one. They would rather receive spiritual guidance from the collective teachings of Scripture and doctrine than to encounter God for themselves in their own depths. In *The Undiscovered Self* Jung wrote of the irony of this:

> The religious person . . . is accustomed to the thought of not being sole master in his own house. He believes that God, and not he himself, decides in the end. But how many of us would dare let the will of God decide, and which of us would not feel embarrassed if he had to say how far the decision came from God himself?

Jung's complaint was a valid one. Most Christians do not want to hear a message from God if it has their own name on it and puts upon them explicit, personal demands, as dreams and synchronicity do. They find it more comfortable to stay within the framework of general admonition. It is a shortcoming of Christianity that it does not ask more than this of its members. It is an even greater shortcoming that it does not ask more of its clergy. By rights, a religious leader should be one who knows the depths of the Spirit as well as the heights, who knows the value of dreams as well as the value of prayer, praise, and Christian community.

In Jung's day this idea was completely unheard of. He could hardly have expected, therefore, that it would be embraced the moment he suggested it. He himself had to produce the framework by which the depths of the Spirit could be grasped. And in his preoccupation with the depths, he lost his own personal connection to the heights, which made it that much more difficult for him to communicate effectively with the keepers of traditional Christianity. Met repeatedly with misunderstanding, he became frustrated and impatient and often answered his critics with disdain and sarcasm. This only made matters worse.

Had Jung followed the example of Jesus, who balanced the individual way with participation in the religious life of the community, he might in his mature years have come to have more love and respect for the Christian community and thus would have been able to speak to it more effectively. People are much more willing to listen to someone who loves them than to someone who holds them in disdain. Jung in his wisdom should have known this. But he was not his wisest when dealing with the Church. This was a shadow area for him.

The reason we have a shadow is because as limited human beings we cannot be well developed in everything. A strong personal quality will always bring with it a correspondingly strong deficit in the opposite quality. Jung was gifted in the spiritual depths. The spiritual heights were his weakness. I am sure, however, that despite his shortcomings, Carl Jung accomplished the basic task God gave him to do. The fact that he had a shadow should not deter us from taking from his writings all the gold that is there to be found.

Many followers of Jung feel that his analytical psychology ushers in a new level of religious life that goes beyond organized Christianity and leaves community religion behind. They see the analyst's office as a viable substitute for the house of public worship. The dream I related at the opening of this chapter suggests, however, that it is Carl Jung who will ultimately be left behind. But the dream also warns that before Christians do leave him behind, they should first accept from him the gifts he has offered them. I believe Jung would be satisfied with that, for he was first and foremost a servant of God. "I am not a Jungian," he often said. Neither do Christians have to be Jungians in order to make use of Jung's work.

The inner landscape Jung described did not belong to him, and it will not disappear with his passing. Consciousness and the unconscious are not Jungian theories—they are phenomena that simply exist. Dreams and their symbolic language did not come from him. He merely observed them in a systematic way and described their regular features. So too is synchronicity a reality that has always been present in the world and always noticed, whether by whole cultures or only by observant individuals. Jung's contribution was to describe this phenomenon and give it a name. Archetypes are universal motifs that anyone can discover for himself by studying the mythologies of the world. Nor did Jung conjure up the symbolic images of transcendence that come to us in dreams, visions, and life experiences. He merely took note of them, categorized them, and gave them in their many manifestations a single name—the Self. Shadow, anima, and animus are his labels, but they refer to true realities that everyone meets as dream images and as living psychological facts. Individuation, that key concept of Jungian psychology, is a true and natural process that comes to us from God. Jung merely recognized its importance and named it. These inner realities could just as well have other names, but his are the ones that

have been presented most comprehensively and successfully and that are
gradually becoming accepted in the educated world.

   Jung's framework offers the conceptual equipment we need to discern
the features of the natural landscape of our inner world. Using these tools,
we can begin to decipher the language of God's feminine voice, which
speaks through natural, created life to shape us into our truest forms and
lead us toward oneness with God.

# PART THREE

# THE
# INDIVIDUATION
# JOURNEY

# CHAPTER NINE

# The Opposites

IN THE LAST FEW paragraphs of the Revelation of John, we read:

> "Alleluia! The reign of the Lord our God Almighty has begun; . . . this is the time for the marriage of the Lamb. His bride is ready. . . ."
>
> Then I saw a new heaven and a new earth. . . . I saw the holy city, the new Jeruasalem, coming down from God out of heaven, as beautiful as a new bride all dressed for her husband. . . .
>
> The Spirit and the Bride say, "Come." Let everyone who listens answer, "Come." Then let all who are thirsty come: All who want it may have the water of life, and have it free.

With this climax the Bible comes to a close. All who want it may have the water of life, symbol of the unconscious, and have it free. And this is linked with the symbolism of mystical marriage.

What does marriage mean fundamentally? It is the union of opposites, the joining together of the basic polarity of life—the masculine and the feminine—those opposing realities whose differences are never resolved except at a transcendent level of conjunction symbolized by the image of marriage.

When a person applies the Jungian tools to his or her individual journey and begins to pay attention to dreams and synchronistic experience, that person will find that the problem of reconciling the masculine and feminine elements of his or her own life rises to prominence in the dialogue that comes from the unconscious. The road toward God is a road toward marriage, not in the outer world but within ourselves. It is a road toward a wedding of opposites that seeks to take place in the depths of our own being.

Chinese Taoists understand that Tao, the ultimate source of life, unknowable and undefinable, contains within itself a basic polarity which they call *yin* and *yang*. In the Tao that precedes existence, the opposites are in an undifferentiated state of primal unity. But when Tao manifests itself, primal unity breaks apart into yin and yang, and it is the interaction of these two poles that produces "the ten thousand things," the profusion of life.

There are many pairs of opposites with which we have to struggle in human life: maturity and youth, culture and nature, tradition and innovation, home and work, spirituality and worldliness. The list could go on and on. But Taoism understands that underneath all these varieties of opposition lies the primal opposition of yin and yang.

Yin is associated with femaleness and yang with maleness, but the idea behind them is more complex than this and their basic meanings do not contain explicit gender references. The original written Chinese character for yin signified "cloud" and carried the idea of a dark cloud that overshadows earth and brings life-giving rain. The original character for yang signified a yak-tail and conveyed the idea of a pennant fluttering in the sun. Later a classifier signifying "mountain slope" was added to each. Yin then became "dark mountain slope," and yang, "light mountain slope." Together they convey the idea of a valley with a shaded slope and a sunny slope. This is the valley of life, which has two sides, dark and light, neither of which can be separated from the other.

A pennant fluttering in the sun is a beautiful image of the masculine principle. This is the principle of inspired activity, of high hopes and exciting ideas, of will and purpose, of ideal and perfection, of objectivity, theory, and abstraction. The masculine principle is the principle of heaven, and as such it is free from the constraints of material reality. Reality is only present in the masculine principle as a seed of desire: the pure idea wants to be realized. But for this it must join itself to the feminine principle of earth and accept the limitations that come with physical being.

When a cloud passes overhead and brings rain for the life of the earth, the pennant's high moment in the sun is interrupted. Wherever darkness is found on earth, something physically real and solid has blocked out or reduced the light of heaven and made a kind of closed in, interior space. That solidity that forms a barrier to the light might be the droplets of water and dust in a cloud, the leaves of a tree, the roof of a cave or a house, or the other side of the earth itself as night begins to fall. The feminine principle is the principle of matter, of solidity and physical reality. It is the principle of the interconnections and relationships that form the complex web of life. It is the principle of nature with its seasons and cycles of birth, growth, and death and its mechanisms of compensation, adaptation, and balance. It is life as it is, healthy or stunted, whole or maimed, easy or difficult, without regard to perfection or ideal but only to overall balance.

The feminine principle is completely absorbed in its own process. Like a cat stalking a bird or a calf frolicking in a field, it is not hampered by consciousness of what it is. It has no outside vantage point from which to view itself, no ideal standard by which to measure itself. And because of that, because the masculine principle is missing, it cannot rise above itself. And yet the seeds of the masculine are present in it. In moments of discomfort or distress, natural life wants to be perfected. Rain-soaked creatures want to be dry. Drought-stricken plants want rain. Parent birds want to keep snakes from raiding their nests. Nature contains this seed of desire to rise above its own limitations. Earth longs for heaven just as heaven longs for earth.

This primal longing and seeking is the image with which the Bible opens. *In the beginning God created the heavens and the earth.* Out of the primal, unknowable, preexistent source that is God comes the first manifestation of Being: the polarity of heaven and earth. *The earth was without form and void, and darkness was upon the face of the deep.* Here is one pole—matter—the realm of reality. But there is no consciousness, no idea by which to grasp or know anything in it, no light of understanding by which one thing can be distinguished from another. It slumbers in its own unknowing, its natural processes shrouded in darkness, unseen and unnamed. *And the Spirit of God was moving over the face of the waters.* Here is the other pole—spirit—the dynamic realm of idea and perfection. The primal unity has been broken apart. The two poles show themselves, hovering together, and for a moment each is distinct from the other. Then they begin their interaction. *God said, "Let there be light," and there was light.* The masculine side of God provides the idea, the feminine side provides the substance, and the world comes into being.

This same principle can also be seen in modern physics where it has been discovered that subatomic particles exist only as waves of probability until they are observed. The observing consciousness is the masculine principle. The waves of probability are the feminine principle. Only when they are joined together does the world as we know it come into being.

It is important to understand that masculine and feminine are divine principles of equal value, each with its part to play as a basic component of creation. Their interaction and balance determine the health and viability of life as we know it. As human beings we carry the opposites within our species as male and female creatures. We also carry both sides of the opposites within our individual selves: each of us struggles to reconcile earthly reality (the feminine) with aspirations and ideals (the masculine). This does not mean, however, that both sexes carry masculinity and femininity in the same way. Ideally, a man carries masculinity on the outside, in his personal identity, and is softened or gentled by femininity as an inner quality, while a woman carries femininity in her personal outer identity and is strengthened or supported by masculinity as an inner quality. This ideal state does not come about automatically, however. To identify oneself superficially with one's own gender is not the same as identifying with the actual properties of that gender principle.

An effort is required to become conscious of the masculine and feminine principles as they exist in our own being, and until we can differentiate between them, they tend to get mixed up. Sorting them out is a difficult task for everyone. It is only because we are conscious beings that we have to grapple with the problem of the opposites. In the rest of creation this dance proceeds unconsciously. If we were nothing more than unconscious creatures of nature, we would do our part instinctively and the balance of life would automatically be maintained. But as conscious beings we have a will that can to some extent put us in opposition to nature and threaten the balance inherent in creation. We can align ourselves too much with the masculine principle—women can do this as well as men—and then life as it is begins to suffer at the expense of our excessive striving toward what could be or ought to be. Or we can cling too tightly to the feminine principle, and then life as it is begins to carry too much weight and to swallow up what could be or what ought to be.

The opposites turn in and out upon themselves. A close look at any polarized situation will reveal its converse present within it. Too much masculine striving, for example, will suddenly flip over and show another side—too much feminine holding hiding underneath it. One is lived consciously, the other unconsciously. Nothing is simple and straightforward when it comes to the problem of the opposites.

Our personal relationship to the masculine and feminine principles, to spirit and matter, is reflected in every aspect of our lives—in our physical and mental health, in our material well-being, in our relationships, in our intellectual life, creativity, and spirituality, in our capacity for initiative and our capacity for contentment. If we are to find redemption and resolution for the problems of our lives and live toward the inner marriage to which the Christian life calls us, we must become conscious of the opposites. We must understand what is feminine in us and what is masculine and allow these two principles to find their right relationship. They cannot be consciously related until they are consciously separated. Each principle must be recognized and honored in its own right. Only then can the two come together in true union.

Physical sexuality is but a small part of our experience of the opposites, much of which takes place in our inner lives and in outer expressions that do not involve sexual intimacy. The full range of human sexuality exists in all of us and is experienced by us in one way or another as we pass through phases of separating and strengthening the opposing principles and then conjoining them. The part of this process that seeks expression through physical sexuality depends upon the make-up of each individual. I once had a dream in regard to the variety of sexual expression:

> *I dreamed of several sexual packages, so to speak, different ways of being sexual. Each one was suited to certain circumstances, thus allowing a person to meet the need to be sexual in a way that goes with the particular person that he is. The idea seemed to be that different human configurations carry different requirements and difficulties in regard to sexuality. Sexuality itself, the dream seemed to say, is not a part of any human configuration but only a package that is compatible with that configuration.*
>
> *Homosexuality was given as an example. It is one of the packages, but it is not a basic human configuration. The basic configuration would be something non-*

*sexual, such as needing not to be overwhelmed by woman, or being a Wise Man*
*[see Chapter Ten], who by first nature is more connected to the spiritual aspect*
*of the feminine than to the physical aspect. When one of these is a man's basic*
*configuration, homosexuality is a sexual package that can fit his needs.*

*The idea was also present that although sexuality at the physical level is not*
*terribly important, everyone needs to spend some time with it. That is why the variety*
*of sexual packages has been made available.*

When we think about the sexuality of our lives, therefore, we should move
away from the limited idea of physical sexuality and begin to notice the
deeper and more meaningful ways in which our experience of the opposites pervades every aspect of our existence.

## Sun and Moon: Symbols of the Opposites

A GOOD WAY TO BEGIN thinking about the opposing attributes of the
masculine and feminine principles is to consider the differences between
the sun and the moon. As the two principle sources of natural light, the
sun and moon symbolize our two principle modes of consciousness. Although some of the world's mythologies have considered the sun to be
feminine and the moon to be masculine, it is much more common to find
the sun linked to the masculine principle and the moon to the feminine.
It is not that one mythology is right and the other is wrong, but rather
that different attributes of the opposites appear depending upon the lens
through which they are being viewed. Using the more common lens, we
can learn much about the polar qualities of the opposites by looking at
the sun as a symbol of masculine consciousness and the moon as a symbol
of feminine consciousness.

Just as sunlight is hard and bright, and moonlight is soft and mellow,
so is masculine consciousness by nature concentrated and focused, while
feminine consciousness is more gentle and diffuse. Masculine consciousness focuses intently on one thing at a time and carries one overriding idea
at a time. Everything else tends to be closed out as extraneous and distract-
ing. This concentration allows accomplishments that might not be pos-

sible by a less focused approach. Feminine consciousness, on the other hand, takes in the whole picture, moves easily from one aspect of a situation to another, and holds many strands together without concentrating exclusively on any one part. This is the consciousness that is needed for tending life, for keeping an eye on children, for taking care of the many details of a household or an office, and for maintaining the cohesion and health of a group by noticing the feelings and needs of all the different members.

Both men and women have access to each kind of consciousness. A man, however, will be more healthy and whole if he meets the world with focused consciousness and cultivates diffuse consciousness as an inner, spiritual quality which balances and tempers his outer way. Similarly, a woman will be more whole if she meets the world with diffuse consciousness and lets focused consciousness arise from within as a spiritual quality that gives her an authority and effectiveness which does not conflict with her feminine being. This same general pattern of outer and inner manifestations holds true for all the properties of the opposites.

Another difference between moon and sun is that moonlight has a melding effect on the world, while sunlight has a differentiating effect. On a moonlit night distinctions between things are blurred and all is united into one undifferentiated landscape. At sunrise, distinctions begin to return. As the sun drives away the darkness, one thing is separated from another. So too does feminine consciousness weave and connect the many strands of life into a whole, while masculine consciousness cuts and divides the world into separate constituent parts. Masculine consciousness carries *logos*, which Jung defined as "objective interest." The realm of logos is the realm of knowledge and discrimination, of separating and naming. Feminine consciousness, on the other hand, carries *eros*, the principle of relationship and feeling, of interweaving and connecting. Feminine consciousness seeks communion and peace. It says, "We are." Masculine consciousness seeks singularity and says, "I am." Competition and conflict come from this masculine preoccupation, but so does individuality, which carries the possibility of the fulfillment of one's unique, God-given path.

Another difference between sun and moon is that the sun's light emanates from its source, while the moon's light is reflected. The surface of the sun is fiery and projecting, flaring out as it hurls its energy into the universe. The surface of the moon is cool and cratered, receptive to the light of the sun, pocketed with interior spaces. So too is the masculine principle oriented toward outer life, and the feminine toward inner life. The masculine is the principle of activity and movement, of dynamic energy. The feminine is the principle of stillness, receptivity, and reflection. The focus of the masculine is on what is outside—outside the body, outside the house, outside in the visible world. The feminine, on the other hand, knows the importance of what is inside—inside the house, inside the body, inside the psychic realm, hidden from the visible world. The feminine understands the veiled and secret world where new life grows and develops, secluded and protected until it is strong enough to emerge into the light. Where the masculine sees nothing of importance, nothing that is dynamic and exciting, the feminine sees the slow, miraculous unfolding of what matters most.

Another notable difference between sun and moon is that the sun always shines with the same steady light, while the moon's light is constantly changing. Masculine consciousness shares with the sun this aspect of constancy. Masculine consciousness tends to be either up or down, light or dark, fully engaged or fully disengaged. There is not much in between. This makes it reliable and steadfast, when it is operative, but it also gives it a certain inflexibility. Masculine consciousness does not move easily from knowing to not knowing, nor even from one idea to another. It has difficulty with ambiguity, paradox, and compromise. When a shift is required, it tends to collapse instead.

Feminine consciousness on the other hand is more comfortable with varying degrees of knowing and perceiving. It knows the limitations on knowing that spring from life itself, and it is guided, rather than stymied, by changing circumstances. Like moonlight, it is able to mingle with darkness.

Sunlight, in contrast, excludes darkness. When the sun comes up, darkness disappears. We are under the light of the masculine principle when we see our goal clearly and move toward it directly, without ambiguity or confusion. This calls for initiative and action, which are masculine properties. When we are aware of the darkness, of the limitations of reality, we are under the light of the feminine principle. In this light we must feel our way toward an unseen goal. Nothing is completely clear, though the degree of darkness can vary. This calls for the feminine qualities of stillness and discernment and of waiting for gradual development rather than charging ahead.

## The Opposites and the Stages of Life

THIS BRIEF LOOK at the sun and moon does not exhaust their symbolic attributes. Much less have we considered all the many aspects of the opposites as they appear in human life. To learn fully about the opposites, we must pay attention to our own experience of them. Each of us is born with a different mixture of masculine and feminine qualities, with particular strengths and weaknesses inherited from our forebears, each of us with special gifts and special problems in this complicated arena. And yet, although each person is different, there is also a shared human pattern in the general development of the opposites in the course of human life.

In early life—in infancy and childhood—we live in the world of the mother, under the sway of undifferentiated feminine consciousness. In this stage of life masculine and feminine co-exist in an unconscious unity suggestive of the primal unity of preexistence. This is the innocence of childhood, when sexuality has not yet become the polarizing and dominating factor that it later will become. In the world of the mother, consciousness is more diffuse than focused, who we are is valued over what we do, gradual development is more important than heroic accomplishment, and imagination and play, which are expressions of the inner world, command more of our energy than do the discipline and achievement required for life in the outer world.

At puberty the undifferentiated unity of the opposites breaks apart into the separate realities of masculine and feminine. We become more strongly identified with one than with the other. Now we are divided against ourselves, and the tension of that division energizes us. Feeling incomplete, we are driven to seek completion. The containing life of the mother, life as it is, must now be left behind in a bid for life as it could be. This adolescent state of polarity is conducive to masculine consciousness, which begins to gain ascendency as we move toward the outside world, the world of the father. This is a time when hopes and aspirations lead us forward. If we are to have any chance of realizing them, we must develop focus and discipline. Masculine consciousness helps us claim a separate identity as we leave the mother world. And it gives us the objective interest we need to learn about the greater world in order to make our way in it.

Just as boys, with their masculinity, live under the domininance of the feminine principle in childhood, so do young women, with their femininity, live under the dominance of the masculine principle in young adulthood. This is true whether the masculine principle is manifest in themselves or in a husband upon whose support they depend. Life does not thrive at this stage if the masculine does not take the lead. A young woman, however, can be hurt if the balance at this time goes too far toward the masculine, just as a boy can be hurt at the earlier stage by too great a dominance by the feminine.

At midlife, when support in the outer world has been secured, another change in consciousness occurs. Our outward striving has helped relieve our sense of incompleteness but has not been able to lay it to rest altogether. In answer to this, the feminine principle reasserts itself. Inner life makes a bid to return. But now, because masculine consciousness has been established, it is possible for the masculine and feminine principles to co-exist in a conscious way rather than in the unconscious, undifferentiated way they co-existed in early life. A woman at this stage is called to rediscover her own feminine value and to learn the effectiveness of the feminine way when supported by the masculine as an inner rather than an outer quality. A man is called to discover the value of the feminine world within himself and to find there the balance he needs to bring his outer life to wholeness and peace.

This view of the unfolding of the opposites in human life is a broad and simplistic one. The real picture is much more complex. Later stages begin their development in earlier stages. Earlier stages carry over into later stages. We stumble at transitions and sometimes bungle them altogether. One stage might usurp another. Our life with the opposites is never smooth or ideal.

Much of our work on the opposites is outer work and lies at the heart of our relationships—with mother and father, sister and brother, girl-friend and boyfriend, husband and wife, lover and would-be lover, son and daughter, boss and co-worker, friend and enemy. Even dog and cat have a part to play as symbols of our masculine and feminine instincts.

Inner work on the opposites is done as we struggle with ourselves, with our sense of belonging and being at one with others, with our need to separate from others and make a unique place for ourselves, and then, in later life, as we struggle to reconcile our separate reality with the world as we find it and to shift our energy from our own striving toward furthering the lives of others.

The true marriage of the opposites does not take place until death, when we leave the manifest world, which depends for its very existence on the polarization of the opposites. Death is often symbolized in dreams as a wedding, for it is only at death that our inner and outer selves can finally be united in true wholeness. Until then, the limitation of time and space, that inescapable condition of life in this world, breaks wholeness apart into its many aspects and prevents us from having a continuous experience of it.

I once had a dream about this:

*I was moving through outer space. It was like flying, although I was not aware of flying, just of moving. There was a man with me, a masculine presence. I was not aware of how he looked or of any particular identity, although I knew him very well. We were in outer space as I have seen it in pictures. Then we were out of it, beyond it. I looked back and saw the universe being folded up like a map. I knew we had gone beyond infinity. I was aware of the love coming from the masculine presence beside me. He was my lover, my companion in a totally satisfying way, the perfect masculine love for the individual woman that I am.*

*So this is where this kind of love is, I thought to myself. Out here, beyond the universe. No wonder I could never find it back there. There could only be parts of it back there in all the men I loved and in all the men my women friends loved.*

It is interesting that when the dream referred to the parts of my masculine lover in the world of space and time, it included the men in the lives of my women friends—masculine lovers one step removed. I also found it instructive that the dream showed me to be distinct from my masculine self. He and I were together, each with an arm around the other, but he was not the same as I. He was my Lover, the Divine Lover, the Beloved. My own feminine consciousness was going into eternity firmly linked and completely loved by my own most perfect masculine Companion, a spiritual quality that was greater than myself. He was not surprised, as I was, to see the universe folded up behind us nor to realize that only in eternity could perfect love be found.

For me this dream was a foretaste of the marriage of the opposites, the goal of our journey toward God. It has helped me to be patient with life on earth and to reconcile my hopes and ideals, my desire for perfect love, with human life as it is. In this way the dream has furthered my journey toward the very goal it depicts, the goal of a perfect union of love between spirit and matter, between heaven and earth.

CHAPTER TEN

# Masculine Wholeness

ISSUES OF MASCULINE and feminine wholeness are so fundamental to human life that they arise immediately in the dreams and synchronistic events of anyone who sets out on the path of individuation. One of the very first dreams that came to a woman who had just joined our church's natural spirituality Journey Group was this:

*I asked a woman friend at work to help me pin some lace on my sweater. I was going to be married.*

The friend at work, in real life, was a recent bride. The dreamer herself had long been married and had raised a family. And yet the dream showed her making an adjustment to her feminine way of being — adding lace, a more conscious femininity — in preparation for an inner wedding with her animus, the true masculine spirit within her.

This is the essence of the individuation process. The unconscious first leads an individuating person step by step through his or her shadow work—a man becomes more effectively masculine, a woman more effectively feminine in the particular way God intended for that individual person to be. This prepares the person for fruitful union with his or her anima or animus—the contrasexual element within. This divine inner marriage rounds out that person as an individual, giving him or her healthy access to both the masculine and feminine aspects of life, enabling that person to serve God with more wisdom, love, and effectiveness than he or she ever before thought possible.

Although this is a lifelong process, never fully completed, a great deal of progress is made in this direction in the first few years of an individuation journey, a time when the individuating person takes a giant leap forward. It is helpful, therefore, to carry in mind at least a rough idea of the elements of masculine and feminine wholeness in order to more easily recognize the themes being raised by the unconscious.

There are many worthwhile books on this topic, a number of which are listed in the Sources section, Appendix A, at the end of this volume. For a thumbnail sketch of the elements of masculine and feminine wholeness, however, I offer here and in the next three chapters a quaternity-based system of understanding that has arisen in my own consciousness during the course of my journey and has proven helpful to many people with whom I have shared it.

Systems of categorization based on quaternities—or four-part divisions of a whole—are probably as old as mankind itself. A natural product of the unconscious, they can be regarded as thought-mandalas, expressions of wholeness and order arising from the organizing principle of the God-center deep within us.

One of the earliest symbols found in the archaeology of the Indians of the American South, for example, is the so-called "sun circle," a circle quartered by an equilateral cross. Virtually all American Indian groups had elaborate cosmological systems based on the four compass directions— sometimes referred to as the Four Winds. Certain colors, qualities, and spiritual properties were associated with each direction.

In the history of European thought at least two quaternities figured prominently: the four elements—earth, air, water, and fire—and the four humors, or bodily fluids—blood, phlegm, choler (yellow bile), and melancholy (black bile). Elaborate early theories of physics, physiology, and personality were based upon these four-part divisions. The rise of rational, scientific thought put these old systems into disfavor, but in the twentieth century Carl Jung reintroduced quaternity-based thinking with his system of the four functions of consciousness—thinking, feeling, sensation, and intuition.

Jung's associate Toni Wolff made her contribution to quaternity-based thinking with a four-part division of feminine wholeness. Although her quaternity is often cited in Jungian literature, I myself have never found it compelling. It has seemed to me unconvincing and not particularly useful, and it played no role in the development of my own version of the feminine quaternity. Once I had constructed my own framework for understanding, however, I was able to go back to Toni Wolff's quaternity and

see that she had in fact described the same four basic categories of feminine wholeness at which I had arrived, although our approaches and de-
scriptions are very different.

Jung himself classified a man's anima, or inner feminine being, into four
stages of development, which he symbolized with the figures of Eve—instinctual woman; Helen of Troy—romantic woman; the Virgin Mary—
spiritual woman; and Sophia—wisdom woman, the highest of the stages.
His treatment of this quaternity in his Collected Works was quite brief,
and when I myself first came upon the formulation, it was in a mere
synopsis—half a paragraph—in *Man and His Symbols*, a collection of essays
by Jung and his colleagues. Even though so briefly described in that synopsis, the truth of his quaternity struck a chord in me—unlike my experience with Wolff's quaternity—and the images of those four women
stayed with me as meaningful stages of development in a man's anima. I
wondered if they could be applied to woman herself.

My own feminine quaternity did not arise from these thoughts but had
a different basis, as I shall presently explain. However, once I began to
perceive the qualities of the four quarters that my system was producing,
I could see that there was a correspondence with Jung's four stages of the
anima. I therefore incorporated the most basic ideas of his system into
mine, using two of his four names for my feminine quarters.

More recently, a masculine quaternity has been put forth by Robert
Moore and Douglas Gillette, Jungians active in the men's movement of
the late twentieth century. Their work became available in published form
after I had already developed and begun teaching my own masculine quaternity. Here, then, were two four-part systems that had been intuited
completely independently. I was pleased to see that Moore and Gillette
had arrived at a quaternity of masculine wholeness that was very close to
my own—especially in the names they used. Where they had the Lover,
the Warrior, the Magician, and the King, I had the Poet, the Soldier, the
Wise Man, and the King. There were some significant differences, however, in the attributes they assigned to the four quarters, and they did not
rest their four-part division on the same foundation upon which I rest
mine. Their system was much more elaborate than mine and claimed more
for itself than mine does. The fact, however, that there is a somewhat close
correspondence between these two independently developed systems seems

to me to be a reassuring affirmation of the fundamental truth of this masculine quaternity.

The basis for the four-part division of the masculine and feminine quaternities that I present here is not to be found in any of the quaternity systems developed by others. It is, I believe, a refinement of understanding that makes the quaternities especially easy to grasp and to carry along in consciousness, thereby increasing their usefulness for ordinary people on their individuation journeys. Before presenting the masculine and feminine quaternities separately in all their detail, I will first combine the two into a single human quaternity for the purpose of putting forth the underlying principles common to both.

This human quaternity is best thought of as a fundamental duality which is then divided again to form a quaternity. The duality is based upon the fact that each of us comes into the world as the offspring of two parents, which means that in a manner of speaking we are each two sons or two daughters. A man is both his mother's son and his father's son, and a woman is both her mother's daughter and her father's daughter. This is true even when one or both parents are unknown.

As our mother's child we receive our relationship to the feminine realm—to the intimate world of home, self, and psyche, of relationship, nature, and physical being. As our father's child we inherit our relationship to the masculine realm, which broadly speaking means the outside world, the world of "others," with its issues of power, achievement, and wealth, and of culture and tradition.

In diagramming either the masculine or the feminine quaternity as I am presenting them here, the mother world is always placed on the righthand side, and the father world on the left.

*Father World*     *Mother World*

Figure 4. Mother World–Father World Duality

This consistency of form makes the ideas behind the quaternity more concrete. One becomes accustomed to analyzing life by holding it up against the diagram, so to speak, looking for the feminine qualities of a situation on the righthand side and the masculine qualities on the lefthand side, checking the balance of the mother world and the father world. This positioning of the two sides might seem contrary to the usual symbolic association of the masculine principle with consciousness and the right-hand side and of the feminine principle with the unconsious and the left-hand side, but in fact it is not. Facing the diagram is like facing a person, which means that for the person represented by the diagram the father world is on the right and the mother world is on the left.

The second division in the quaternity is based on the fact that "mother" and "father" are each experienced on two distinct levels of reality. Every person is not only the child of a personal father but also of the heavenly Father, the masculine spiritual principle. This is a living reality in each of us, whether we are well related to it or not. Likewise, we are the child both of a personal mother and of Mother Nature, the feminine spiritual principle. The spirit of heaven and the spirit of nature are forces in the world that are larger than we are and to which, therefore, we are subject, giving us a relationship to them of child to parent.

|  |  |
|---|---|
| *Personal*<br>*Father* | *Personal*<br>*Mother* |
| *Spiritual*<br>*Father* | *Spiritual*<br>*Mother* |

Figure 5. Mother World–Father World Quaternity

Generally speaking, the first half of life takes place on the personal level of the mother world and father world, a level that could be called the ego's world. When we are young, it is our personal mothers and fathers, and their surrogates, whom we directly experience as powers higher than ourselves. Our task is to grow up to their level, to become what they are and assume their positions of responsibility. When we do that, we ourselves become the mother and the father, no longer the child looking up to others.

This attainment automatically issues in the call for transcendance to the next level, where God rather than the ego is central. Again we find ourselves looking up to a higher power, to God as heavenly spirit on the masculine side and as the wisdom of nature on the feminine side. Again our task is to learn the way of the higher order and to take our place in life as effective carriers of God's spirit. We are called upon to grow up to a partnership with God. As Jesus puts it in John's Gospel, God wants us not as lowly servants, who know nothing of His business, but as friends and confidants.

When diagramming the quaternities, the youthful, ego level is located above the horizontal line, and the mature, spiritual level is located below. Again, this seems contrary to symbolic language, which portrays the spiritual level above the ego level. The position in the diagram, however, is in accord with the fact that the spiritual level follows the ego level as the central focus of life. As the diagram is read from top to bottom, the ego level comes first, as it does in life.

The diagram shown here of the human quaternity (figure 6) includes some of the aspects of life that belong to each of the four quarters. Although certain aspects of each quarter belong particularly to the masculine or feminine version of that quarter, we all have the qualities of both the masculine and feminine quaternities within our own being, one of them reflecting our same sex aspect and the other our anima or animus.

All aspects of the quaternities belong to all men and women, regardless of their sexual orientation. Sexuality is one expression of the dynamics between the different parts of the quaternities, and it is as varied as the dynamics themselves.

## The Masculine Quaternity

THE MASCULINE QUATERNITY begins with the basic dichotomy of father's son and mother's son. Every man, and every woman's animus, can be seen in these terms. Although the divisions of the masculine quaternity are universally valid, the names given them for the purpose of discussion are arbitrary and necessarily imperfect. The names I present here are simply

| FATHER WORLD | | MOTHER WORLD | |
| :---: | :---: | :---: | :---: |
| *Personal Father* | | *Personal Mother* | |
| *(Outside World)* | | *(Home)* | |
| man | mastery | woman | physical life |
| will | expansion | love | pleasure |
| boundary | mind | nurture | play |
| competition | knowledge | tending | novelty |
| ambition | analysis | children | creativity |
| focus | protection | family | art |
| discipline | support | intimacy | song |
| work | fidelity | relationship | self |
| *Spiritual Father* | | *Spiritual Mother* | |
| *(Heaven)* | | *(Nature)* | |
| ideal | order, timing | wilderness | dreams |
| perfection | structure | garden | synchronicity |
| purity | limitation | color | meaning |
| justice | hierarchy | variety | solitude |
| civilization | unity | life process | depth |
| community | theology | healing | inner life |
| brotherly love | worship | wisdom | death |
| servant leadership | vocation | psyche | transformation |

Figure 6. Human Wholeness

the ones that seem most useful to me. On the ego level I call the father's son the *Soldier* and the mother's son the *Poet.* Every man experiences the tension between these two parts of himself, between the "hard man," who can handle himself in the harsh reality of the outside world, and the "soft man," for whom love, pleasure, and creative expression are important. At the God-centered level, I call the son of the spiritual father the *King,* and the son of the spiritual mother the *Wise Man.* In these two parts of himself a man is divided between the need to play a responsible role in community life and the need to seek the mystery of life in solitude and communion with his soul.

Every man has a "star" in one of the four quarters. By nature he might

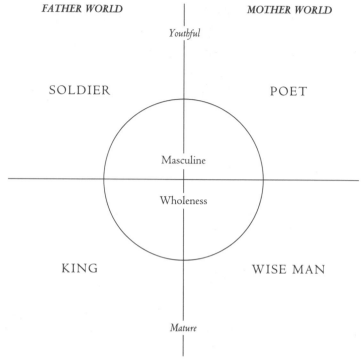

Figure 7. The Masculine Quaternity

be more a Soldier than anything else, or he might be more a Wise Man. His effectiveness in life, however, will depend on how well he integrates into his conscious being all four aspects of masculine wholeness. A man whose strongest flow of energy comes from the King quarter, for example, but who has not developed the Poet, the Soldier, and the Wise Man in himself, will not be all that a King can be.

## The Poet

GENERALLY SPEAKING, a man begins life in the Poet quarter. Early childhood takes place in the world of the personal mother. As the son of his mother, a boy experiences his basic relationship to woman and to life, for at a deep, symbolic level woman *is* life. The dominant themes of the Poet quarter are love and imagination. Love is so large a part of it that Moore and Gillette name this part of the masculine quaternity the Lover, a term that can be very useful when thinking about the quarter, although in my opinion it is ultimately too limiting. The world of the personal mother is not only the world of love and relationship but also of imagination and play, the zone of life from which creativity comes.

| *Soldier* | **POET** |
|-----------|----------|
| *King* | *Wise Man* |

Figure 8. Poet Quarter

The artist, the dreamer, and the visionary all have their home in this quarter. The new and the novel arise here. The son of the personal mother could be called the Artist or the Dreamer, but that would leave out the image of the lover. Poet—although it, too, can be an overly narrow term if taken too literally—comes closer than any other to combining the images of creativity and love. The Poet, archetypically, is a romantic, a lover of woman and of life. He is non-analytical, using words as song, attending to and expressing the feelings and images which arise from the depths of his being. The Poet knows his creative expression to be valuable for its own sake, just because it comes from himself. He loves it as a mother loves her child.

The Poet as lover has to do with personal and intimate relationship, not with the broad love of mankind, which belongs to the King quarter, nor with the love of feminine wisdom, which is the province of the Wise Man. The Poet's love is that first experienced with the mother, the love found in home and family, a love based on unity, inclusion, and sharing, not on doing and proving. It is a love centered on pleasing the other and being pleased, on meeting the needs of the other and having one's own needs met. A man whose Poet aspect is healthy can express his feelings to another person. He can embrace another, man or woman, without embarrassment. He can relate easily to his own children. And he can make a stranger feel at home.

A man's connection to his body life comes from the Poet quarter. His body is an important part of his own feminine reality. It is the vessel of his spirit, his "mother" at a deep symbolic level. It is the Poet in a man, the son of the personal mother, who savors and values the physical experience of life on earth.

Although the Poet and Soldier belong generally to the youthful level of life, and the Wise Man and the King to the mature level, each of the four quarters has within itself a youthful, or instinctual, expression and a mature, or achieved, expression. The youthful expression of the Poet quarter reflects that of the boy in relationship to his mother. The youthful Poet in a man says, "Love me. Please me. Watch me." In his healthy aspect the youthful Poet knows himself to be worthy of love, knows how to take pleasure in life, and knows that that which comes from his own being is valuable.

The mature Poet, on the other hand, no longer needs to be mothered. He says, "I love you. I please you. I watch you." In relationship, he goes beyond emotional gratification to the hard work of love, setting aside his own needs when necessary. He seeks to please others for their sake rather than his own. And he is able to value and nurture the creativity of others. A balanced Poet is both of these—youthful and mature—in an integrated whole.

As is true with all the quarters, the shadow of the Poet is to be found in its unconscious and unbalanced manifestations. The man who seeks only his own pleasure without regard for others, and the man who seeks too much to please others—both are shadow manifestations of the Poet. So too the man who is obsessed with problems of love and the man who can never commit himself to another; the man who lives always in his imagination and dreams, never facing reality, and the man who is so consumed with reality that he has no time for play.

The list of shadow possibilities could go on endlessly and would include not only blatant manifestations but extremely subtle ones. But no such list would be of much help for anyone on an individuation journey. Through dreams and synchronicity the unconscious itself teaches each of us in an individual way about the many aspects of our own shadow. This process unfolds slowly over time, as we are gradually able to understand the ways in which we have been off balance and can make the necessary responses. While the quaternities can be helpful in recognizing our shadow parts as they are revealed to us, this help can only be general in nature. There is no magic formula for shadow work.

# The Soldier

LIFE BEGINS in the Poet quarter with love, imagination, and play, the gifts of the mother world—valuable gifts, the lack of which is always crippling. But valuable as they are, they will not carry a man far unless he also receives the gifts of the father world. He must be able to take his sense of his own worth and potential which he receives in the mother world and turn it into reality in the organized world of competitive interests that lies outside the intimate family circle. In the father world, the world of "others," nothing is granted unless it is proven, nothing gained unless it is won. Where love counts for all in the mother world, it is will that counts in the father world. And will is a quality that is as elusive and mysterious as love itself.

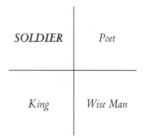

Figure 9. Soldier Quarter

The father world at the ego level is the realm of the Soldier. Here the will is trained and guided with the help and support of the personal father, and of father surrogates. In the intimate mother world a man can relax and be himself. But if he is to succeed in the outside world of the father, he must learn its ways and adapt himself to its requirements, however foreign and unnatural they may seem. To do this he must gradually gain control of his own will and use it to counter his natural impulse to fall back into the ease and comfort of the mother world.

The Soldier trains his will into an effective force with which, first of all, he guards his personal ego boundaries. It is the Soldier in a man who must stand up for his separate reality against outsiders and loved ones alike. The Soldier is always on the lookout for the enemy, for anyone who would encroach upon the territory of his being and threaten his sense of who he is. The more a man knows himself, the more effective he will be in differentiating between friendly and unfriendly elements that come toward him, a distinction that is not always obvious.

The Soldier trains his will to work, to accomplish necessary tasks, however difficult and unpleasant. A strong will is required to override the body's natural inclination to stop and rest, to give up, or to take an easier way. A youthful will is not disciplined enough to carry a boy or young man successfully through the difficult requirements of the early stages of life. It is the will of the father, or father surrogates, including the mother's animus, that must make up the difference and supply the needed inspiration, direction, and discipline. A Soldier obeys his superiors, accepting training and mentorship from those who are established in whatever aspect of the organized, collective world he seeks to join. Ultimately he serves the King, the highest principle of that realm.

The masculine world is the world of consciousness, of ordered reality constructed slowly over time from the creative chaos of the unconscious natural world. It is the structure side of life, a work against nature, difficult to achieve and to maintain. Each life has something new to bring to it. That newness, which arises in the mother world, must find a way to establish itself in the powerfully conservative world of the father, the constructed world of culture and tradition. It is the Soldier who prepares the way for this by embracing some aspect of tradition and seeking to serve it. To the degree that it is necessary, the Soldier part of a man puts on a uniform and becomes a team player. He learns to march in a straight line, in step with the collective world into which his individual contribution will eventually be absorbed. It is only by engaging in the life of the father world that a man can find an effective way to make his contribution to it.

There are times, however, when the Soldier must be a rebel and fight against a father world that has grown dark and is no longer open to the creative contributions that seek to come from the mother world. There is always some resistance in the father world to new ways of understanding and doing things. Sometimes that resistance becomes so unyielding that protests and uprisings are necessary. But the rebel must be careful not to become permanently antagonistic to the father world. The world of the dark father is a distortion, a departure from the true spirit of the father, which seeks to support new life, not to crush it. If a Soldier is always a rebel, standing forever outside the traditional system, feeling hopelessly overpowered by it, railing against it just because it is a system and does not include or go along with everything that he himself is, then he will die with the special gift of his life unrealized. Such a rebellion is actually against the outside world itself and the sacrifices it requires. It amounts to a refusal to leave home and enter adult life.

The Soldier is the part of a man that wields a weapon. If the enemy is starvation, a hoe is a weapon. If chaos is the enemy, a plan is a weapon. A Soldier arms himself with whatever tool enables him to exercise his will upon the world and gain an advantage over the forces that oppose him. A stone spearpoint, a wheeled cart, a windmill, a rifle, a saber saw, a book, a violin, a computer—anything that gives him a competitive edge. The ultimate weapon is the mind itself with its rational, analytic power. The word and the sword are symbolically akin, both able to cut and dissect, to wound and to conquer.

Training, practice, and skill; mastery and craftsmanship—all fall within the realm of the Soldier. Learning based on established knowledge also belongs in this quarter. Creative vision and natural talent come from the Poet, but it is the Soldier who applies the discipline that is necessary to bring that potential forward against all rivals and establish it in the world.

The youthful Soldier is the one who guards the territory. A boy's task is to defend what is his by natural right. He must be strong enough to maintain his essential being against anyone who would encroach upon it. The mature Soldier expands that territory through training and mastery. Becoming better at what he does, he gains effectiveness in a larger sphere.

Both the youthful and the mature aspects of the Soldier are necessary for masculine wholeness.

## The Wise Man

IN THE EGO-CENTERED WORLD of the Poet and the Soldier, the basic problem of life is that of the individual in relationship to the human world. In the God-centered world of the Wise Man and the King, the problem is that of the human world in relationship to God, a problem that includes the individual's personal role in that greater drama. We do not have to subscribe to a theology that names heaven and nature as divine aspects of life in order to experience them as such. Named or unnamed, the ideal of perfect life (the spirit of heaven) both inspires and oppresses everyone. We are continually called forth by it, and we continually struggle beneath the impossibility of it, unable wholly to satisfy or escape its demands. So too does nature make her overpowering presence felt, though she is noticed more when she blocks and defeats our will than when she moves in accord with it and helps us along. In droughts, floods, and storms, in illness, disability, and death, and in the intractability of human nature itself, we are faced, whether we like it or not, with the mighty power of the feminine aspect of God.

Figure 10. Wise Man Quarter

It is the Wise Man who accepts and respects the feminine aspect of the divine. He seeks to understand its wisdom, to learn from it and work with it in its endless unfolding of life on earth. The Wise Man is that part of a man who loves nature, an attitude which draws him into solitude. Whether fishing, hunting, hiking, gardening, or watching a sunset, a true engagement with nature draws a man away from his fellow humans into communion with his soul.

The youthful Wise Man brings masculine consciousness to his experience of nature as a physical phenomenon. He learns the way of things— where the fish bite and when to plant the corn, how to keep a cut from becoming infected and in what part of the sky to look for the Big Dipper. If he has strength in this quarter, he will go deeper and become a natural philosopher. Drawing analogies between nature and human life, he comes to understand for himself such eternal human verities as: the seasons of a person's life are like the seasons of the year; wherever there is human prey, there will be human predators; individual growth takes time, it cannot be rushed.

The mature Wise Man is the rare individual who goes even deeper and sees *beneath* the physical surface of nature to the divine wisdom that underlies it, the living spirit of God that uses natural life as the language and process of spiritual growth. At this level the Wise Man sees in nature not only analogies of eternal truths but also explicit manifestations of particular truths concerning the human drama in which he is presently participating. He understands that through natural occurances God speaks to us personally, guiding us through the moments of our lives. The mature Wise Man pays attention to dreams, synchronicity, and the murmuring undercurrents of his own consciousness. He recognizes the reality of natural spirituality.

The Wise Man uses his masculine consciousness to bring system and order to the feminine truth of the divine wisdom of nature. The Jungian concepts I discussed in the first part of this book are an example of such a system, perceived and developed by the Wise Man aspect of Carl Jung. Another example is the *I Ching*, the Chinese book of wisdom, an orderly system perceived and constructed by several generations of Chinese sages. The masculine and feminine quaternities as I am presenting them here are a system perceived by the Wise Man in me, an aspect of my animus. Such systems put a grid in front of the natural spiritual process that underlies conscious life, making it possible for us to understand the process more clearly, to work with it more intelligently, and to convey its nature to others.

It is the mature Wise Man who takes the individuation journey, follow-ing the feminine wisdom in himself into the unknown world of the un-conscious. He leaves behind his identification with collective conscious-ness in order to find his own unique truth, submitting to the death of his ego-centered self and experiencing resurrection to a new and more mean-ingful life centered in God. Once a man has made this journey, he becomes available to others as a guide—a sage, a wise old man. The Wise Man is solitary, off to himself, strongly connected to earth and nature. Commu-nity life does not belong to this quarter. This is the side of spiritual life that does not reach out to others but waits, in the way of the feminine, for seekers to find it. It is a well-known aspect of wisdom that when the student is ready, he will find the right teacher, the one to whom he be-longs through a deep and mysterious connection. The meeting of student and teacher is inevitable. Fate brings it about in response to the readiness of both.

## The King

SPIRITUALITY that is more extraverted and oriented toward community life is located in the King quarter. Here the masculine ideal of perfection seeks realization in human life. This ideal comes from God, the source of all perfection, the Father of all. The King is that part of a man who, as the son of the masculine spirit, is dedicated, consciously or unconsciously, to the heavenly ideal. The last pages of the Bible describe a vision of heaven, an image that can be seen as a symbolic statement from the un-conscious about heaven's true nature. In this vision, heaven is described as a holy city where God lives in the midst of humankind, a community in which there is no death and no sadness. The city is perfectly square and is made of gold and precious gems. Rising from the throne of God and running through the middle of the city is the crystal-clear river of life, its banks lined with trees of life bearing fruit in every season. The city is radiant with the glory of God and needs no other light.

Figure 11. King Quarter

The desciption is of a perfect union of God and humanity, which includes a perfect union of masculine culture (the square-walled city) and feminine nature (the river and the trees of life). Gold and jewels symbolize the highest earthly values. Radiant light symbolizes the highest spiritual values. The best of heaven and earth are wed. This is a symbolic statement about a potential state of being that can only be fully attained in the eternal realm. And yet it lives dynamically within each of us and seeks to find as much expression as possible in our temporal lives.

This drive from within does not come to us in a neat, integrated, and self-explanatory package, but rather as a jumbled and unrealistic sense of what life should be. The more unconscious a person is of its true and deeper meaning, the more it gives him a powerful desire for its literal realization, for a world in which everyone is always good, in which bad things do not happen, and in which he never has to die, which means he never has to be transformed. It fills him with a desire for the highest earthly values—for riches (literal gold and jewels) and for perfect structures (grand houses and magnificent public buildings, perfect families and institutions). He finds himself wanting literally to sit in luxurious accomodations beside crystal-clear waters and be served the best fruits of the earth in every season. And he seeks the highest plane of spirituality, the ever-present radiance of God, all goodness and light, no darkness.

It is the youthful King in a man who is seized by the ideal and cannot see it objectively or distinguish his own reality from it. The youthful King unconsciously identifies himself with the masculine aspect of God. He feels himself to be the one above all others, the smartest, the fastest, the highest, the best. He expects perfection from himself, from those around him, and from life itself. Whether he admits it or not, the youthful King expects to save the world. His attention is ever drawn to the national and international levels of human life. He knows himself, though unrecognized, to be the best in the country, the best in the world, at what he does or wants to do.

These ideals inspire him and draw him forward into life. They help him find what is best in himself. If he is strong in this quarter, these ideals help the youthful King lead and inspire others. But they also set him up for inevitable disappointment and accompanying feelings of rage and despondency.

The mature King is the rare individual who ceases to identify unconsciously with divine kingship. He no longer feels he is the one above all others—though neither does he feel he is the lowest of the low, which is simply a shadow aspect of the youthful King. The mature King understands who he truly is in his limited human reality, and he knows in the depths of himself, not merely as a high and shining ideal, that it is God who is King of all. The mature King is at one with his kingdom—with earth, nature, and reality. He recognizes the bounded realm to which God has called him, with his particular talents, to be a servant leader. He knows that his role is not to be the savior of the world, but merely to help bring forth in an actual, limited community the best life possible, which is perfect in its own way but not in an ideal way.

The mature King is the culmination of a man's development. Different in quality from the other three quarters, the King incorporates them all and unifies them into a new, transcendent level of life. He has within the kingdom of his own being a Poet who, ideally, loves people and is open to creative vision; a Soldier who is strong, brave, and disciplined; and a Wise Man who is connected to earth, soul, and meaning.

The King brings order to his world not by force and decree but by the simple fact of being present in that world with his depth and clarity of consciousness and his wholeness of being. He sees how things fit together. He has a sense of timing, of when to move forward into new expressions of life and when to wait for slower elements to catch up. He loves all the inhabitants of his kingdom and sees them with clear eyes, recognizing both the value and the limitations of each and understanding the role each has to play. That love and recognition confer blessing. Order and blessing are the two primary functions of the King.

In the King quarter inner realities are made manifest in outer life in a way that is healthy for the human community. Civilization belongs to this quarter. Houses and public institutions, manners and mores, customs and rituals—both civic and religious—are manifestations of the King. Charity and religious outreach make manifest the King's blessing.

If the King quarter is too strong or too weak, distortions occur. There can be too much kingly structure and not enough natural chaos, or too much naturalness and not enough structure. There can be too much heavenly spirituality and not enough recognition of earthly darkness, or there can be too much attention to earth's darkness and not enough openness to heavenly light. As with the other quarters, the shadow possibilities of the King are endless.

Few men undergo *conscious* development of both levels in all four quarters of the masculine quaternity. But whether they are experienced consciously or unconsciously, all four quarters manifest themselves in every human life. Whether these manifestations are for good or ill depends on their degree of consciousness and on the overall balance of the whole.

# CHAPTER ELEVEN

# The Beatles and the Masculine Quaternity

THE TRUTH of the masculine quaternity and the fundamental importance of the human wholeness it represents are clearly illustrated in an image of it that arose in the second half of the twentieth century with so much energy that the whole world was affected by it. In the two decades after World War II, the value of the father world was at its height in the hearts and minds of people everywhere. The Soldier, with his courage, discipline, and sacrifice, had saved civilization from fascism. The ideals of the youthful King, an Edwardian ideal of perfect civilization, of all light and no darkness, had a strong, though weakening, grip on the post-war world.

Everyone participating in the collective consciousness of that time was extremely mannerly and constrained. People in all areas of life knew where they fit in the order of things. Every hair was in place, every instinct in check. Families tried their best to give the appearance of perfection, repressing and denying all darkness. Truth had an almost exclusively rational basis. There was little real conversation between men and women. Nature was falling out of the picture as farming ceased to be a widespread occupation. Man was becoming one-sided to the extreme—all father world, all Soldier and King.

Gone almost completely from collective consciousness was the Poet and the Wise Man, that side of a man that loves woman and wisdom, that has heart and feeling, that is natural, relaxed, and open to creative play and new expressions of life. Gone was the part of a man that accepts the non-rational and looks beneath the surface of reality to find meaning and guidance, that acknowledges and honors the darkness of life, that accepts death and transformation. Feminine values, half of what it means to be human, had been driven underground.

Into this world in the early 1960s came the phenomenon of the Beatles, an all male rock'n'roll band from the rough port city of Liverpool. Though obviously carrying the masculine toughness of their Liverpool roots, the Beatles had long hair that fell around their faces in a feminine way, a shocking spectacle in the Soldier world of 1963. Their music was hard and driving, and yet joyful and open—a strange and appealing combination of darkness and light. Their personalities were charming and natural, spontaneous, fun-loving and witty, outrageous, and yet in their own way polite and respectful. Adults as well as teenagers were fascinated by them.

The Fab Four they were nicknamed by the press. John, Paul, George, and Ringo. Even as I write, almost forty years later, most people in the world still know their names. They were the four who were one, the one that was four. Everyone knew that the Beatles could not be the Beatles without each of these particular men. It was the four of them in combination that made them what they were. But although everyone knew that this was true, no one knew why it was true.

Everyone who was open to it could *feel* what it was about the Beatles. It could be felt that they were special, earthshaking, soul-searing, heart-freeing. They meant something important, they brought something desperately needed. Young women especially felt it and screamed and wept in their presence, caught up in an ecstatic joy, seeing something in these four men, hearing something in their music, that belonged to them as women and honored them, something that had been missing in the world and without which they no longer wanted to live. Everyone could feel what it was about the Beatles, but no one could *understand* what it was.

That is the way truth comes in the mother world—nonrationally, as feeling or deep knowing. It cannot at first be rationally stated. New consciousness must be developed in the father world before that is possible. For the most part the new truth that arises in the mother world is kept inside, held close, treasured, believed in. If conveyed to others it can only be through emotion, art, music, poetry, or mystical language. The truth from the mother world nourishes the soul. It gives meaning to life, makes it new again and worth living. An awareness of this feminine side of human truth was returning to collective consciousness in the 1960s, and the Beatles were the four-part image of masculine wholeness that heralded that return.

At the height of the Beatles' career, Paul McCartney said of the group, "The thing is, we're all really the same person. We're just four parts of the one. We're individuals, but we make up together The Mates, which is one person. . . . We all add something different to the whole." The Beatles as a single "person" was a Poet personality. Just as every individual whose special strength is in the Poet quarter has within himself all four quarters, conscious or unconscious, so did the Beatles have all four quarters participating together to make them a whole Poet.

John Lennon was a Soldier poet, a hard man, a man's man. Words and humor were the weapons with which he channeled and tempered the anger and aggression that were never far beneath the surface of his otherwise appealing personality. He himself said that his political advocacy of peace and nonviolence was a counteraction to his own violent temper, an attempt to get beyond it. He was the Beatle who was most devoted to the hard, masculine rock'n'roll music that inspired the Beatles' teenage beginnings in Liverpool. It was his tough, brazen energy that led them from obscurity to fame.

John, however, was also the most wounded of the four, having been abandoned by his father essentially at birth and by his adored mother off and on throughout his childhood until her accidental death when he was sixteen. Loss seemed to have been his fate. The uncle who helped raise him had died a few years before his mother, and in the following decade death claimed his closest friend—Stu Sutcliffe, a former Beatle—and Brian Epstein, the Beatles' manager and surrogate father. John's wound was deepest in the realm of the father, which made him a dark, unconscious Soldier, rebellious and antagonistic toward the outside world and given to bouts of paralysing depression, when his will would abandon him altogether.

His mother's family, however, in which he had been brought up, had been lively, loving, and well-meaning, if somewhat disfunctional. That produced a core of love and goodness in John that always came through and tempered the effects of his undeniable darkness. He did not try to deny his darkness but put much of it out for the world to see, which meant that the Beatles as a whole personality did not try to deny its shadow side but faced it squarely and sought to work with it and integrate it. This added much to their depth, complexity, and authenticity.

Although all members of the group were poets, it was Paul McCartney who occupied the Poet quarter in the greater Beatles personality. Melody flowed through him in a natural, unending stream. He was a woman's man, soft and romantic, a true lover of woman. Good relationships were important to him, and he was mannerly and thoughtful toward others. Even though his mother died when he was fourteen, Paul's experience of his childhood was generally a happy one, and his basic outlook on life was positive and optimistic. Because it was difficult for him to see darkness in the world or in himself, he was prone to sentimentality and superficiality in his creativity, and he also tended at times to be covertly mean and manipulative in his dealings with others. John Lennon's dedication to the truth about the hard side of life checked these shadow tendencies in Paul and brought out the best in him as a songwriter and musician. Though John had been the evident leader of the Beatles in their early years, it was Paul who emerged as the leader in the end.

George Harrison occupied the Wise Man quarter in the Beatles personality. He, too, came from a relatively healthy home, where he was the youngest of four siblings and was especially close to his mother. Though younger than the other Beatles, he was from the beginning more self-possessed and thoughtful than the rest. He spoke as if from a higher vantage point, somewhat removed from the fray. His energy was not so ego-driven as that of Paul and John, and he stood back from their competition for supremacy and center stage. Naturally introverted, he preferred solitude to the company of others. It was George who brought the music and spirituality of India to the Beatles. With great discipline, he learned to play the sitar, a difficult instrument to master. He was strongly drawn to Hindu wisdom, of which he became a devoted student. Indian spirituality was an interest and orientation that he never abandoned. George was also a dedicated gardener, especially in his later years.

Ringo Starr (born Richard Starkey) was the poet King of the Beatles. Even less ego-driven than George, Ringo was a true "servant leader" in the way he ordered and unified the group musically with his drumming, keeping perfect time, never calling attention to himself, serving every song differently according to its individual nature. True to the King's characteristic of being different in quality from the other three quarters, Ringo joined the group just at the moment the Beatles were moving from the Liverpool stage to the world stage, whereas the others had been together since the beginning. Ringo's very name suggests the symbolism of the Self, of whom the King is a human image. The several rings he characteristically wore on his fingers suggested kingship, as did his enthronement among his drums on a platform above the other three during their performances.

Most important to Ringo's kingship, however, was the depth of love he had for the other Beatles and for people in general, a love that conferred blessing on those around him. The other Beatles responded in kind, loving him more than they loved each other. Ringo was the one thing on which they could all agree. He was the nicest and most decent one of them, the most truly loving. His noble spirit unified them and became their ruling spirit. It is because the Beatles carried this basically decent spirit that the world continues to love them, despite their evident weaknesses and follies.

Ringo's spirit seems to have come from a family life that was fundamentally loving, even though his parents divorced when he was very young and his father went out of his life. Unlike John, he grew up close to his father's family as well as his mother's, and he was particularly close to his paternal grandfather. So while he shared John's wound in the father realm, he also shared Paul's happy family life, including a connection to the father world. His childhood, however, was marked by two long hospital stays, several years length in all, which served to initiate him into the solitude and depth of the Wise Man's realm. It was presumably from this experience that he emerged with the qualities of humility, loving-kindness, centeredness, and servanthood that belong to the mature King.

By himself, Ringo Starr was not a whole and individuated man. None of the Beatles were. None were authentically God-centered during this period of their lives, not even George with his dedication to Hindu wisdom. But archetypal forces were shaping their experience, making of them an illusion, a living myth for their time. Together they constituted an *image* of wholeness, and together they took a journey that *looked* like an individuation journey. It was because it carried that image that so many people were fascinated by it, although few, if any, consciously understood this. It is only as I have been looking at the Beatles in connection with this book that I myself have come to realize that not only did their personalities and their life together illustrate the masculine quaternity and the individuation journey, but so did their music itself.

## Beatles Music: A Dream of Individuation

LIKE SO MUCH ARTISTIC EXPRESSION in the twentieth century, the music of the Beatles is a relatively raw expression of the unconscious and is therefore quite close to dream language. It can be analyzed as if it were dream material. If we follow the music through time as the symbolic expression of the life of this Beatles "person," we can see in it the portrayal of a masculine life that rises from youth to a midlife crisis, discovers the unconscious, and individuates in a journey that passes through each of the masculine quarters, culminating in its fullest expression in the King quarter as it accepts and approaches its own death.

The Beatles' music is dramatically divided into roughly two halves, usually referred to simply as early Beatles and late Beatles. The early Beatles music began in Liverpool and lasted almost to the end of the group's world-touring days in 1966. This was the era of Beatlemania, when mobs besieged them wherever they went and the screaming of their fans often rendered their stage performances inaudible. Virtually all their songs in this period were simple teenage love songs set to rock'n'roll music that, though definitely innovative and fresh, was not greatly different from other rock'n'roll music of the time.

As they neared the end of the early period, the Beatles had achieved more fame and fortune than they had ever dreamed possible. As rock stars, they had reached the absolute top. Predictably, this brought with it a crisis of spirit. What next? Like an individual entering a midlife crisis, their music began to show a growing soberness, self-reflection, and even despondency. Then came the song that marks the break between the early and late periods. Its origin reveals the touch of grace that is always offered to a life in need of transformation. The song's melody came to Paul in a dream. He woke up the next morning and went immediately to his piano and played "Yesterday," whole and entire as it had arisen in the night. No other song ever came to him so completely intact.

"Yesterday" was not rock'n'roll. When it was recorded on the *Help!* album, surrounded by rock'n'roll songs, Paul sang it alone accompanied by an acoustic guitar and *a string quartet!* Something new was happening. Existing consciousness, however, always resists transformation. Their next album, *Rubber Soul,* was a transition album, the old music trying to reassert itself but losing ground to the growing new sound that departed from the usual rock beat and incorporated a greater variety of instruments. The song lyrics were also becoming more sophisticated.

It was the next album, *Revolver,* that marked the true beginning of the late Beatles. With *Revolver* the Beatles went completely beyond the boundaries of rock'n'roll, expanding to a new level of richness and complexity in lyrics, music, and instrumentation. It is this later music that carries the image of a conscious individuation journey, the kind of spiritual journey that takes place when a person discovers and integrates the unconscious.

The Beatles had in fact discovered the unconscious, although not in a legitimate way. Through psychedelic drugs they had artificially broken down their structures of conscious perception, allowing themselves to perceive psychedelically the nuances of spiritual reality that underlie physical reality. Carl Jung was careful to point out that such an approach to the unconscious always becomes poisonous and destructive. The unconscious brings with it a moral obligation to understand it and integrate it into consciousness. Drug users almost never have a moral attitude toward the unconscious, and even if they did, they would be unable to integrate such a large amount of artificially induced unconscious material. The result is a disintegration of personality rather than integration and wholeness. This effect can be seen in varying degrees in the Beatles as individuals, especially in John Lennon.

The music of the late Beatles shows, however, that they did manage to integrate some of the lessons coming to them in that period, at least to the extent that this could be put into song. The unconscious was clearly using them more than they were using it. In a rather amazing example of synchronicity, the four great albums of that period—*Revolver, Sgt. Pepper's Lonely Hearts Club Band, Magical Mystery Tour,* and *Abbey Road*—each carried songs that, when taken altogether, were wholly related to a different quarter of the masculine quaternity. Furthermore, the albums appeared in a sequence that followed the masculine individuation sequence of Poet, Soldier, Wise Man, and King.

This certainly was not intentional on the part of the Beatles. They knew nothing at all of the masculine quaternity, which had not yet been formulated by anyone, and they could have had only the vaguest notion, if any, of the process of individuation. Therefore, as I examine these albums through this particular lens, I will not be concerned with what the Beatles *thought* they were saying, but with what their songs actually do say to us as listeners. As in dream analysis, these interpretations are to be held lightly, allowing for revisions and further insights, and always with the understanding that it is impossible to grasp all that the unconscious is trying to express.

## *Revolver:* The Poet Quarter

*Revolver* begins with "Taxman," a song written by George and for which he is the lead singer. (The Beatle who contributed most to the writing of a Beatles song was almost always its lead singer.) In "Taxman" the Beatle Wise Man lays out the hard truth about the steep taxes always demanded by the government. Symbolically, God is the government, and when we have made advances on the ego level, God demands a payment of energy and attention to the spiritual level. If someone reaches the top, as the Beatles had, the payment demanded in conscious growth is proportionately large. So it is time for the Beatles to pay up. There is a noticeable influence of the music of India in "Taxman," indicating the spiritual turn the Beatles' journey has now taken. But there is also anger in George's voice. The journey is just beginning—he is not yet fully wise. No one at the outset wants to pay the price of individuation. It is only as the journey proceeds that its demands begin to seem worthwhile.

The rest of the album focuses on themes related to the Poet quarter—

issues of love and of regression into the mother world. I will group together the songs written and led by each individual Beatle and look at these groupings separately to see how each of the four masculine parts experiences this journey through the Poet's realm, beginning with Paul, the primary Poet voice.

Paul's first song, "Eleanor Rigby," is the second song on the album, and along with "Taxman," it has a special, flagship quality. Like an initial dream, it sets out the overall problem that this individuation journey is going to address, a problem that sets the Beatles' journey into a wider context than themselves.

There is a real way in which every individuation journey is important for the salvation of the world—more important than collective actions and mass movements. This is because of the true insight and centering that the journey brings to the individuating person, an advance in consciousness which spreads to his immediate environment and out from there in a ripple effect. The outer-life developments which arise from this are sound and lasting, and they help give answer to the challenge of the times in which the individuating person is living.

In "Eleanor Rigby," the Beatle Poet speaks of the loneliness in the world in the 1960s, and he names as loneliest of all a married woman who is lost in a dream world and a priest whose sermons are irrelevant and who lives alone, mending his own socks. Married women, disappointed in the romantic ideal (most of the mothers of those in the Beatles generation), and a father world whose spirituality has grown sterile through separation from the feminine. The two problems were connected.

Paul's next song is "Here, There, and Everywhere," considered by many to be the most beautiful of his love songs. All the love songs he sings on this album are especially lovely, as befits the Poet's quarter. In this one he sings of a woman whose physical presence makes him a better person. She improves his life so much that he wants her with him always and everywhere. This is a nice sentiment, but few women would actually welcome it as a reality. This Poet needs a relationship with his inner feminine so that he can get along without a woman always by his side.

The Beatle Poet does not yet realize it, but it is in his dependence on the physical presence of a woman that his personal problem intersects the larger problems put forth in "Eleanor Rigby." When a man discovers and integrates the feminine realm within himself—the unconscious—his spirituality deepens and becomes more relevant to life, while at the same time he becomes a better companion to woman, able to allow her a separate reality and to appreciate her depth and complexity. But the Poet will not be able to achieve this integration of the feminine by drawing only on Poet energy. He needs the analytical ability and disciplined will of the Soldier, the Wise Man's openness to the depths, and the King's capacity to pull all these parts together and make them viable in the context of this particular human life.

The Poet's other songs on the album—"Good Day Sunshine," "For No One," and "Got to Get You Into My Life"—show him basking in a sunny, rather shallow, outer-world experience of love; then rejected by a self-possessed lover who no longer needs him, presumably because of his shallow approach; and then finally awakened to his need to find a new way to relate to woman. This individuation journey has brought to consciousness the Poet's issues having to do with the Poet quarter. He has been operating instinctually in this realm, which is his gifted area. The instinctual way served him well in young life, but more is now required. His determined attitude in "Got to Get You Into My Life" is a strong and healthy one that gives us hope that he will do well in meeting the challenge that has been put before him.

The Poet, however, is only one part in four of the "person" that is the Beatles. As we turn to the songs written and led by John, we see that the Beatle Soldier has experiences of an entirely different nature on his journey through the Poet quarter. This variety of experience is true of each of us on our own journeys. As the unconscious unfolds for us the truth about a certain aspect of our lives, we are almost always given a series of dreams and life events which show us the situation from several different points of view, all of which belong to parts of ourselves, revealing the complexity of our total inner experience.

John's first song on the album is "I'm Only Sleeping," a pleasing evocation of what it feels like to stay in bed in the morning, heavy with dreaming, while the world outside bustles about its business. This is an important aspect of the Poet's mother world—rest, leisure, restoration of physical and mental energy. A Soldier, however, is supposed to be up and at it in the morning, sacrificing his body's needs, if necessary, to do what has to be done. Is this the Beatle Soldier's day off? If not, there may be trouble here. The Beatle Soldier might lack the discipline of will necessary to extricate himself from the powerful pull of the mother world, which he seems to be experiencing in a sleepy, unconscious state rather than with his eyes open.

John's next song, "She Said She Said," confirms our fears in this regard. He sings of a woman whose conversation with him is going too deep. When she tells him that she knows what death feels like, it overwhelms him and makes him feel crazy. The feminine world is too much for his Soldier consciousness, which does not have a strong enough grip on masculine outer reality to stand firm in the face of what seems like the terrifying nothingness of inner reality. His Soldier mind should be thinking about what she is saying, analyzing it and fitting it into a conscious structure. But he is not up to it. He lacks a structure that can hold it. He speaks of the simpler mother world of his childhood, where his present consciousness was sufficient. This indicates a tendency to regression, to turning away from the challenge of expanding his consciousness to the point of being able to *relate* to woman and the feminine side of life, instead of falling into it and being carried along by it.

In the rest of the Soldier's songs on the album—"And My Bird Can Sing," "Doctor Robert," and "Tomorrow Never Knows"—we see him break relationship with a woman and then turn to drugs, completing his regression into the mother world. Instead of getting busy and equipping himself for a healthy conversation between masculine consciousness and the feminine unconscious, the Beatle Soldier has given up, surrendered to the feminine realm. He hopes to remain an unconscious boy, cared for and indulged by his mother, who is no longer a human woman but the unconscious itself, into whose arms he unwisely entrusts himself through mood altering substances.

We would be very worried about this "person" that is the Beatles were it not for the strength we have already seen in Paul, the Poet part of the personality. Paul is having troubles in love, but he has taken them in hand and is going forward to meet them, not letting himself be washed downstream, like John, into the cosmic void. The fact is that Poet personalities are characterized by weakness in the Soldier quarter. That is what throws the weight of their experience of life toward the creativity of the mother world. Therefore, while some worry is justified, there is also reason to be cautiously optimistic.

The Beatles were once asked how they were able to keep their psychic balance. George, the Wise Man, answered, "There's four of us, so if one goes a little potty, it's all right." The same is true for everyone. We all have parts of ourselves that are wounded and unhealthy and that are helped along by the parts of us that are sound. Our wounded parts play necessary roles in our personalities and help make us who we are.

As a Poet, the Beatles "person" is basically a youthful personality. His ego parts, the Poet and the Soldier, have the strongest voices, writing and singing the lead for most of the songs. The mature parts—the Wise Man and the King—play strong supporting roles. They are the major instrumental voices—the Wise Man plays the lead guitar, the King plays the drums. The Wise Man also writes and is lead singer for a few songs on each album, while the King usually sings the lead on only one song per album, often one written for him by the Poet.

On *Revolver* the Wise Man sees the individuation journey coming and announces it with "Taxman." But he also has issues of his own to be dealt with in the Poet quarter. The Wise Man's energy arises from the side of a man that relates to the feminine principle, but in the Wise Man that relationship is a spiritual one, and this estranges him somewhat from his physical passion for woman. All of George's love songs in the early Beatles period showed a notable lack of passion. This love problem of the Wise Man rises to consciousness on the *Revolver* album.

His first song after "Taxman" is "Love to You," which has an outright Eastern sound with heavy Indian instrumentation. The Eastern music tells us that the Wise Man is in a decidedly spiritual mode. He says he is awfully busy—with his spiritual life, no doubt—but if this woman wants him to, he will make love to her. Here is his typical lack of passion. But in his last song on the album, "I Want to Tell You," he acknowledges this problem. He sings to a woman that he has so much he wants to tell her. It fills him up when he is not with her, but when he gets near her, it leaves him, and he can no longer find the words. He hopes that in time this will change and he will be able to relate to her more fully. So, like the Poet, the Wise Man leaves this quarter conscious of his problems in love and in search of a solution.

The one song on this album led by the Beatle King is "Yellow Submarine." In surrendering to the feminine world, the Soldier part of the Beatles has abandoned the dry land of consciousness. But the King comes to the rescue with a vehicle to carry the Beatles through their submergence in the unconscious. A submarine is a human way of going through a nonhuman realm. Ringo tells us that the sea through which the Yellow Submarine travels is in the sky. We also note that the music and imagery of the song are happy and sunny. These are indications that heaven is being included in this individuation journey. We can therefore be hopeful about its outcome, despite the troubles we have seen with the Soldier.

## *Sgt. Pepper:* The Soldier Quarter

THE ALBUM that follows *Revolver* is *Sgt. Pepper's Lonely Hearts Club Band.* The very name suggests the Soldier theme. Now we are in the world of the personal father, the competitive outside world of collective consciousness. We have already seen, however, that the Beatle Soldier has regressed into the mother world. It is not surprising, therefore, that in his first song on this album, "Lucy in the Sky with Diamonds," John describes his outside world as a psychedelic fantasyland with flowers as tall as trees, taxis made of newspapers, and train stations with surreal porters. Instead of seeking a masculine mentor from the father world, the Beatle Soldier searches through this psychedelic landscape for a magical woman, perhaps feeling she could help him solve his problems.

His next song, "Being for the Benefit of Mr. Kite," is a circus poster set to music. Joining a circus might be the Beatle Soldier's answer to making a living. This could be all right. Poet personalities often support themselves as performers. But there is a question of whether the Beatle Soldier can take on the discipline that comes with any occupation, even one that looks like fun. The antique sound of this song suggests he is still in a state of regression.

The Soldier's next song, "Good Morning Good Morning," confirms that he is not adapting to the dailiness required by life in the outside world. He is, however, at least beginning to face the here and now. He sings of a depressed man going through the motions of life, poorly related to his wife and child, bored with his job, with his town, with everything. And finally, in his last song, "A Day in the Life," he sings of his alienation from the greater world as he reads a newspaper, unable to see the point of anything in it.

The Beatle Soldier has shown himself to be highly resistant to his own realm of life. The only gain in consciousness he has made in this quarter has been to come back from the world of fantasy and face his depression in the reality of the outside world.

The Wise Man also makes a poor showing in this quarter, although as a basic introvert, whose true home is the inner world, he is not required to shine in the competitive outer world of the Soldier. George's one contribution to this album is "Within You Without You," another song with a strong Eastern sound. In it he looks at the outside world with introverted eyes and proclaims that all those busy people who are so outwardly occupied with life know nothing of the inner life. They are empty inside, unconscious of true reality, and barren of real love. His tone is preachy. Even though there is some validity to his observations, he nonetheless fails to appreciate the value of collective life. All that busyness (business) keeps the world going. The faithfulness of ordinary people to the requirements of their daily lives has more nobility in it than the Wise Man realizes.

Ringo's one song on the album, "A Little Help from My Friends," gives us a ray of hope in this rather dismal phase of the Beatles' individuation journey. The Beatle King has a willing attitude, even though he admits he is not strong in this quarter. Kings do not have ordinary occupations in the outer world, but this King is not above doing his share. If necessary, he will sing for his supper, hoping to be forgiven if he goes off key, trusting that with the help of his friends he will get by.

Three of the Beatles have now sung their parts. The Beatle Soldier is depressed in the competitive outside world of the father. The Wise Man is aloof. The King is willing but in need of help. This puts the weight of the journey on the shoulders of the Poet, who fortunately rises to the occasion. In the opening song, "Sgt. Pepper's Lonely Hearts Club Band," Paul embraces the Soldier theme. The Lonely Hearts Club suggests the organized collective life of the father world. This particular segment of society is one to which the Poet has evidently been drawn by the love problems he encountered in the Poet quarter.

In his next song, "Getting Better," the Poet tells of several Soldier problems on which he is making some progress. One has to do with the difficulty he has had conforming to a school environment, and the others have to do with controlling his masculine anger and violence. In "Fixing a Hole," he tells us he has taken on the Soldier's task of strengthening his boundaries: fixing a hole in the roof and cracks in the door to keep out disagreeable people. In "She's Leaving Home," he sings of the Soldier's challenge to break out of the mother world. He puts it in terms of a young woman—his anima, or feminine, relating side—who resolutely and grimly steps out on her own, leaving her distressed parents behind.

In "When I'm Sixty-Four," Paul sings a Soldier's love song about the practical and mundane aspects of long term marriage. Poets, who are strong on the passionate and romantic side of love, are often weak when it comes to day-to-day commitment. In this song the Beatle Poet finds in himself a Soldier's fidelity as he asks his beloved if she will share with him the ordinary outcome of love—a house and children, faithful companionship, and mutual support to the end of their days. Finally, in "Lovely Rita," we see the Beatle Poet trying to use his charm to woo a meter maid, presumably to evade a parking ticket. This shows a certain darkness in his approach to the law, although the infraction is not great.

For the most part Paul has done well enough in the Soldier quarter. Being basically a Poet, he is not as strong as a Soldier can be, but we hope he is strong enough to carry the Beatles forward despite the heavy weight that John's shadow is beginning to exert. In the last song on the album, "A Day in the Life," we see the delicate balancing act of these light and dark sides of the Beatles personality. While John sings about his alienation from the outer world, Paul comes in with a little song within the song and sings of getting up in the morning, combing his hair, and catching a bus, show-ing an adequate acceptance of life's daily grind. On the upper level of the bus he handles his boredom by looking out the window and daydreaming. The Poet's soundness balances the Soldier's brokenness, though just barely. The Soldier's failure in his own quarter, however, remains troubling.

## *Magical Mystery Tour:* The Wise Man Quarter

THE NEXT ALBUM IS *Magical Mystery Tour,* and it takes us, as its name implies, into the realm of the Wise Man. Paul opens with the title song, inviting us to join the Magical Mystery Tour, which *wants* to take us away. The unconscious is an automonous reality which seeks relationship with us. This is a truth to which our ego consciousness has great resistance, since the ego fears being eclipsed by the much greater power of the un-conscious. It tries to hold off the unconscious by denying that it actually has a separate existence of its own. The Beatle Poet, however, has gained strength in the Soldier quarter, and he feels ready now to take on a con-scious relationship with the unconscious.

In "The Fool on the Hill," the Poet sings about the wisdom to be gained in the Wise Man quarter, an inner wisdom which seems foolish to people in the outside world. In "Your Mother Should Know" he pays tribute to the wisdom of the mother world, acknowledging that youth does not know everything and that there is a wisdom of the ages carried by the feminine side of life. In "Hello Goodbye" the Poet sings about the problem of reconciling the opposites, a major task to be accomplished in the Wise Man quarter. It could be said he is coming to terms with the compensatory nature of the unconscious, which says yes when he says no, high when he says low, and goodbye when he says hello.

Then in "Penny Lane" the Beatle Poet is led by the unconscious to revisit his childhood. When a person's individuation journey brings up from the depths long-buried issues from his childhood, it is to help him understand and accept himself as a particular, unique individual who springs from a certain time, place, and set of circumstances. Some of the wounds that have long existed in him can now be healed. Others must simply be accepted. Inherited gifts and tasks must also be accepted. It is these special features of his life that make him the person that he is and none other. In accepting the truth of his life, an individuating person recognizes and honors his individual reality and thereby comes into his true inheritance. The question then becomes, what is he going to do with that inheritance? The Poet sings about this in his last song, which he shares with the Soldier. We will look at that after we have followed the Soldier's progress through this realm.

Knowing the burden under which the Beatle Soldier has been laboring, it is not surprising that John makes a ragged start in the Wise Man quarter. "I Am the Walrus" is all babble and gobbeldygook. While he was in the Soldier quarter, John failed to develop a disciplined consciousness with which to take this tour of the depths. As a result, the nonrational language of the unconscious now seems to get the best of him. However, it is possible that this nonsensical song actually shows a positive development in the fact that the Beatle Soldier is neither protesting against the feminine depths and turning away, nor dreamily surrendering, as he did in the Poet quarter. Rather, he hangs in there this time and tries to express what he understands is coming to him from this foreign realm, however absurd it may seem. Perhaps he glimpses behind it the magical woman he was looking for earlier, the one he hopes may be able to help him. Though it is true that his consciousness is undisciplined, it is possible that his native intelligence will be enough to get him through this encounter with the unconscious.

His next song affirms this positive assessment by showing further progress. In "Strawberry Fields Forever," the Soldier, too, goes down into his childhood, a darker and more troubled world than the Poet's. (Both Penny Lane and Strawberry Fields were familiar places in the Liverpool boyhoods of John and Paul.) In this song the Beatle Soldier is feeling easier with the strangeness of the inner realm, and he is actually beginning to learn things there. He is sorting some things out.

From this comes a breakthrough in his next song when he sings, "All You Need Is Love." Coming from the Beatles, this is a somewhat naive statement, since love also needs a disciplined will to go along with it. Nonetheless, it does seem that in his brokenness the Beatle Soldier has found his way to something important. Because of his deep wounds in the father realm, the greatest answer for the Beatle Soldier *is* love, even if it is not completely centered and balanced by a healthy will.

The Beatle Soldier has been unable to embrace will, but it seems that he can embrace love. In that he has finally found at least one sound leg upon which to stand. It is none other than the weak leg of the father world into which the Beatles were born, the very leg that needs strengthening through more concentrated use. The correction of an imbalance almost always means a temporary imbalance in the other direction. The Beatles and their generation embodied a correction of the world's spirit toward love, away from an overdependence on disciplined will. It was the task of that generation to embrace and retrieve the lost value of love, a task which necessarily entailed letting go of other values that would themselves have to be retrieved by future generations.

This is the way it is with each of us as individuals. Through the process of individuation we gradually come to realize that we have a specific purpose in life, not so much by choice but by force of circumstance. We were not put on earth to be all things to all men. We can only hope to do a few things well, while many things we can barely do adequately, and at some things we must fail miserably. It is when we can understand and accept the value of our particular, individual strengths that we can also understand and accept our shortcomings.

"Baby You're a Rich Man" is the duet the Soldier sings with the Poet, mixing two songs into one. They sing it after they have visited their childhoods. They ask what they are going to do now that they have discovered who they are. Having become rich with the inner treasure of self-knowledge, they are ready to leave the solitary world of the Wise Man and go out into the active world of the King to make use of what they have gained.

The Wise Man has been more quiet than usual in this quarter, seeming to be already familiar with the territory. He waits for the others, anxious for them to learn their lessons and move on with him to the King's realm, where, perhaps he knows, he himself will finally come into his own. But he is worried about their progress. His one song on this album is "Blue Jay Way." The bird imagery in the title symbolizes the part of the natural spirit that soars away from the earth of the Wise Man's quarter toward heaven and the King's realm of perfected outer life. In this song the Wise Man waits late into a foggy night for the expected arrival of his friends. Though he gave them directions, he fears they have gotten lost. The Wise Man seems to see a problem here that no one else can see.

There are moments like this in every individuation journey. Just when things seem to be going well, a dream speaks of trouble that has not yet shown itself in outer life. Dreams usually project forward in time. They often refer to developments whose seeds are present but that have yet to break through into the light.

The King does not seem to share the Wise Man's concern. Though Ringo sings no song of his own on this album, he co-composes an instrumental number with the other three. This is the only song the four of them ever composed together. Its title, "Flying," suggests movement toward the King, as does their unity of effort in composing the song. This balances the Wise Man's concern that the Beatles might be hopelessly lost in the foggy night.

## The White Album: A False Move

IT TURNS OUT, however, that the Wise Man's concern is at least partly justified. The next album to appear is a double album whose cover design is all white, so pure in concept that its minimalist title, *The Beatles,* is visible only in raised relief. Immediately dubbed The White Album by the public, it is the first Beatles album to be met with widespread disappointment. Something has gone wrong. The total effect of the album is ragged, uneven, and undistinguished. There is no unified mood or atmosphere. Few of the songs are deeply pleasing.

The White Album is a false move into the King quarter. The Beatle ego parts—John, Paul, and to some extent George—have become inflated, which is to say, unconsciously identified with God, the One above all. Each thinks he is the best, that he can do what the Beatles do all by himself, entirely in his own way. They are no longer collaborating with each other, but each merely uses the others as a back-up band, with little give and take among them as each records his own songs.

In order to understand what is happening, we will have to look more closely at what is actually going on in the real life of the Beatles. This change of viewpoint comes in with the King, who in his mature phase brings with him earth's reality, an awakening from our unconscious dreams of life to life itself. What we see here are real life events that parallel the themes we have been watching in the music.

At the heart of the problem is a major rift that has grown between John and Paul. John was the ego leader of the early Beatles, back when they sang simple rock'n'roll and made albums of unrelated songs that were put together without regard for any connection between them. The new level of music that became the late Beatles arose primarily through Paul's inspiration. These later albums were "concept" albums, characterized by an intentional interweaving of themes, with some of the songs actually linked together, no silence between them. With this and the inclusion of orchestral instruments, these albums seemed to be moving toward a synthesis of popular and classical music.

This called for an expansion of technique, knowledge, and ability— the disciplined work of the mature Soldier. But the demand was too much for John. He could only be a youthful Soldier and defend his original territory. He wanted to go back to their old style. While Paul was taking piano lessons and learning classical music, John turned heavily to drugs. He went along only reluctantly with Paul's leadership through the later albums, dragging his feet and feeling alternately resentful and guilty. The weight he exerted on the Beatles was great. Paul's own Soldier aspect was healthier than John's, and with it he had carried the Beatles this far. But John's Soldier energy, though dark, was stronger than Paul's, and the downward pull of it was making it increasingly difficult for the Beatles to go on.

The situation came to a head when John fell in love with Yoko Ono. This was a deep and powerful attraction like none John had ever known before. Yoko replaced the Beatles as the center of his life. She was the magical woman he had been looking for, a dark wisdom woman who became the guide for his experience in the Wise Man quarter. She was an avant garde artist whose work was intended to make conscious structure meaningless, in the spirit of "I Am the Walrus." She knew about the wisdom systems that underlie nature and introduced John to astrology, Tarot cards, and the *I Ching.* She helped him grapple with the issues of his childhood and inspired him to believe in love as the ultimate answer to his life. But Yoko was dark in the sense that she, too, was alienated from the father world, which she viewed as hostile and life destroying. Unwilling to avail herself of legitimate masculine power, she sought to use love and wisdom as means of power, an approach to the feminine that always undermines life.

Following Yoko's lead, John found earth's depths, but with her he was confined to its darkness, unable to open himself at the same time to the sun and sky of collective consciousness and true community. He had made it as far as the Wise Man quarter, but in the end he could go no further. In one of his better songs on The White Album he sings, "I'm So Tired."

Ringo, the King, actually quit the Beatles during the making of The White Album. Beginning to doubt himself in the face of their disunity, Ringo felt unloved and left out by the other three. The others went after him, reassured him of their love, and convinced him to come back. When he returned, he found they had covered his drums with flowers. On The White Album the Beatle King for the first time sings a song that he himself has written. Its title was his plea to the others: "Don't Pass Me By."

George sings what is perhaps the most powerful song on The White Album. In "While My Guitar Gently Weeps" he sings to the others that it saddens him to see their love miscarrying to such an extent, because he knows how much love is really there.

Paul's best song on the album, the one that most touches the soul, is "Blackbird." In it he creates a haunting image of a crippled blackbird trying to rise into flight in a night sky. This is its moment, he sings. It must fly despite the brokenness of its wings. This song gives us hope that the inflation of this album will be overcome and a centered experience of the King might still be had.

## *Abbey Road:* The King Quarter

THE PUBLIC'S REACTION to The White Album made the Beatles realize they had lost their center. They tried to regain it by getting back to their roots and recording an album that was more down to earth, more like the old days in Liverpool when they were of one mind and spirit. But this effort ended in more acrimony than ever. They could not even bear to mix the tapes to make them into a finished album. (*Let It Be*, the album released just after their breakup, was finally pulled together from these tapes.) From this experience they knew that their days were numbered. The "person" that was the Beatles was dying. Their broken parts were making their reality unsustainable. Without a sound Soldier component they could not live forward into the next required phase, the King's world of human community.

The Beatles embodied the spirit of a generation. It is the fate of every generation to pass away, hopefully before its shortcomings have undermined the gifts it has brought. With more grace than the generations just before it, the Beatles recognized the end of their time and acquiesed to it. Their journey had brought them face to face with their own death. In full knowledge and acceptance of this fact, they let Paul lead them through one last effort, an album that they hoped would be like the great albums of the *Sgt. Pepper* days, one that would redeem the failure of The White Album. They wanted to show that they could still pull together into one and that, despite their impending death, they really did still love each other. To meet this challenge, even John rose on his crippled wings and flew toward the King, who came to meet him halfway. The album they made was *Abbey Road*, which many consider to be their best. It is the one that reflects the true essence of the King.

The effectiveness of the King does not belong to the ego. It comes from the Self and is only present when we let it be in us without trying to claim it for our own. As so many Christian hymns proclaim, it is Christ who is the true King. Christ the King is the image of earth's reality and heaven's spirit joined together into one. The King within us takes us as we actually are, without idealization, and blesses us—our shortcomings as well as our strengths, our sorrows as well as our joys. He shows us that, despite our limitations, we are perfect for the part we were meant to play in our particular time and place to meet a particular need in the unfolding of the world. This only makes sense when we know ourselves to be one with the intricate web of the human community.

Abbey Road was the street on which the Beatles' recording studio was located. It was their real life kingdom as mortal men. The album cover shows them crossing from one side of Abbey Road to the other, an ordinary street scene, four rather colorful men in London in 1969. The Beatle myth is dissolving into reality.

The music on the *Abbey Road* album has a unified sound, but within that unity it is divided into two distinct parts to accommodate the different approaches of John and Paul, a solution that reveals the mediating presence of the King. Side One is for John and is made up of separate songs which have no intended connection between them. (This was in the days of LP records, but the two sides can still be distinguished on compact disc by the abrupt break at the end of the last song on the original Side One.) Side Two is Paul's and has the connected, rock-symphony style that the Beatles probably would have continued to develop had they been able to go on.

Because this is the King quarter, the symbolic content of this album has a different quality from the albums of the other three quarters. Reality has come in with the King, and the album seems to be about John and Paul as the real individuals who are the ego carriers of the dying Beatles. Because the unification of all the parts is the theme of the King, our best understanding of the album comes from leaving the songs in their given sequence rather than breaking them apart and grouping them according to the separate Beatle voices.

On Side One it seems that all the Beatles come together in spirit to sing a blessing on John's life. He actually asks them to do this in the first song, the title of which is "Come Together." John seems to be asking them to unify in spite of him, or because of him, or for the sake of him.

In the second song, "Something," George surprises us with a beautiful love song about a woman whose movement and smile attract him like none other ever has. The Beatle Wise Man is finally able to give voice to deep love for a woman. He sings with the passion of a Poet, but also with the Wise Man's ability to leave space in a relationship. With this the Beatles "person" has become a better lover, a development which goes far to resolve the love problems presented in the Poet quarter. The quality of George's songwriting has also increased enormously, showing that he has integrated the creative aspect of the Poet's quarter as well. If we look at

"Something" in terms of this being John's side of the album, we see in it John's love for Yoko, which for him was like no other because it reached down to the depths of feminine wisdom. The drumming, especially the use of hollow tom-toms, is particularly compelling in this song, giving us a strong sense of the King's presence. Throughout this album Ringo is more present in his drumming than on any other album.

The rest of the songs on John's side of the album can be seen as commentaries on his life, the shadow aspects of it as well as the light aspects. The songs are sung without judgement, but also with a clear eye to consequences. Paul sings "Maxwell's Silver Hammer," a cheery song about a serial killer—a shadow side of John—who murders a student, a teacher, and a judge, all symbols of the father world. In "Oh! Darling," a stirring tribute to John's rock'n'roll spirit, Paul sings of someone who is excessively dependent on his lover and yet must repeatedly assure her that he will not harm her. These relationship problems are consequences of John's rejection of the father world, and they were mirrored in his life with Yoko.

In "Octopus's Garden," Ringo sings of a free and protected life beneath the sea in the realm of a friendly octopus. As a monarch with roundness of form, the octopus symbolizes a benevolent but unconscious aspect of the Self. The Beatle King seems to be granting John his own kingdom, an inner one submerged in the feminine realm. It reminds us of John's secluded life as a househusband in the final years before his death.

John himself sings the last song on his side of the album. "I Want You (She's So Heavy)" speaks of his strong attachment to Yoko but also of the burden of his life under the domination of the feminine realm. The heaviness of the song seems to reflect the long depressions he often suffered. At the end there is a protracted and increasingly ominous instrumental refrain that goes on and on and on until it finally ends abruptly, midmeasure. As we listen now to this sudden end, it evokes the image of John's murder in 1980 by a young fan who was more alienated from the father world than John himself was. In the way of the unconscious, which is not bound by time, it probably does refer to that. John's life, though blessed by the King, will be what it will be.

It is with great relief that we hear George open Side Two with "Here Comes the Sun," another surprisingly beautiful song by the Beatle Wise

Man. The sun is a symbol of consciousness and of the King. The Beatles have finally come through into the full daylight of the world of masculine consciousness. This is Paul's side of the album, and in the next song, "Because," John pays tribute to Paul's optimism. He sings of the roundness of the world, the blueness of the sky, and the highness of the wind, all of which move him and lift his spirits just because they are what they are.

Paul, more than the rest, carries within himself the spirit of the Beatles. The remaining songs on his side of the album are connected together in his own creative style and have to do with his life with the Beatles and with the end they now face. He begins with "You Never Give Me Your Money," in which he alludes to the irreconcilable differences that have arisen among them on the business side of their relationship. Then he reviews their lives together, from when they were fresh out of school with no money and no prospects, through their rise to fame, and then to a death—someone has gone to heaven. We think of the death of Brian Epstein, their manager.

In the next song John picks up the story and shows us Paul's shadow, just as Paul showed us John's shadow on the album's other side. We surmise that the "Sun King," of whom John now sings, is Paul trying to lead the Beatles in the wake of Epstein's death. It is obvious from the flatness of their voices that the Sun King's subjects only pretend to be happy with him. In the next two songs John explains why. He sings of "Mean Mr. Mustard," a mean, low man who stands in contrast to Paul's over-niceness and perfectionism. This is Paul's shadow, poorly hidden beneath his pleasant surface. Whenever Mean Mr. Mustard goes out to see the Queen of England—the ruling monarch—he hurls obscenities at her. So Paul carries in his shadow the same antipathy to the father world that John carries openly. Then there is "Polythene Pam," a rather bizarre woman with a muddled gender identity who inhabits the sexual underworld. We presume this to be a dark side of Paul's anima, or inner feminine self.

Paul seems to be strong enough to accept these judgements from the others. His next song, "She Came in Through the Bathroom Window," is vigorous and upbeat. He sings of resigning from the police force (the thankless job of trying to lead the Beatles), of getting a regular job and making a life with an intriguing woman who has burst into his life. We assume this refers to his recent marriage to Linda Eastman and his decision to leave the group and start a new career with her. In "Golden Slumbers" Paul sings a lullaby as if to a dying loved one, poignantly accepting the breakup of the Beatles as a reality that cannot be turned back. "Carry That Weight" seems to be about the burden of the dark Soldier, which all of the Beatles will have to face in themselves when John is no longer present to carry it for them.

Having accepted that, they come to "The End." In this song Paul makes an important breakthrough by inviting the others to come into his dream-life. The Beatles meant wholeness to Paul, and if he cannot have these other three parts of himself in his outer life, he would like to have them in his inner life. In this he opens himself to integration of the essence of the others as parts of his own psyche.

This puts the Beatles' death in perspective and shows why it has turned out to be the goal of their individuation journey. Every outer reality to which we cling must eventually be surrendered in order to be replaced by an inner reality that truly belongs to us and from which we can never again be separated. It was in this spirit that Jesus accepted his own crucifixion, explaining to his disciples that he must leave them in order for them to discover his reality within themselves. It is in this same spirit that we are called upon in our own individuation journeys to let go of outer realities that feel to us as if they are life itself. Death in this context is a painful but transformative process.

The King responds to Paul's request for inner wholeness with a triumphant drum solo, virtually the only protracted solo he ever played on any Beatles album. After this the Beatles sing their last line, telling us what they have learned about love. Ultimately, they say, it comes down to the fact that what you receive in love is in direct proportion to what you give. This, then, is their answer to the problem of loneliness in "Eleanor Rigby." The lonely woman and the empty priest must undertake the task of reconciling life's opposites through the real work of love in order for their own lives to become rich and meaningful.

## Paul Is Dead: An Outbreak of Synchronicity

*Abbey Road* was a huge success with the public. Its music resonated deeply, although no one yet knew that the Beatles had recorded their last album. Looking back on it with what we now know, we can see the farewell element in it, but in the fall of 1969, this was not so obvious. However, the truth of the matter was picked up unconsciously, and it led to the strange "Paul is dead" episode, which was actually an outbreak of synchronistic awareness, although it was not consciously understood in those terms nor was the true nature of synchronicity correctly perceived.

Immediately after the release of *Abbey Road*, the rumor began to spread among the public that Paul (who, as the Poet, most personified the Beatles) had died in 1966, when the Beatles stopped touring. According to the rumor, a look-alike and sound-alike had secretly been put in his place, for fear the fans would turn away if the knowledge of his death became known. However, the later albums (the individuation albums) were supposedly strewn with clues about Paul's death, as if it were the Beatles' handlers who wanted to keep the secret, while the Beatles themselves wanted to reveal it.

The perceived clues were endless. On the *Revolver* album Paul was said to be referring to his own death in an auto accident when he sings in "Got to Get You Into My Life" that he made a right turn and found a surprise there. More details about the wreck were believed to have been given in "A Day in the Life" on the *Sgt. Pepper* album. On that album cover, which was now believed to depict Paul's funeral, there is a raised hand, with palm outward, above Paul's head: this was interpreted as the Mafia sign for death. In another picture on that album, Paul stands tellingly with his back to the camera while the other three face forward.

On the *Magical Mystery Tour* album, in the electronically distorted words at the end of "Strawberry Fields Forever," John can supposedly be heard to say, "I buried Paul." (He actually says, "Cranberry sauce.") As the Beatles cross the street in single file on the cover of *Abbey Road*, Paul's presumed stand-in is barefooted while the others have on shoes, supposedly indicating that Paul is the corpse in his own funeral procession. George, dressed in bluejeans, is the gravedigger; Ringo, in a formal suit, is the undertaker; and John, dressed all in white, is the minister. A Volkswagen Beetle (!) parked just beyond the crosswalk has a license tag that reads *28 IF,* interpreted as a cryptic reference to the fact that Paul would be *twenty-eight* years old *if* he were still alive. And on and on.

People sensed that something odd had been going on with the Beatles ever since *Revolver.* Because the Beatles carried the image of wholeness, and therefore of the Self, the "Paul is dead" believers projected onto them the Self's use of synchronicity in revealing to us in ordinary daily events the unrealized truths of our own lives. As we have seen, there actually *was* something unusual going on in those later albums, although the public did not have a conscious framework by which to understand it and describe it.

Not even the Beatles themselves could see the degree to which they and their times were leading the collective consciousness of the world toward the fuller love and wisdom that come from the feminine realm. But they did not need to see the big picture. Because of their basic good-heartedness and their openness to the creativity of the unconscious, these four men from Liverpool proved to be adequate vessels for a truly synchronistic display of a particular image of masculine wholeness, one that stresses the lost feminine side of human life, including the process of individuation. And thus, as is true of any individuating person, the Beatles "person" helped to answer the challenge of his times.

## Jung's Liverpool Dream

IN LIGHT OF THIS ANALYSIS of the Beatles, it is interesting to look at a dream that came to Carl Jung at the end of the intense phase of his own individuation journey in 1927. This dream is recorded in his autobiography, *Memories, Dreams, Reflections,* which was published posthumously in 1963, the very year the Beatles were emerging onto the world stage:

> This is the dream: . . . I found myself in a dirty, sooty city. It was night, and winter, and dark, and raining. I was in Liverpool. With a number of Swiss—say, half a dozen—I walked through the dark streets. I had the feeling that there we were coming from the har-

bor, and that the real city was actually up above, on the cliffs. We climbed up there. It reminded me of Basel, where the market is down below and then you go up through the Totengässchen ("Alley of the Dead"), which leads to a plateau above and so to the Petersplatz and the Peterskirche. When we reached the plateau, we found a broad square dimly illuminated by street lights, into which many streets converged. The various quarters of the city were arranged radially around the square. In the center was a round pool, and in the middle of it a small island. While everything round about was obscured by rain, fog, smoke, and dimly lit darkness, the little island blazed with sunlight. On it stood a single tree, a magnolia, in a shower of reddish blossoms. It was as though the tree stood in the sunlight and were at the same time the source of light. My companions commented on the abominable weather, and obviously did not see the tree. They spoke of another Swiss who was living in Liverpool, and expressed surprise that he should have settled there. I was carried away by the beauty of the flowering tree and the sunlit island, and thought, "I know very well why he has settled here." Then I awoke.

On one detail of the dream I must add a supplementary comment: the individual quarters of the city were themselves arranged radially around a central point. This point formed a small open square illuminated by a larger street lamp, and constituted a small replica of the island. I knew that the "other Swiss" lived in the vicinity of one of these secondary centers. . . .

This dream brought with it a sense of finality. I saw that here the goal had been revealed. One could not go beyond the center. The center is the goal, and everything is directed toward the center. Through this dream I understood that the self is the principle and archetype of orientation and meaning. Therein lies its healing function.

This was a dream about the quarters of the psyche, the tree of life, the center, and the Self, all found in the unlikely setting of Liverpool. It follows the pattern revealed by Christ that new life from God arises in unlikely places and thus often goes unrecognized. Jung received prophetic dreams about World War I shortly before it broke out, and about World War II many years before it occurred. Therefore, while it is remarkable, it is not strange that the dream that confirmed for him the nature of the Self would contain imagery that is linked to the Beatles, that four-part image of human wholeness that rose up in the second half of the twentieth century and swept the world before it. It is fitting that on the cover of *Sgt. Pepper's Lonely Hearts Club Band,* Carl Jung's photograph is among those pictured looking on from the crowd.

# CHAPTER TWELVE

# *Feminine Wholeness*

THE MASCULINE QUATERNITY of Poet, Soldier, Wise Man, and King belongs to woman as well as man. A woman's Poet must be healthy and in good relationship to her outer feminine being if she is to be playful and creative. If her Soldier is strong and brave, she will be focused and disciplined. Her Wise Man must be awake and aware if she is to deal consciously and rationally with nature and the unconscious. And when her King is well balanced and sound, she can be an effective leader in the outside world. These aspects of life, however, are not the ones that are most fundamental to her.

Feminine life is of a different quality than masculine life. It is concerned with the human experience of being rather than doing, with personal story rather than public achievement, with life as it is rather than as it is conceptualized, with relationship rather than power, with openness and receptivity rather than defense and conquest, with being at one with the process of life rather than analyzing it and naming it, and with establishing and maintaining the forms of community life rather than with leadership.

The names I use for the quarters of the feminine quaternity reflect this difference in quality. The masculine quarters were given impersonal, occupational names—Poet, Soldier, and so on. But for the feminine quaternity it seems best to use women's names, mythically based for wide application and recognizable meaning, but names that suggest feminine embodiment and personal story.

Every woman—and every man's anima, or inner feminine self—is two daughters: her mother's daughter and her father's daughter. At the youthful, ego level of life I call the mother's daughter *Eve*, after the mother of humankind, and the father's daughter *Scarlett*, after the strong-willed heroine of *Gone With the Wind*. Young womanhood is lived in tension between these two sides of feminine being, between the personal mother's world of relationship and physical life, with all its many details, and the personal father's world outside the home where a woman must establish a relationship with power in order to insure her own survival.

At the mature, God-centered level I call the father's daughter *Athena*, after the Greek goddess who sprang full grown from the head of Zeus, the sky father. I call the mother's daughter *Sophia*, the Greek name for wisdom. Here the tension is between that part of woman that is dedicated to the masculine ideal of civilization and high principle and that part that is oriented toward the natural processes and deep meaning of unfolding life.

Every woman has all four of these feminine parts within herself, although by nature they are not present in equal degrees of consciousness. One quarter will be stronger than the others—a woman's "star" will be there. This is the arena in which she will shine most brightly in her life.

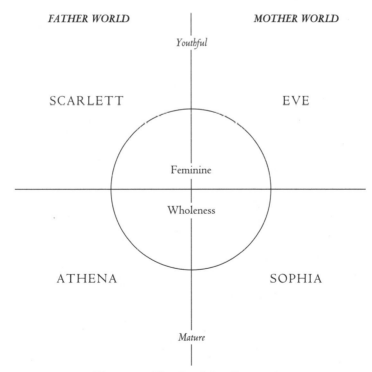

Figure 12. The Feminine Quaternity

But all four quarters must eventually be recognized and lived in order for her life to be complete.

## Eve

EVE is the part of a woman—and of a man's anima—that identifies with the personal mother and is at home at the fundamental level of life that the mother oversees. Eve is woman in her most basic nature, woman as creature, vessel of physical life. My own dream voice once said to me, unaccompanied by image: *The important thing about the feminine vessel is that you are never to forget about it.*

Figure 13. Eve Quarter

The requirements and limitations of physical life are easily forgotten, swept aside by our ideas and expectations, our dreams and enthusiasms, and by our aversion to physical exertion—our laziness. It is the Eve in us, the natural mother, who understands and accepts the requirements of physical life.

The essence of this principle is captured in the simple problem of trying to find a jar of mustard in the refrigerator. It is not unusual for a man or a child to open the refrigerator door, take a brief look inside, and then wail helplessly, "Where is the mustard?" It is the Eve in a person who knows it is not enough to stand before the open door wishing that the mustard would appear. Eve takes it for granted that time and effort must be spent looking carefully on each shelf, moving larger objects aside in order to look behind them until at last the mustard is located. This might sound elementary, but the fact is that people by nature seem almost incapable of accepting the basic physical requirements of life unless the Eve within them is conscious and developed.

Eve is the part of a woman that tends physical life with all its many details. She provides the foundation for life on earth. Without her a woman will not be healthy and balanced in the other three aspects of her feminine being. To forget about or denigrate Eve is to turn away from the very essence of the feminine principle.

It is in her Eve aspect that a woman maintains relationship through physical connections. Purely spiritual love does not belong to this quarter. Eve wants the real thing, the physical presence of the other. Eve's love is offered with outstretched arms, with a telephone call or a visit, with eyes that caress the reality of the other, with ears that take in the voice, the words, the experience of the other. Her love is a hands-on love, expressed in food, gifts, and other physical ministrations.

Until Eve matures, her relationship with others is the instinctual relationship of unconscious identity. She is one with those she loves. There are no boundaries. The youthful, instinctual Eve lives in and through others, dependent upon them for her experience of life. Her own individual personality is largely unknown and undeveloped. But ironically, to the degree to which she fails to know herself, she will fail to know others, unconsciously seeing them as projections of unknown parts of her own personality and not as the individuals they truly are. The more unconscious she is in her relationships, the more her efforts to meet the needs of others will miss the mark.

The Eve aspect of a woman matures as the other feminine aspects are developed. The mature Eve knows herself as a separate individual. She is not dependent on those with whom she is in relationship, and she is able to recognize their individual needs and the degree of her own responsibility toward them. A balance of the youthful and the mature aspects of Eve are necessary for a woman's wholeness. Without the mature Eve, a woman would be too dependent in her relationships, clinging to and smothering the ones she loves. But without a measure of the youthful Eve, she would be too cool and distant. Some unconscious identification is always present in every deeply felt relationship. It is the permeation of boundaries that provides the warmth of human connection.

Not only must the Eve aspect of every person find balance between its youthful and mature qualities, but so must Eve be balanced with the Poet, the masculine expression of this same quarter. Both men and women have the problem of balancing within themselves the dual expression of each quarter. Here, the playful, creative, and romantic activity of the Poet is in direct competition with Eve's attention to the immediate needs of physical life and real relationship. In this same way, the masculine and feminine expressions of life vie for the energy available to each of the other quarters, even as the different quarters vie with each other.

## Scarlett

A GIRL is not only her mother's daughter and heir to the mother world, but she is also the daughter of her father and heir to his world outside the home. The father wields power in the greater world in order to wrest away from it what is needed to support life in the intimate, noncompetitive world of the mother. The father's daughter is the part of a woman that comes to grips with this necessity of drawing support from the greater world outside the home.

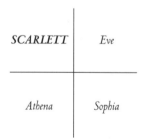

Figure 14. Scarlett Quarter

The daughter of the personal father is an aspect of woman that has taken a great developmental leap forward in recent times. The modern mythological figure of Scarlett, therefore, is an especially appropriate one. *Gone With the Wind,* the American novel in which Scarlett's character is drawn, was published in 1936 and has since sold more copies worldwide than any other book except the Bible—this despite the fact that it is not particularly well written and is rather mean-spirited. Such a large and long-standing popularity attests to the power of the book's archetypal content and its relevance to its time as this particular aspect of feminine life has arisen to new consciousness.

While the daughter of the personal mother focuses on the needs of others, thereby failing to become conscious of herself as an individual, the daughter of the personal father turns her attention to herself and her own potential for winning recognition and security. From the point of view of the mother's daughter, the father's daughter seems self-centered and estranged from her basic feminine nature of providing love and nurture. Yet every woman has the father's daughter in her, and this part of her is just as necessary for feminine wholeness as is the mother's daughter.

When Scarlett is not consciously present, she is present *unconsciously*, undermining Eve's work in the mother world with unrecognized motives of self-seeking and competition. An important component of the new feminine development heralded by *Gone With the Wind* can be seen in the way the character of Scarlett consciously and unapologetically embraces her own ego-centered nature. It is healthier to be conscious of one's instinctual ego-centeredness than to be unconscious of it. When it is conscious, it can be directed toward useful ends and checked when it begins to become destructive.

The consciously ego-centered orientation to life that comes from the Scarlett quarter makes a woman more companionable to men, especially youthful men, who carry this quality as their own first nature. It is Scarlett who can relate to a man on his own terms of competitive striving for power and recognition in the outside world. She also relates to him on his own sexual terms through her inborn readiness to make herself into the image of his desires.

In the early chapters of *Gone With the Wind*, Scarlett portrays the youthful, instinctual father's daughter, wielding the power of her femininity to draw support—suitors—from the masculine world. Although she is not particularly admirable in her calculated approach to this, she nonetheless partakes of an aspect of feminine life that is important and cannot be left out of a woman's wholeness.

There is a natural instinct for the masculine to support the feminine. It is based upon the fact that the pure feminine is softer, kinder, less competitive, less active, and physically weaker than the pure masculine. In her feminine being a woman carries the image of soul, an intangible inner reality from which comes the grace, beauty, and loving-kindness of life. As the carrier of soul a woman needs masculine support—from without and from within—in order for this fragile quality to survive in the greater world. If it does not survive, if it is crushed and driven into the unconscious, the world becomes a hard and ruthless place.

The instinct to give and receive masculine support for feminine soul is rooted in the relationship of father and daughter. It begins in the little girl as the "frilly" feminine, an accentuation of femininity that is healthy and instinctual and draws to it the masculine instinct to support it. The frilly feminine forms the foundation for the development in adolescence of conscious sexual attractiveness. Here again the feminine represents the soul, which seeks to draw men into relationship and connection to life.

Women who miss this development, who were never able as girls to identify with the frilly feminine or, later, with the authentic attracting power of sexuality, often find themselves living lives in which they give support to the masculine world to a greater degree than they receive support from it. In the absence of a healthy measure of masculine support, a woman often tries to become the father, taking on this role in her outer being and growing more and more distant from her own feminine softness and grace. This is an overbalance toward the mature Scarlett, who, as we shall see, develops the masculinity of her own being in order to stand on her own in the greater world.

The instinctual needs of the youthful Scarlett to be soft and graceful and supported by the masculine do not go away just because they have been skipped over. Instead, they appear darkly in the overbalanced mature Scarlett and undermine her strength, making her soft and passive in unconscious and destructive ways, despite her seeming hardness. When such a woman undertakes an individuation journey, her dreams and life experience lead her first to the frilly feminine and unblock her resistance to it. Acceptance of the frilly feminine moves a woman quickly to a conscious experience of the power of her sexual attractiveness, which she then must learn how to handle in a God-centered way. It is only on this instinctual foundation that a healthy mature Scarlett can arise.

The mature Scarlett is the part of a woman who develops her own inner masculine potential. Ideally it is the father who first encourages this development in his daughter, although to do it in the right way, he must be careful not to withdraw support for the soft side of her feminine being—a balance on his part that is not easy to achieve. If the development of the mature Scarlett fails to take place in due course, fate will often step in and try to arrange it by pulling away a woman's outer masculine support in an attempt to force her to find strength and independence within herself.

Through education and training the mature Scarlett acquires the knowledge, discipline, and skill that are necessary to wield her own masculine power and handle in her own right the competitive reality of the outside world. When this development is balanced, a woman's masculine energy does not take over her outer personality, but rather it comes to her from within, bringing authentic focus, strength, and courage that complement her feminine reality without burying it. Both the youthful and the mature aspects of Scarlett are needed for wholeness—the first to bring a woman the masculine support she needs to retain her feminine softness and grace, and the second to give her strength, independence, and the satisfaction of achievement in the outside world.

## Athena

THE FATHER'S DAUGHTER at the higher, God-centered level of life is symbolized by Athena, the Greek goddess who was born fully mature from the head of Zeus. Clothed in armor and carrying a spear, Athena sprang into the world with a war cry. Her father gave her the use of his thunderbolt and shield, conferring upon her the agency of his mighty power. She of all the gods and goddesses on Mount Olympus stood closest to his throne. Athena was the protectoress of cities and of the soldiers who fought for them, the guardian of culture and civilization.

Figure 15. Athena Quarter

The Athena quarter has to do with the part of woman that strives to give form to the masculine ideal of heaven on earth. The heavenly ideal requires the vessel of physical reality to hold it and give it tangible life. This attempt to shape the components of nature into an expression of heaven's truth is the essence of culture and the basis of civilization.

It is the Athena in a woman, or in a man's anima, who tells us to take our elbows off the table and our shod feet off the sofa, to use the correct fork, to wear clothing appropriate to the occasion, and to make sure our verbs agree with their subjects. The goddess Athena introduced the bridle to humankind. The Athena aspect of woman helps us bridle our natural instincts and turn our energy toward the effort that is required to give the best possible shape to civilization and community life.

The Athena in us invests her energy in churches, schools, libraries, and other public institutions. She helps establish the structures and forms that carry cultural life. She is the teacher, the seamstress, the interior decorator, the book publisher, the hostess, the nun. She needs her armor, her spear, her warlike determination, and the shielded protection of the spirit of heaven to effect her purpose against the tendency of natural life to return to chaos. Without health in the Athena quarter, civilization devolves.

The youthful, instinctual aspect of Athena can be seen in a woman's preoccupation with perfection of form in her own being, especially in regard to her body, her hair, and her clothes. This preoccupation extends to her house and everything else that she feels is a reflection of herself, including her family, her school, church, neighborhood, and town. It also applies to her personal performance in every situation. *She* is the feminine vessel whose form she feels compelled to make perfect. This very strong compulsion is one with which every woman must contend.

The standard to which the youthful Athena holds herself is a collective one. It is also a masculine standard, coming as it does from the outside world. And yet a woman's compulsion to meet it does not come from the collective culture nor from men, but from her own Athena self, an inescapable part of her being that is born of the father's masculine spirit and seeks to serve that spirit with fierce loyalty.

In order to bring the Athena quarter into balance, a woman must develop her other feminine aspects, since all the quarters counterweigh and balance each other's demands. It is also necessary that a woman become conscious of that *voice within herself* which belongs to the father of her youthful Athena. This is the judging voice of her animus, which so easily becomes dark, or negative. It is the part of her inner self that always holds up the *collective* standard, the voice that says "ought" and "should" and makes her feel guilty for not measuring up to the prevailing ideals of whatever collective spirit she is serving. It often speaks with the voice of a particular man in her life, usually husband, lover, father, or the animus voice of her mother. But it is not that person who is actually speaking or who has any real control over her. Rather it is an unrecognized part of her own being. When a woman can recognize that natural, instinctual, and potentially oppressive inner judge and consciously distinguish it from her true, individual self, she is ready for a healthy development of the mature Athena.

In the mature Athena, service to the collective ideal is replaced by service to God. The mature Athena still seeks to be a vessel of perfection, but she chooses God's perfection over man's, a perfection that is more merciful than man's because it includes the natural limitations of unfolding life on earth. This is the Virgin Mary saying yes to God, agreeing to become the physical vehicle for His appearance in the world. The birth of Mary's son in the rough, earthy stable instead of in a well-appointed inn illustrates the difference between God's perfection and man's.

A woman's wholeness is not served, however, if she embodies only the mature Athena. The youthful Athena is always present, whether conscious or not. If the youthful Athena is unconscious, she will distort the mature Athena's service to God by substituting the voice of collective religion for the voice of the living God. If the mature Athena has not learned how to recognize, and separate herself from, the judging voice of her negative animus, her compulsion to perfection will enslave her to unrealistic collective standards of religion that are no less destructive than unrealistic standards of secular life.

Both the youthful and the mature aspects of Athena are needed in human life. The youthful Athena helps a woman shape herself and her surroundings into an effective vehicle for service to the human community. She accepts the training and coaching that come from the masculine ideal. The mature Athena takes the form she has gained from that training and turns it over to God. In allowing the prepared vessel of her life to be filled with the spirit of the living God, for His purpose alone, she accepts her true vocation, rather than one placed upon her by outside expectations.

## Sophia

BALANCE between the youthful and mature aspects of the various feminine quarters and between the quarters themselves does not come about automatically. It is Sophia, the fourth quarter in the feminine quaternity, who, like the King in the masculine quaternity, is of a different quality than the other three quarters and oversees the health and balance of the whole.

Figure 16. Sophia Quarter

"Sophia," wrote Carl Jung, "is the woman wisdom of God." In Greek translations of the Bible, *sophia* is the word used to translate the Hebrew word *chokhmah*, which refers to divine wisdom. Both the Greek and Hebrew words are feminine in gender. This *chokhmah*, or *sophia*, or wisdom, as revealed in Scripture is a mysterious primeval order, a manifestation of divine meaning that is found in the heart of created life. This is not the blindness and cruelty that characterizes nature when no consciousness of God is present. True Wisdom is marked by her benevolence toward humankind. It is through her that the love of God flows into creation. In the following passage from Ecclesiasticus (The Wisdom of Jesus Ben Sirach), Wisdom takes on the image of a sheltering tree—protective, benevolent nature imbued with the glory of God:

> Happy the man who meditates on wisdom . . .
> who studies her ways in his heart,
> and ponders her secrets. . . .
> He pitches his tent at her side,
> and lodges in an excellent lodging;
> he sets his children in her shade
> and camps beneath her branches;
> he is sheltered by her from the heat,
> and in her glory he makes his home.

It is this woman wisdom of God, unfolding from the natural life process, that brings everything in life into balance—not without pain, but always with mercy. Life provides its own corrections, but whether we are protected and aided by that process, or trampled and crushed, depends upon our relationship to wisdom.

Sophia is the part of a woman who is the daughter of the feminine aspect of God. Like every daughter she has an instinct to identify with her mother. A woman who is particularly strong in the Sophia quarter will tend to identify with nature itself. She is the woman who likes things the natural way, who shuns technology and elaborate manifestations of culture. She gardens, hangs her clothes in the sun, takes walks in the woods, and says whatever comes to her mind.

It is the Sophia aspect of woman who finds interest in every twist and turn of unfolding life. She does not necessarily understand the meaning of all that happens to herself and those around her, but she senses importance in it and feels a great need to talk about it. This is the teenager spending endless hours on the telephone, the neighbors lingering at the backyard fence, and the long lunches of women who are friends. When these conversations are going well, there is an element of eternity in them—they take place in a timeless realm. Meaning constellates from them. Insights are received, and health and balance are restored. An hour flies by like a minute, and a woman comes away from them blinking her eyes as she readjusts to the here and now, her hair dripping a little with the waters of the stream of life.

When the Sophia quarter is not lived consciously, it can become more a refuge from life than a source of healing and balance. Gossip, soap operas, television talk shows, and romance novels appeal to an unconscious Sophia. So do astrological predictions, psychic readings, and tabloid newspapers.

In her Sophia aspect, a woman not only identifies with nature and the process of life but also with wisdom itself. She feels that she herself is the one who knows how life should unfold and what would be best for everyone in her circle, and she tries earnestly to control things and make them come out that way. She truly thinks that she is the one who can solve the problems of all her family members, who can mend the broken hearts of her friends, and who knows which way her children's lives should go.

Sometimes she is seized with genuine intuitions, with knowing that comes to her not through her mind but through her body. She knows in her heart or in her gut or perhaps through a dream she has had. If she is unconsciously identified with the feminine side of God, she will think that this kind of knowing is a special power which belongs to her and which she is supposed to use to influence the course of events in her world.

The mature Sophia, like the mature King, is relatively rare. She is the woman who awakens to the fact that the wisdom of God does not come from her but from life itself. It is life that knows what is needed and how to bring that about. It is life that provides the answers and makes things unfold. The mature Sophia knows that although her intuition may be a gift, it is not a special power. She cannot control life. She may see wonderful possibilities, but that does not mean she has the power to bring them about. She may see disaster looming, but that does not mean she has the power to stop it. The mature Sophia knows that wisdom gives her understanding but not power. Her task is to try to recognize as best she can the true stream of life, to trust it, and to work with it where possible to help it bring healing and wholeness to herself and the world around her.

It is the mature Sophia who understands the unconscious and feels comfortable in that realm. She presides over the inner journey. She needs a Wise Man's map, a trustworthy cultural understanding of the nature of the unconscious, to keep herself safely connected to human reality, but the territory of the unconscious itself is not strange to her. A man approaching the unconscious in his Wise Man aspect will always have an anima figure in his dreams or outer life—a Sophia—who leads him into the realm of mystery that the unconscious appears to him to be. But the Sophia part of a woman does not experience the unconscious as a mysterious realm. It feels familiar to her. She does need the help of her animus, but it is for the order and meaning he imparts, and even more it is for his watchful and protecting love, a mediation to her of the love of God.

It is in a fully developed Sophia that all the other aspects of woman come together and express themselves in the truest love of which the human heart is capable. This is a love that does not seek to control or to hold but only to know and to further the will of God as it unfolds from the process of life. Sophia accepts whatever comes, knowing with the fourteenth century anchoress Julian of Norwich that, "All shall be well, and all shall be well, and all manner of things shall be well." As with Julian, the mature Sophia's love for God is at the center of her being. While Athena loves God with a daughter's love, Sophia loves Him as a Spouse, as her other half, her completion, the masculine complement of her feminine being. And because of her love for God, God's love flows through her to others, not by her design but by her faithful attention to God's unfolding purpose.

All four quarters of the feminine quaternity are active within every woman's personality, whether their manifestations are conscious or unconscious. It is the goal of life's journey to bring the four quarters into consciousness and balance, an end that can only be attained when life is fully lived.

# CHAPTER THIRTEEN

# Psyche and Eros and The Feminine Quaternity

WHEN A WOMAN accepts the task of individuation, she enters into a conscious experience of the natural process by which the four quarters of the feminine quaternity are brought into balance in her own being, a development which readies her ultimately for union with God. An illustration of this process can be seen in the classical myth of Psyche and Eros.

The story of Psyche and Eros is a tale within a tale, an ancient Greek myth recounted in the *Metamorphoses* or *Golden Ass,* a novel written by Lucius Apuleius, a second-century Roman. Psyche, whose name means "soul," is a human woman and the main protagonist of the myth. Her love involvement is with Eros, the mythical god of love (also known as Cupid or Amor), a personification of divine love.

As the story of soul and love, the myth of Psyche and Eros is a particularly compelling one, and a number of writers in both religion and psychology have taken their turns at wresting the meaning from it. C.S. Lewis made his contribution by transposing the story into his interpretive novel *Till We Have Faces.* Three Jungian analysts have also devoted books to it. Erich Neumann presents a particularly insightful treatment in his work, *Amor and Psyche.* Somewhat easier to approach and also containing much insight is Robert Johnson's *She. The Golden Ass of Apuleius,* by Marie-Louise von Franz, is an analysis of the entire novel within which the myth is situated. Von Franz makes a valuable contribution to the Psyche and Eros literature by looking at Psyche's story in terms of a man's anima. Psyche as anima is certainly one way in which the myth should be viewed—men should see this as the story of their own souls. But because the soul is feminine, it is carried more consciously by women than by men, and so, for the purpose of analysis, I will speak of the myth as a woman's tale. While my own analysis includes or shares some elements from all three of the Jungian works cited above, much of it is not found in those sources, especially the connection drawn between Psyche's four tasks and the feminine quaternity.

## Psyche Is Sacrificed

THE TALE OPENS with Psyche as a maiden, one of three beautiful daughters of a king and queen. While her sisters are beautiful in an ordinary way, Psyche's beauty is of a higher order, so much so that she begins to attract the adoration and devotion that formerly was reserved for Aphrodite, the goddess of love. "Here is a *new* Aphrodite," people say, "an Aphrodite who is flesh and blood and lives among us." This, of course, excites the jealousy of Aphrodite, who determines to rid Psyche of the special quality of her beauty.

Aphrodite summons her son Eros, whose arrows inflame with love whomever they strike without regard for rules, bounds, or standards of suitability. She instructs him to make Psyche fall in love with and marry the vilest of men, the lowest of the low. Certain that this will take care of her rival, Aphrodite departs for an extended holiday in Poisidon's realm beneath the sea.

Meanwhile, Psyche's two sisters make happy marriages to kings in other lands, but no one asks for Psyche's hand. Men hold her in awe and pay homage to her beauty, but none wants to marry her. Her father becomes concerned and consults an oracle of Apollo. To his dismay he is told that he must take Psyche to a lonely mountaintop where she will meet the one for whom she is destined. But this will be her funeral rather than her wedding, for the one who will come to claim her for his own will be a fierce, winged dragon.

As terrible as this is, the gods must be obeyed, and so, with great sorrow, Psyche's father and mother take her to her doom on the wild mountaintop. Accepting her fate, Psyche does her best to comfort her grieving parents. They leave her there, darkness falls, and she waits in fear and trembling. But no dreadful beast comes to claim her. Instead, the gentle West Wind wafts her down into a hidden paradise deep in the valley below. Here she finds a beautiful palace filled with all the treasure of the world. Disembodied servants, known to her only by their voices, minister to all her needs. Then in the darkness of night the one to whom she has been wed enters her bridal chamber. She hears him and feels him, but she cannot see him. He is tender in his love, and though he leaves before daylight can reveal his identity, she is content to be his wife. He continues to return in the same way every night. As she settles into life in paradise, she comes to love her unseen husband, as he loves her.

## Two Streams of Life and Love

THIS THEN, is the beginning of the tale, which we now interrupt to look at its meaning so far. I will interpret it as if it were a dream.

Psyche is one of three sisters, the others ordinary, she extraordinary. It can be assumed that these are three parts of one woman—the two sisters representing ordinary consciousness, perhaps mother's daughter and father's daughter, and Psyche representing the inner life of the soul.

Every woman carries the radiance of Psyche in her being. This is the pure feminine light that glows in her most noticeably when she is a young woman moving full of hope toward adult life, her dreams of love and fulfillment still intact. The radiance of Psyche comes from within and is beyond the beauty of ordinary flesh. Although physically real, Psyche's beauty has a spiritual quality, and to those who are discerning, the presence of God is clearly evident in it. It can be seen in a woman at any time in her life when she is centered in herself, when her spirit, soul, and body are knit together in harmony.

Psyche's beauty calls forth from man a positive response, an admiring, adoring, even worshipful regard. But it does not call forth a physically sexual response. There are two streams of love and attraction between the masculine and the feminine, both coming from the unconscious. One is experienced at the surface of life and involves romantic fantasy and physical desire. The other comes from a deeper level where the human soul and the spirit of God are ever drawn to each other. The union that seeks realization at this deeper level is the union of feminine wisdom and masculine godliness.

It is not easy to think about these two streams of human life and love. I have had a number of dreams that shed light on this subject, three of the clearer ones coming as understanding, with no images. The first of these speaks of a split in consciousness between body and spirit. The dream said:

> *We have a body mind and a spirit mind. While we are in our body minds, absorbed in our bodies, we cannot commune with the God of heaven, the God of the Old and New Testaments.*

The dream seems to suggest that this split is general in the human condition—consciousness of one level obscures consciousness of the other.

The next dream came several years after the one above:

> *I dreamed that Sigmund Freud was estranged from sexuality. He did not know what it was. This was because he did not know about the deeper, truer level where real sexuality takes place.*

Freud, of course, was virtually fixated on sexuality, but the only stream of the unconscious of which he was aware was the stream of wish-fulfilling fantasy and physical desire that connects us to the surface of life. This dream makes it clear, however, that sexuality has a truer reality at a deeper, more spiritual level than the level with which Freud was concerned. What Freud failed to understand was that sexuality at the surface of life is a symbolic language that refers to our journey toward wholeness at the deeper level.

A few weeks after the dream about Freud, I received a further clarification about the two levels:

> *While dreaming deeply, I had a clear realization about the surface of life, about how limited it is. And a sense of the level below the surface where the real life is—where God is present all the time.*

This dream suggests a correspondence between the deeper level of life and the kingdom of God, which, as Jesus pointed out, is always with us though seldom recognized. The surface of life, on the other hand, is understood in the dream to be more like what Jesus referred to as This World, a limited reality that is not as important as it seems.

These, then, are the two levels of life, each with its stream of love. The two streams tend to be experienced as mutually exclusive, especially by the focused consciousness of men, and this gives rise to the difficulty a man typically has in approaching woman on the physical level of sexuality while he is loving her for the beauty and wisdom of her soul. In our story, therefore, Psyche, who carries the beauty of the deeper stream, is loved and even worshipped by men, and yet she has no suitors and no offer of marriage.

Aphrodite symbolizes the romantic and physically sexual stream of love. This stream leads to an outer world enactment of the union of the opposites with all its joys, difficulties, and varied consequences, but it does not necessarily lead to a corresponding inner union.

Aphrodite's requirement for consciousness is minimal. Love strikes and entangles two people, and, if conditions allow, sets them on a course together. No effort by the participants is needed to assemble the components of this situation—it all happens automatically through the archetypal effect that Aphrodite symbolizes. The woman always appears beautiful, the man always appears strong and full of potential. Their love for each other always seems destined from the beginning of time and sure to last forever. Romantic fantasy and physical desire carry them forward. But after this initial experience has done its work of entangling them in new life together, a change begins to occur. The romantic feelings dissipate and sexual desire begins to wane. If there is no *real* love coming to them from the second, deeper stream—if there is no awareness of God, no nourishment from the soul—then the initial love that seemed so sure and lasting takes a downward turn and may not stop in its decline until it finally turns into its opposite, hate.

The two sisters in the story carry the ordinary consciousness of the surface of life and thus make ordinary marriages in the Aphrodite way. Psyche, the soul of the woman represented by the three sisters, sinks down into the unconscious, submerged by the intensity of the early stage of ordinary love. It is as if she has died. But she has not died. She has in fact been wed to a mysterious but loving husband whose kingdom is a virtual paradise.

This tells us that a potential for deeper love exists in the Aphrodite experience. A woman's soul, forced into the unconscious, finds there a rich love hiding beneath the everyday reality of physical love and romantic illusion. But it is a love upon which the light of ordinary consciousness does not fall. It lives only at the deeper level, separate and apart from life on the surface. The soul of woman is not disturbed by this in the beginning. She accepts love where she has found it and is content.

We now continue with the story.

## Psyche Is Banished from Paradise

IN DUE COURSE Psyche's sisters hear about her supposed death and come to the mountaintop to grieve for her. Psyche's husband is distressed at this. In the darkness of his nightly visits he warns Psyche not to reveal herself to them, for they will not rest until they have persuaded her to try to find out who he is. And if ever she looks upon him, she will lose him forever. Furthermore, the child she now carries—for she has become pregnant—will be divine if she goes along with things as they are, but if she tries to see her husband's face, the child will be born a mortal.

Psyche now falls into despair as she realizes for the first time how completely she has been cut off from human company. She wants to see her sisters. She is inconsolable, until at last her husband gives in and allows the West Wind to waft the sisters down into the valley for a visit. Their grief immediately gives way to envy when they see Psyche's paradise and hear about the great love she enjoys with her husband. Their own husbands, who at first had seemed such happy matches, have turned out to be old and sickly and stingy with their money, no longer regarding their wives as lovers but as nursemaids. Why should Psyche be so happy and they so miserable?

The two sisters set about to undo Psyche's situation. They try to persuade her that her husband is an evil monster and that she should shine a light on him to see this for herself and kill him. Because Psyche has never seen him, she cannot be sure that her sisters are wrong. He may indeed be the dreadful monster to whom she was originally betrothed. So the next night as her husband sleeps, Psyche approaches him with a lamp in one hand and a knife in the other. When she holds the lamp above him, however, what she sees is not a monster but beautiful, winged Eros, the god of love himself. She drops the knife and at that same moment accidently pricks herself on one of his arrows and falls more deeply in love with him than ever.

As she swoons with this deeper love, a drop of hot oil spills from the lamp onto Eros' shoulder, wounding and awakening him. Upon seeing her transgression—the lamp and the fallen knife—he flies away. But as he rises, she catches hold of him and is carried out of paradise into the wide world, where finally she can hold on no longer and drops to earth. Eros alights in a nearby tree and speaks to her, explaining that his mother Aphrodite had told him to unite her with a foul husband, but that on seeing her, he had pricked himself with his own arrow and taken her for his wife, loving her dearly. Now, however, she has betrayed him and he must fly away from her. And with this he disappears into the heavens.

## Reuniting the Two Streams of Life

AGAIN WE PAUSE to examine the meaning of what has occurred.

The deeper love that can be sensed beneath the surface of physical and romantic love turns out to be nothing less than the love of God itself. Ordinary consciousness is responsible for bringing this to light. It is the two sisters who realize that the soul is missing and presumed dead and who go to mourn for her at the place where she was lost. Only then does the soul remember ordinary consciousness and wish to be reunited with it. It is when the effects of Aphrodite have worn off that a woman realizes that she has lost track of the deeper, truer part of herself and begins to mourn its loss. This crisis comes at midlife, if not before, and sets in motion a response from the soul that, when given the right circumstances, can lead a woman into the individuation process.

The chief impediment to this development in consciousness turns out to be Eros himself. The love of God as it first arises in the unconscious cannot be lived consciously at the surface of life. It is too divine, too blissful, too demanding that life be paradise. In order for the divine to live in human life, it must sacrifice some of its glory, let go of its expectation of perfect fulfillment, and accept the limitations of outer reality, which even at best can hold and express only a small portion of God's love. In the same way, as we shall see, the human soul must endure sacrifice and suffering in order to be integrated into ordinary life. This development of the soul is a human task, a work to be consciously engaged. Love, meanwhile, retreats more deeply into the unconscious, where in its own mysterious way it will be transformed in tandem with the soul's progress.

The story now continues.

## Psyche Searches for Eros

WITH GREAT LAMENTATION Psyche watches Eros fly away until he is out of sight. Then in her despair she heads straight for a nearby river and throws herself in. But the river, knowing she belongs to Eros and is under his protection, disgorges her back onto the shore. There she meets Pan, the god of nature, who comforts her, telling her not to despair but to go find Eros and address him with her prayers, for he is soft-hearted and will reconcile with her. So Psyche sets out to find him. But first she settles the score with her sisters, whose envy broke up her paradise. She tricks them into dying of their own greed by throwing themselves headlong into the valley of paradise without waiting for the aid of the West Wind.

Meanwhile, Aphrodite returns from her holiday beneath the sea. The world has fared badly while she was playing in Poisidon's realm and while Eros was secluded in paradise with Psyche. Because of their absence, there is no longer any joy and love to be found in the world. Relationships of every kind have fallen into neglect and ruin. Hate and loathing are running rampant. The reason for Aphrodite's return, however, is not that she is particularly concerned about this. She comes back to wreak her vengeance on Psyche for stealing the heart of her son Eros, who has returned to his mother's house to recover from the wound he suffered from the hot oil. Because his love for Psyche has not abated, Aphrodite puts him under guard to keep the lovers from reuniting.

Psyche does not know where Eros has gone. She looks for him first in the temple of Demeter, the divine earth mother. There she hears that Aphrodite is after her, and she begs Demeter for refuge. The earth goddess sympathizes with her, but she fears Aphrodite and will not let Psyche stay in her temple. Psyche goes next to Hera, the wife of Zeus, but Eros is not here either, and again Psyche is refused refuge. Now she realizes that she has no choice but to go to Aphrodite and throw herself on the goddess's mercy. She hopes that at least she might find Eros at his mother's house. This decision is driven home when Aphrodite sends Hermes, the messenger of the gods, to stir up all the world in a universal search for Psyche. There is no longer any possibility for escape.

So Psyche goes to the house of Aphrodite. There she is met at the door by the servant Habit, who grabs her by her hair and drags her to the goddess of love. Aphrodite greets her with scorn and turns her over to her handmaidens Trouble and Sorrow, who whip her and torment her in various other ways. When they have finished, Aphrodite beats her some more and then assigns her an impossible task to be completed by the end of the day.

## Stillness and Surrender: The Feminine Way

BEFORE WE GO ON with Psyche's first task, we will stop once again to examine the meaning of what has unfolded.

Psyche is desolate at the loss of Eros. Here, symbolically, is a woman whose ordinary consciousness has penetrated the depths of her own being and glimpsed the living reality of the love of God. She has recognized God as her own inner Spouse, her Beloved, her highest value. From this point on, she will allow nothing to come between herself and the fulfillment of that love. It is this, and only this, that gives her the strength and courage for a true individuation journey.

When a woman's consciousness pierces the depths and finds the love of God within herself, her soul, no longer separated from consciousness, is

drawn out of the paradise of the unconscious. As the soul enters the ordinary world, the surface and the depths are conjoined, creating a new
level of consciousness. But the surface and the depths, though bridged, are
still very far apart. The surface of life has suffered from having lost track
of its soul. Discord and difficulty have replaced the hopefulness of youth.
Ordinary relationships, with their unexamined shadow sides, carry little of
the tender love of God that the soul has come to know in her secluded
paradise. Much change and transformation will be necessary in order to
integrate the two worlds, each of which needs what the other has to offer.
The surface of life needs the tender love and saving grace of the depths,
and the spiritual depths need the surface of life in order to be fully known
and truly lived.

At the outset the two realities are so far apart that Psyche despairs of
ever seeing Eros again. She first collapses in a fit of weeping, and then she
tries to drown herself. This collapse and impulse to die is Psyche's hallmark. We will see it again and again as the story proceeds. It is the way of
the soul, the feminine way of growth and change. An individuation journey that is not marked by episodes of deep weeping and the soul-felt
willingness to die to one's old way of being is not a true journey of transformation. The masculine aspect of the journey involves heroic action,
but the feminine aspect involves stillness and surrender in the face of the
seeming impossibility of effective action. It is this feminine surrender that
opens us to the depths of the spirit and to the help that is always available
from that realm when our own strength is no longer enough.

The river refuses Psyche's bid for death. Because it knows that she belongs to Eros, whose power the river honors and fears, it will not drown
her and instead puts her back onto the shore. This is the first of many
indications in the story that although Eros is not present in an obvious
way, he is in fact present insofar as nature itself has consciousness of him
and of Psyche's relationship to him and gives her special aid and protection
in his name. This symbolizes nothing less than natural spirituality as it is
experienced by us when we approach it in the context of a conscious
relationship with the love of God.

The idea of natural spirituality is reinforced by the appearance of Pan,
the god of nature. Pan, who knows Eros to be tender and forgiving, assures

Psyche that she can draw him back to her with her prayers. With this encouragement, Psyche sets out to find her husband. The meeting with Pan tells us in symbolic language that the individuation journey begins when we meet the living spirit of nature and establish dialogue with it. This cinches the new level of consciousness, making permanent the connection that has been achieved between the surface of life and the spiritual depths. The center of this new consciousness is the love of God, which can also be called the Christ, or the Self, or the God-center within. It alone can bring about the unification of the two competing streams of life.

The new, integrative consciousness brings an end to ordinary consciousness, which has the ego at its center. This is symbolized in the story by the death of the two sisters, whose tendency to envy and greed show the overriding dominance of the ego. Psyche will now be required to carry in herself the ordinary consciousness of the sisters as well as the deep consciousness of the soul. Symbolically, this is a woman who has become one with her soul and who must now integrate the deeper awareness of her soul with the reality of everyday life and love.

For Psyche to integrate the two levels of consciousness, she must enter the world of Aphrodite and submit to the consequences of ordinary love just as her sisters did. But resistance always accompanies any movement toward new consciousness. Psyche, who undertakes this journey both as mother-to-be and as wife, tries to hide from Aphrodite in the temples of Demeter and Hera, symbols of archetypal motherhood and wifehood. The call to individuation, however, is a call away from the central identification a woman has found as the mother of her children or the wife of her husband. These are important relationships, but a woman must eventually move beyond them to become, like the Virgin Mary, the spouse and mother of God, both within the depths of her own being and in a way that has reality in the ordinary world.

It is important to understand, however, that we cannot move beyond what we have never attained. Psyche's visits to Demeter and Hera might also be seen as homage paid to these instinctual realms of womanhood as she enters the individuation process. A woman who by midlife has not consciously lived as wife or mother will find as an aspect of her individuation journey that these parts of herself must come awake and gain some kind of outlet in her life, however attenuated. Instinctual life must be accepted and valued in its own right before it can be sacrificed and transformed into a higher reality.

A complete surrender to the individuation process can no longer be evaded when Hermes stirs up the whole world in a search for Psyche. This symbolizes the point at which the unconscious breaks out in a display of synchronicity and archetypal dreams that have a powerful effect on the ego, breaking down its resistance. At this moment a woman realizes that she has no choice but to go along with the change in consciousness that is arising in her. New life is coming, a life she cannot imagine and yet cannot refuse. With this submission of the ego, the way is open for transformation.

In the story Psyche submits to Aphrodite. The part of a woman that was created to be deeply loved and truly understood in a way that only God can do consents to enter the context of ordinary human life and love. Though she agrees to this because she has no other option, she also hopes to find there the divine love that she seeks. What she finds, however, is suffering at the hands of Habit, Trouble, and Sorrow. The daily requirements of mundane life and the twists, turns, and seeming reverses of its slow development feel like torture to the soul, which longs for the fulfillment of the deep love that it knows to be its rightful due. But that perfect love that has been known in the depths has lacked outer reality, and the only way to make it real is to integrate it with the surface of life. A beginning to this must be made, even though the quality of love first encountered in everyday life is so far from perfection that the soul feels nothing but torment.

It is, in the first place, life's burden of Habit, Trouble, and Sorrow that has driven a woman to seek her soul in the hope of finding a better way to live. But reconnection with her soul brings with it the requirement to learn life all over again in a way that accords with the soul's way. This is what the individuation journey accomplishes. In the story this relearning is symbolized by four seemingly impossible tasks imposed upon Psyche by Aphrodite. These four tasks can be correlated with the four quarters of the feminine quaternity. With each task the soul faces the seemingly impossible challenge of living a whole and healthy feminine life in the face of the overwhelming demands of everyday reality. But where ordinary consciousness found only Habit, Trouble, and Sorrow, the soul finds a way that is eased by the love of God and that leads ever closer to the ultimate fulfillment of that love in a manifestation that is as human as it is divine.

We now return to the story.

## Psyche's First Task

APHRODITE is jealous of the deep love between Psyche and Eros and resentful of their secret marriage, from which a child is soon to be born. The goddess of love considers Psyche to be an upstart, a mere mortal who is not worthy of her divine son. To prove Psyche's unworthiness, Aphrodite gives her a task that no mortal woman could accomplish. She shows her a great heap of jumbled seeds: wheat, barley, millet, poppy seeds, chick peas, lentils, and beans. She tells Psyche that she is so low and ugly that she could only attract a lover by being his drudge, and so now it will be seen how worthy a drudge she is. Before night has fallen, she must sort all these seeds into separate piles according to their kind. Certain that she has gotten the best of Psyche, Aphrodite leaves to attend a wedding feast.

Psyche sits down in a stupor, overwhelmed by the impossibility of the task. But a little ant sees her and feels sorry for her, knowing that she is the beloved spouse of the great god Eros. The ant goes out into the fields and calls together all the other ants in the vicinity. Addressing them as nurslings of mother earth, he urges them to pity Psyche in her plight and come to her aid. So they all go in, a great host of tiny beings, and separate the seeds one by one, accomplishing the task before nightfall.

### Relearning Eve's Quarter

LOOKING NOW at the meaning of Psyche's first task, we see that as the soul enters ordinary life, it comes up against the challenge of the Eve quarter of the feminine quaternity, with its requirement for the endless tending of physical life. This is the realm of the personal mother, the aspect of the feminine that is instinctual mother, or earth mother. She is symbolized in Greek mythology by Demeter, who was closely associated with grain and other cultivated fruits of the earth. The heap of seeds of cultivated foodplants can be seen as an image of the many small details which accompany the living of life and require the attention of the feminine in the Eve quarter. Whether in a man or a woman, it is Eve energy that is needed for keeping a house or an office, preparing food, tending children, and in general overseeing the physical details of life.

"You are nothing but a drudge," says Aphrodite. This is true of a woman who lives the Eve quarter in a purely Aphrodite way. Earthly love begets earthly life, which must be tended. How is one to take care of all the many details of fundamental earth life? Overwhelmed by the task, Psyche cannot do a thing. She just sits there. As we have seen, this is her hallmark. When the soul is overwhelmed, her answer is to *do nothing*. But this nothing is actually something. It creates an opening for help from the spiritual depths, which is just what happens in the story. To Psyche's aid comes an army of ants—friends of Eros, nurslings of mother earth. The problem of the seeds arises from life on earth, and so does the solution. The ants symbolize little bits of earth energy, coming naturally. They are the little impulses and urges that can be felt coming to us through our bodies, saying: *Do this. Now this. Now this.*

When faced with an overwhelming task—as for example, when we have been tied up with a project at work, the house is a mess, and twenty relatives are descending the next day for Thanksgiving dinner—the answer at first is to sit down and be still. Wait. Keep waiting until a little impulse comes, a tiny jolt of energy from somewhere deep inside that says: *Go make the cranberry sauce.* The impetus, the will to engage, is only for that task and no other. And so we get up and do it. Then we clean up where the bubbling sauce has splattered on the stove. Then we feel moved to clean the entire stovetop. Then the countertops. Now we take a magazine from a countertop to the coffee table in the living room, where we do some straightening. Then take a dirty glass back to the kitchen and wash up some dishes. One task leads to another, each with its own energy that says, *Yes, do it.* The little impulses know that perfection is not the goal. *Do this. Leave that.* There is a solution that fits the time and energy available, and the ant helpers know what it is. They guide a woman to just the right efforts in just the right order. She needs no overall plan. She simply follows the guiding spirit from within, the Holy Spirit manifest in the earth of her being.

The answer to an overwhelming task in the Eve quarter is not one big, focused effort but a diffuse, interwoven effort from woman's diffuse, interweaving consciousness. If a woman puts on a masculine mind and focuses her consciousness too much into organized effort, she will lose her ant helpers. Their little impulses will be overwhelmed, unfelt. Driven by ideas of perfection, she will wear herself out by doing too much, or else she will give up in the face of all she thinks she has to do and therefore will do too little. But when the ants are helping her, she moves from this to that at an even pace, taking time for herself and others when needed, and yet never losing her forward momentum.

With the help of the soul, Eve's realm is relearned. When Aphrodite is in charge of this quarter, a woman is at the mercy of her nurturing instincts, which, when unchecked by reflection and consciousness, make her feel she must give of herself and keep on giving until she has met all the needs and expectations, real and imagined, of those for whom she feels responsible. But when a woman is at one with her soul, the Eve part of her is no longer driven by unconscious instinct or the expectations of others. The spirit of God, which loves her and understands her and comes to her individually from the depths of her own being, guides her in the ordering of her life. It tells her what needs to be done, and it tells her when she has done enough, according to her particular circumstances. It frees her from drudgery and awakens her to the beauty and value of tending life in a God-centered way.

With this development, the Eve aspect of life is no longer an unwelcome chore. It becomes an important and valued part of a woman's feminine being, fundamental to all the other parts of herself. It is especially fundamental to the wisdom quarter of Sophia, since a woman's willingness to tend her home can be an outward reflection of her willingness to tend her inner life, where the same neverending attention is required.

We now continue the story.

## Psyche's Second Task

IN THE EVENING the goddess of love returns from the wedding feast and finds to her dismay that all the seeds have been sorted. "This is not your work!" cries Aphrodite. "It is the work of Eros!" And so the next morning she gives Psyche a second impossible task. She tells her to go fetch some golden fleece from the terrible rams that wander in a grove beside a certain river.

Psyche knows this cannot be done. The rams are too fierce to be approached. She goes to the river as she was told, but her intent is to throw herself into the water and drown herself. She is stopped, however, by the gentle murmur of a green reed growing at the river's edge. Like a panpipe blown upon by divine breath, the reed speaks to her and tells her not to kill herself.

It is true, the reed says, that the rams are dangerous. They draw blazing heat from the sun, which maddens them with a wild frenzy. Their horns are sharp and their foreheads are like stone, and even their bite is sometimes poisonous. If Psyche tries to approach them now, as the sun moves toward its zenith, they will kill her. But if she waits until noon has passed and the sun has begun to cool and the rams have been lulled to sleep by the soft river breeze, then she can go to the grove, where earlier the rams were charging about, and gather there the wisps of golden fleece that she will find clinging to the twigs and brambles.

So Psyche waits in the shade of a tree until the heat of the sun begins to wane. Then when the rams have grown quiet, she goes out and easily gathers all the golden fleece she needs and takes it back to Aphrodite.

### *Relearning Scarlett's Quarter*

PSYCHE'S SECOND TASK sends her to the second quarter of the feminine quaternity, to Scarlett's realm, where she must get some masculine power. Scarlett is the father's daughter at the ego level, the one who must learn how to handle herself in the competitive outside world.

Aphrodite wants to see Psyche do some work of her own. Rams, who battle each other with their heads, symbolize the effectiveness of masculine consciousness in achieving a place for oneself in the world. With their massive, spiraled horns, rams could be said to represent masculine-mindedness, man's instinctual attitude toward power and achievement. The rams' golden fleece is linked symbolically to the fiery power of the sun, the hot blaze of consciousness.

A woman needs a measure of masculine power to free herself from a one-sided, all-feminine existence. Without it she will have no life of her own in the outside world nor will she have any basis for relating to man except as mother to son. So Psyche must go into the realm of masculine consciousness and get from it what she needs for her own wholeness and fulfillment of life. But how can she, as feminine soul, take on this danger-ous masculine power, heated as it is by the energy of the sun to the point of mad frenzy? How can she hope even to approach it? Overwhelmed again, she goes to the river to kill herself, a symbolic recognition of her need to sacrifice her present state of consciousness in order to make room for a new way of understanding things.

Her surrender opens her to help from the spiritual realm. This time it is a reed that speaks to Psyche from the shallow water at the river's edge. The river symbolizes the unconscious, the feminine counterbalance to blazing masculine consciousness. The reed is of the river, and yet its phal-lic shape and its associations with Pan and with breath, or spirit, make it a masculine symbol. This cool and gentle masculine element from the unconscious tells Psyche how to approach hot, fierce masculine power. She is not to confront it directly. The feminine will be destroyed if it tries to seize power in a direct struggle with the masculine. A woman who takes on masculine power in this way does so at the cost of her feminine being. The threat to her is not only from masculine power in the outer world but from the fiery masculine energies within herself. If a woman identifies too strongly with her masculine side, her feminine side will be eclipsed.

The reed tells Psyche to wait until the intensity of the noon sun has passed. This means symbolically that instead of entering into a direct struggle for power, a woman should bide her time and watch for oppor-tunities which might otherwise be overlooked, unanticipated avenues that open to her from life itself and offer all the power she needs to lead a balanced and whole feminine life. When she approaches power in this way, without direct confrontation and competition, she will find enough of it lying about the edges of things, opportunities that are hers for the taking and that fit well her need to have a satisfying life in the outside world while maintaining the essence of her feminine reality.

When living the Scarlett quarter unconsciously, in a purely Aphrodite way, a woman will either approach it too passively and never make any legitimate bid for consciousness, identity, and power, or else she will approach it too actively and wound her feminine being by meeting masculine consciousness and power head on. Psyche's way, the way of the soul, is supported by the love of God and leads a woman to a life in the outside world that is balanced, healthy, and fulfilling. The masculine power that she gathers for herself in this way will be enough.

## Psyche's Third Task

AS WE CONTINUE with the story, we find that Aphrodite is not at all pleased with Psyche's success at gathering the golden fleece. She now proposes to test whether Psyche has prudence and stoutness of heart beyond that of a mortal woman. She tells her to go to the peak of a certain high mountain, from which peak a black stream flows down a channel worn deeply into the steep and slippery rock face of the mountain. The stream is guarded by fierce dragons that never sleep, and its waters continually cry out, "Beware! Doom! Get Away!" The black water descends in an inapproachable chasm to the Stygian swamps in the valley below, where it feeds the streams of the underworld. Aphrodite gives Psyche a small crystal urn and tells her to fill it with water from the place where the stream emerges on the mountaintop.

Psyche goes to the mountain with no hope of getting water from the stream. Instead she intends to throw herself from the high peak and put an end to her suffering. When she arrives at the foot of the mountain, however, she sees that it is impossible even to climb its steep face. This realization paralyzes her, as if she were turned to stone. All her senses leave her body and she cannot even weep. But the watchful eyes of kindly Providence see the anguish of her soul, and the eagle, the royal bird of Zeus, recognizes her as the bride of Eros and flies down from the heavenly heights to give her aid.

The eagle tells Psyche that even the gods fear the Stygian waters, which are both holy and cruel. Just as mortals swear by the divinity of the gods, the gods swear by the majesty of the River Styx. But even so, the eagle knows what to do. He takes the crystal urn in his talons and flies to the peak, where he tells the guarding dragons that he comes at Aphrodite's bidding to fetch some water. The dragons grudgingly allow him to fill the urn. The eagle returns to Psyche, who receives the urn with joy and carries it back to Aphrodite.

## Waiting in Athena's Quarter

WITH THE THIRD TASK, we have not only entered a new quarter of the feminine quaternity, but we have ascended to a new level of human life, one that goes beyond nature to include culture. With the first two tasks Psyche mastered the youthful level of instinctual feminine life. All the elements in those earlier tasks were natural: seeds, ants, rams, reeds. But with the third task a cultural element—the crystal urn—is introduced, symbolizing civilization. Psyche has entered the quarter of Athena, the daughter of the spiritual father. She is now in the realm of service to life beyond her personal life, the realm of community and civilized humanity. Here Aphrodite tests her for prudence and strength of heart, qualities which are associated with the heavenly ideals of the masculine spirit.

The crystal urn represents the purified vessel of Psyche's physical being. Her completion of the first two tasks was symbolically equivalent to integrating her shadow. She is no longer an unconscious creature of nature, but has transcended to a higher level of human life. She has become, like the crystal urn, a solid reality through which the light of consciousness can shine. Now the purified vessel of her being is ready to be filled with her own limited portion of the divine purpose that runs through the heart of life.

The black river represents this vital stream of the divine. It is none other than the unconscious itself. As the source of all divinity, all mystery, and all life, it is experienced as both holy and cruel. The gods and goddesses of Olympus are but archetypes produced by the unconscious, which is greater than they are. Thus even they are in awe of it.

Everything spiritual comes from the unconscious. The part of the river involved in this third task runs from the mountaintop to the valley and symbolizes the upper, or masculine, spirit. The waters that run from the swamp down into the underworld would symbolize the lower, or feminine, spirit. Psyche is told to fill her urn at the place of highest spirit. But to approach directly the living stream of the divine is dangerous to the extreme. Frail human consciousness could easily be shattered by an unmediated engagement with the unconscious. Normally it is religious structure that provides the necessary mediation for human contact with the divine. In this task, however, Psyche is asked to seek a direct experience with the divine spirit outside of any established structure.

What is symbolized here is a woman who has taken time out of her life to do her shadow work and purify her natural being. But for what purpose? Though she has become a new person, she does not yet know what this means for her at life's higher level. She has the feeling that she is meant to partake of the heart of life itself, that she is supposed to carry forward into the greater world something important from the divine source of things. She feels she has something of value to offer. But with her new connection to the home side of life and her understanding that competition for power is not good for her and is not her way, how is her cup of life to be filled?

Psyche does absolutely nothing to fill her cup except to go stony still and wait. As her body life shuts down, she becomes open to the upper spirit. A woman on her individuation journey must wait in this way for her assignment for the second half of life, which is not a matter of career but of vocation. Because her shadow work has been done, her ego desires are no longer at the center of her being. She is not waiting to find out how to become rich and famous, but how to serve greater life as she was meant to serve it, however great or small that realm of service might be. The shape of this is not something she can decide for herself. It can only be discerned. It comes from God, and she must wait for it to announce itself and become apparent. Like the Virgin Mary, she awaits her annunciation.

Zeus's eagle, symbol of the masculine spirit of heaven, comes and fills

Psyche's urn for her. This would be the moment in a woman's journey when the way opens to her, both within herself and in the world outside. Her special value is recognized, her path is clear, and she accepts her true vocation of effective service to life beyond her personal life.

We now return to the story.

## Psyche's Fourth Task

APHRODITE is not pleased that Psyche has successfully accomplished the first three tasks. "You must be a great sorceress!" Aphrodite says sarcastically. And so she assigns a final task. Handing Psyche a small wooden lockbox, she tells her to take it to Persephone, the queen of the underworld, and ask Persephone to fill it with a day's worth of beauty for Aphrodite, whose own beauty is getting worn out from all her cares.

Psyche is now sure that she is doomed. Knowing she could never survive a journey into the underworld, she heads straight for a high tower from which to hurl herself to her death. But before she can throw herself down, the tower begins to speak, telling her that it makes no sense to kill herself, for then she would still have to go to the underworld, but with no hope of return. Instead, she should follow the tower's instructions for how to accomplish the task she has been given.

The tower tells Psyche where to find the hidden entrance to the underworld. And it tells her that she must not enter the underworld empty-handed, but must carry a barley cake in each hand and two coins in her mouth. As she proceeds along the path through the underworld, she will meet a lame man with a lame donkey loaded with wood. The man will ask her to do him the favor of picking up some twigs that have fallen from the donkey's load. But she must not help him, for to do so she would have to put down a barley cake. Nor must she speak, for that would mean dropping her coins. Instead, she must pass by in silence.

Then, says the tower, she will come to the river of the dead, where she must pay the boatman his toll. She is to do this by letting him take one of the coins from her mouth. As the boatman ferries her across the river, a dead man floating in the water will beseech her to pull him aboard, but she must turn a deaf ear and resist taking pity on him. Once across the river and on her way again she will encounter three old weaving women, who will ask her to lend a hand in the weaving of their web. But she must refuse, lest one of the cakes fall from her hand.

All these temptations to put down the barley cakes are Aphrodite's traps for her, says the tower. If she is ever to see the light of day again, she must hold onto the cakes until she reaches the three-headed hound which keeps sleepless guard over the house of Persephone. The awful baying of this creature terrifies even the dead, though they are past all hurt. But a barley cake will silence him. She must throw him one of the cakes and slip past as he eats it.

Once past the dog, she will be in Persephone's hall. The queen of the underworld will welcome her and offer her a seat and a sumptuous feast. But Psyche must sit on the ground and ask for coarse bread to eat. She is to give Persephone the box, explaining why she has come, and Persephone will fill the box and return it to her. Then Psyche must retrace her steps, giving the other barley cake to the hound and paying the boatman with the last coin. Once back across the river, she must hurry out to the open world beneath the sky.

Now the tower gives Psyche a final warning. Above all, it tells her, she must not open the box to see the treasure of divine beauty that Persephone has put into it. She must instead take the box straight to Aphrodite.

Having listened carefully, Psyche proceeds on her way according to instructions. Armed with barley cakes and coins, she finds the entrance to the underworld and successfully makes her way to Persephone's hall, avoiding all temptations and pitfalls. Persephone fills the box in secret, and Psyche carries it back through the gloom of the underworld and emerges into the light of day.

Now all she has to do is take the box to Aphrodite. But as she walks along, she thinks about what she is carrying in her hands. It is nothing less than the gift of divine beauty. If she could have just one drop of this for herself, she could be sure of winning Eros back again. How could she forego such an opportunity and risk losing her beloved? She would be a fool to pass this up. And so Psyche opens the box. But what she finds inside is a hellish sleep, which rushes out and covers her like a cloud, and she falls to the ground unconscious.

## The Inner Journey through Sophia's Quarter

THE FOURTH TASK takes Psyche on a conscious journey into the fourth quarter of the feminine quaternity. This is Sophia's realm, the inner world of the feminine spirit, the realm of wisdom and natural spirituality. A woman on her individuation journey has actually been engaged in this task from the beginning. Like the King quarter in the masculine quaternity, the Sophia quarter is different in quality from the first three quarters. It overlies the others, and when it is consciously lived, it coordinates them and brings them together into wholeness and balance. It is the conscious journey through the fourth quarter that has made possible the conscious journey through the other three.

That is why when Psyche completes the first three tasks, Aphrodite accuses her of being a sorceress. Sorcery, which is the shadow side of Sophia, is an attempt to use the feminine spirit for personal power. Although Psyche is not a sorceress, she is tempted in the end to try a bit of sorcery—to steal some divine beauty for her own use—and it is this that proves to be her undoing.

For the fourth task Psyche must go into the underworld and fetch back some divine beauty from Persephone, who is the daughter of Demeter and a symbol of the eternal maiden. It was Persephone who, while picking flowers in spring, was abducted by Hades and carried down into the underworld, from which she regularly returns for half of every year. As the eternal daughter of the earth mother, Persephone symbolizes the natural beauty of young womanhood, the beauty that fuels love at the surface of life. As the wife of Hades, she is the queen of the underworld.

With this new assignment from Aphrodite, Psyche despairs, as always, and as always, help appears. A tower begins to speak to her. For the first time, her helper is not a natural being—not a plant or an animal. It is not even a divine being. It is a cultural element, symbolizing a human understanding of the journey she has to make. We can see it as a Wise Man's map, a systematized understanding of the nature of the unconscious. In our day, the tower might be Jungian psychology. The mystical traditions of Christianity and Judaism are towers that were built in the past and still stand. No one should attempt a direct experience with the depths of the unconscious without guidance from a well-constructed tower. It is the tower that can tell Psyche where to find the hidden entrance to the underworld. Jungian psychology does the same when it tells us to pay attention to dreams and synchronicity, entryways to the unconscious that are in plain sight, yet hidden to the unaware.

Psyche is told to carry two barley cakes in her hands and two coins in her teeth. (It is not explained how she carries the lockbox—perhaps tucked in her clothing.) The barley cakes and coins effectively tie up her hands and require her to keep her mouth shut. She must make the journey as one who is powerless and wordless. When a woman begins a conscious relationship with the unconscious, she must direct her attention to the journey. It is necessary that she allow her energy to turn inward, away from outer engagement with the world. This means pulling back from a fully active life. Furthermore, she must be quiet. In most contexts of her life, she must refrain from trying to explain herself and from telling very much about what she is learning.

These requirements are difficult. Though her energy has turned inward, she continues to live in the outer world, where she must meet certain responsibilities. Most people around her are unaware of what she is going through, and yet for the most part she cannot explain it to them. If she should try, they would not understand. Even worse, they might think her unbalanced, which she is in a way—unbalanced toward inwardness. She is in a different place from where they are and from where she herself will later be. So it is best if she says nothing. This is what it means to keep the coins safe.

It is important to understand that turning inward for the inner journey does not mean a complete withdrawal from the outer world. One needs the mundane routine of daily life to balance the potentially disintegrating influence of the unconscious. As the *I Ching,* the Chinese book of wisdom, would put it, small undertakings in outer life can be accomplished at this time, but great undertakings should not be attempted.

The trials Psyche faces along the path through the underworld—the lame man and donkey, the drowning dead man, and the three old weaving women—have to do with the necessity for the individuating woman to overcome her instinct to help and tend life indiscriminately. If she is to save her energy for her journey, she can no longer afford to be pulled by every need that presents itself to her. If she were not on an individuation journey, it would not necessarily be the right thing for her to refuse in this way to let her feminine nature be of general service to the world. But her journey is leading her to a new kind of usefulness, one that is uniquely her own and more precisely guided by God than any collective assignment could be. There is something of this in what Jesus meant when he said, "Let the dead bury the dead." In order to follow an individual call from God, one must turn a deaf ear to the collective call from the world.

When Psyche pays the boatman his coins, she symbolizes a woman who, by remaining inactive and silent, has saved enough energy—symbolized by money—to meet the requirements of the inner journey. The three-headed dog that guards the halls of Persephone can be seen as a symbol of the anxiety which is normally experienced as one advances toward a true engagement with the unconscious. The dog terrifies the dead, even though they are past all hurt. So, too, is the anxiety which surrounds the unconscious ultimately harmless, provided we have saved our barley cakes by keeping our conscious energy available for reflection upon our inner journey.

Psyche is told to refuse the lavish hospitality offered to her in the underworld. Accepting only the simplest food and sitting on the ground to eat it is symbolic of a balanced approach to the unconscious. When we tap the unconscious, we tap a stream of mystery and meaning that can easily carry us much further and deeper than our human life requires. Our challenge is to stay grounded in solid reality and accept only the insights that offer aid to the immediate living of our lives. If a woman on her individuation journey tries to take too much from the unconscious, she will lose her connection to life in the greater community, which will come to regard her as strange and incomprehensible, while she will come to regard it as hopelessly shallow and benighted.

Psyche, however, follows her instructions and avoids this pitfall. Her wooden box having been filled by Persephone, she returns safely to life in the outer world. But now, after almost completing the task, Psyche inexplicably disregards the tower's final warning and opens the forbidden box. We will delay our discussion of this until after we have heard the conclusion of the story.

## The Wedding of Psyche and Eros

PSYCHE lies unconscious on the ground. All seems to be lost. But now Eros arises from his bed in his mother's house, his wound healed at last. No longer can he bear his separation from his beloved Psyche. His mother has posted a guard at his door, but Eros slips away through a high window and flies swiftly to Psyche's side. Kneeling beside her, he wipes off the deadly sleep and puts it back into the box. As Psyche awakens, Eros tells her to take the box to his mother and leave the rest to him.

While Psyche is taking Persephone's beauty to Aphrodite, Eros goes to his father Zeus to seek protection from his mother's continuing wrath. Zeus, the giver of law and civility, responds by speaking of the perpetual trouble Eros has caused him with his arrows of love that so often upset the laws of heaven and violate public order. But the sky father acknowledges his love for this son of his, remembering how Eros grew up in his own arms and was reared by his own hands. As he listens to the story of the love between Eros and Psyche, he begins to see a solution to the problem of his troublesome son.

Zeus calls an assembly of all the gods and goddesses, including Aphrodite. He explains to them that Eros needs to be married in a public way, rather than in the secret way of his marriage in paradise. A proper marriage will settle him down, fetter his lustful boyhood spirit, and bring him into full maturity. Since Eros has chosen Psyche, let him keep her and hold her in his arms for all eternity.

Zeus turns then to Aphrodite and assures her that this will not be an unworthy match for her son, that he will insure that it accords with the laws of civility. With this, he sends Hermes to fetch Psyche up to heaven. When Psyche arrives, Zeus offers her a cup of ambrosia, inviting her to drink it and become immortal so that she can join with Eros in a marriage that will endure forever. Psyche accepts the cup and becomes immortal.

A grand wedding now takes place in the presence of all the company of heaven. A mollified Aphrodite provides the orchestra for the wedding feast and even joins in the dancing, while Pan plays his pipe of reeds. After the wedding Psyche and Eros make their home in the heavenly community, and before long their child is born, a daughter whose name is Pleasure.

## Feminine Wholeness in the Outer World

WE HAVE SEEN that at the end of the fourth task, which symbolizes the inner journey, Psyche opens the box and falls into a deadly sleep, finally meeting her defeat. I once had a dream that said, in meaning with no images: *Outer life and inner life meet their limits in each other. Neither can go on and on without end.* The idea conveyed in the dream was that consciousness oriented toward inner life cannot expand indefinitely, but will eventually be brought up short by the outer world, just as the expansion of consciousness that is oriented toward outer life will be finally brought to a halt by the inner world.

This limitation of inner life by the outer world is what is symbolized by Psyche's failure at the end of the story. Psyche represents a woman who has taken the inner journey. She has learned the way of the unconscious and found healing for the four quarters of her feminine being by allowing the spiritual depths and the surface of life to become integrated in her consciousness. She has found the treasure of the inner world, the beauty of the feminine aspect of God. It has required the most desperate struggle of her life to gain consciousness of the unconscious and learn its value.

It is therefore not at all obvious to her that she cannot keep that feminine spirit as a part of her outer world identity. There is a difference, however, between *identification* and *relationship*. Although a woman can and should have a continuing relationship with the unconscious, she must guard against identifying with it. For if she tries to take even a drop of that identity for herself, she cancels out her own conscious being. She can only be a human woman, not a goddess.

When a woman turns away from the outer world and identifies herself with the feminine spirit of the inner world, she loses sight of her own common humanity. The human community is an outer world community, and she cannot live in it effectively if she feels herself to be at one with the wisdom of the inner world. The inner world of the feminine spirit is meant to heal outer life, but not to replace it. It is meant to assist it and serve it, but not to preside over it. If outer life is to thrive, it must be led by the masculine spirit of consciousness, the heavenly spirit of law and civilization. The final hurdle on a woman's individuation journey is to come to the realization of this truth: that the inner journey itself is not the goal, that the inner journey is meant to lead back to the outer world of conscious structure, order, and civilization, just as the outer journey will always lead back to the inner world of rest, healing, and transformation.

Psyche's failure is a human one, and the myth seems to suggest it is inevitable. But at the very moment when human effort and understanding meet their limit, divine love breaks free from its confinement in the unconscious and reappears in outer life. Healed of the wound it received when it first encountered consciousness, it is now ready for a higher, more developed relationship with the soul, one that is more in harmony with heavenly order and community than was the immature love that could live only in paradise.

When Eros removes Persephone's beauty from Psyche and puts it back into the box, he lets Psyche know that her own humanity is enough, that he loves her fully and completely just as she is. After all, from the very beginning her own beauty has been greater than that of any goddess for the very reason that it is human and real. But a woman cannot arrive at this truth all alone. It must be conveyed to her by her personal experience of love in life itself. Once she has experienced it and learned it, she is ready to be consciously joined to God's love forever and to live a life that reflects her experience of that love and her confidence in it.

The wedding of Psyche and Eros brings the story to a close. All the gods and goddesses are in attendance, symbolizing the state of wholeness that has been attained. This is an image of the divine marriage, the same union of opposites—of heaven and earth, of divine love and human soul, of feminine wisdom and masculine godliness—that is portrayed in the

Song of Solomon and the Revelation of John. Although the divine marriage can never be fully realized within the limits of earthly life, it can be partially realized to the extent that the two streams of human life and love—the depths of the spirit and the surface of life—are brought together into one. In that union the temporal is elevated by the eternal, and the eternal is made real by the temporal. The fruit of the divine marriage is the pleasure of the fullness of life, both in heaven and on earth.

CHAPTER FOURTEEN

# Individuation as Church Mission

WHEN ATTENTION is turned to dreams and synchronicity, the dialogue that begins to come to us from the unconscious contains certain regular features. Noteworthy among these is the language of the opposites, which symbolizes the human struggle to bring nature and spirit into balance and ultimate union. This underlying process at the deeper level of life is as real and observable in the inner world as are the forces of nature in the outer world. The deeper level of life is, in fact, a part of nature, and like its outer-world counterpart, its laws can be discovered and systematically described.

A hundred years ago the geological antiquity of the earth and the long prehistory of mankind were new ideas, while subatomic particles, DNA, and many other aspects of outer-world nature that we now take for granted had yet to be discovered and described. Today it is the natural reality of the inner world that is just beginning to enter human consciousness. Our understanding of the masculine and feminine quaternities, for example, is not yet complete, and some of the ideas I have presented here will undoubtedly be refined and modified as time goes on. But the essential validity of the quaternity model is demonstrated in the way it so closely fits and helps to explain the real-world phenomenon of the Beatles. In the example of the Beatles it can be clearly seen that the natural reality of the inner world has a strong influence on the outward shape of human life. So too does this natural inner reality find expression in mythology, both secular and sacred, as can be seen in the ancient myth of Psyche and Eros and in the imagery contained in Holy Scripture.

It is in the observable reality of the inner world that the secular and sacred come together in a way that is much more apparent than in the outer world. In the inner world, divine reality is a given, not a mere idea to be accepted or rejected. Although the imagery of dreams and synchronistic events may at first glance seem anything but divine, the fact is that the symbolic language of the inner world is about our journey to God and about nothing else. If the journey is going badly, if we reject the divine guidance that God seeks to reveal in both our conscious and unconscious lives, then the images from our inner world will reflect back to us the underlying truth of the barrenness or chaos or horror in which we are living in relation to God's intent for us. But even terrifying nightmares have a divine purpose and are meant to move our conscious attitude toward a position that is more closely aligned with God.

Therefore, although the inner world is as real and describable as the natural history of the outer world, it is at the same time religious territory, and the journey taken in dialogue with it is a spiritual journey. The fruitfulness of that journey depends on the quality of a person's conscious relationship to God. To the degree that God is acknowledged and loved as the highest value in one's life, the inner process is found to be the pilgrim's way, a journey to a closer union with God than can ever be achieved by conscious means alone.

## Stages of the Individuation Journey

THE INDIVIDUATION JOURNEY, when fully engaged, unfolds in recognizable stages that can be roughly described. Although there is no end to the journey, the most intense experience of it takes place in about the first ten years. By the time the ten-year point has been reached, the journeyer feels that he or she has come to an established place in a new world that was completely unknown before the journey began. This is true despite the fact that much of the journeyer's life in the outer world looks just the same as it did before. What is different is the way in which the world is experienced and the ways in which the individuated person operates within it. In sketching out the stages of the journey, I will restrict the discussion to this approximate ten year period. The stages presented here are meant only as a rough guideline, the purpose of which is to offer some idea of what is to be expected when a person becomes open to the individuation process.

The first stage of the individuation journey consists of entering into the process and becoming accustomed to the reality of the unconscious. This stage lasts at least a year, even when the *idea* of the unconscious is embraced right away. There is a difference between assent to an idea and the personal changes that are required to recognize and accept the autonomous reality of a new, inner center of authority and truth. For some people, their enthusiasm for the journey runs considerably ahead of their actual readiness, in which case this stage is extended for months or even years while the ego retains its position at the center of consciousness and grows strong enough to recognize the real autonomy and primacy of the Self.

When dream work and other attempts at dialogue with the unconscious are undertaken outside the framework of traditional monotheistic religion, this life-giving shift of the center of consciousness from the ego to the Self is greatly jeopardized. This is especially true when work with the unconscious is seen as a substitute for a traditional understanding of God. Despite our ego's wish that it could be otherwise, it is in the end an inescapable fact that it requires a regular practice of devotion through prayer, praise, and the study of Scripture to direct our hearts and minds toward the full knowledge and love of God.

It is only God in His oneness who is capable of bringing about the reconciliation of all the conflicting parts of ourselves and of the world around us. In traditional religious practice we continually remind ourselves that God is the highest value in human life, and we repeatedly affirm our intention to place Him at the center of our being and surrender ourselves to His service. It is quite true that one can say these words forever and still remain basically ego-centered. But that does not negate the fundamental truth that it is almost impossible to make the shift from the ego to the Self without the deeply ingrained intention that can only come with active devotional practice.

It is a mistake, therefore, to substitute dream work for a straightforward concept of God, shying away from the word "God" and putting perma-

nently in its place an idea less burdensome to the ego, like "the unconscious" or "the Self" or "the universe." But it is also possible to make the
mistake of accepting the concept of "God" in a devotional and theological
context that is outside the bounds of deeply rooted religious tradition, as
is done, for example, in some of today's New Age philosophies, or in
radical revisions of traditional religion.

When individuation is attempted from this position—in devotion to
a newly constructed version of "God"—there is a danger that the shift in
consciousness from the ego to the Self will go too far, in which case the
ego is submerged by a version of the Self, or of "God," that is overbalanced
toward the unconscious. The result then is not individuation but possession by archetypal religious ideas. Traditional religion has over the course
of several thousand years worked out man's conscious relationship to God
in a way that honors, upholds, and safeguards the humanness of our individual lives. Even though religious freedom gives us great leeway to follow whatever spiritual path appeals to us, not all religion is equally good
for us. A person must be careful of the inner forces to which he would
surrender himself. The more unconscious they are, the more his individual
reality will be negated and swept aside by their blind, cosmic purposes.

Thus, the progress of the first stage of the individuation journey depends on the readiness (strength) of the ego and the soundness of the
journeyer's religious framework. Even under the best of circumstances
this stage lasts about a year. Many dreams during this period have to do
with the unconscious itself—with its peculiar nature, which is so different
from consciousness, and with the journeyer's progress and difficulties in
learning to relate to it.

Other dreams during this first stage raise fundamental themes to be
addressed by the journey, and initial work on them is begun. This also
takes place through synchronicity. It is usual for there to be a heightening
of synchronistic experience during this time. Outer world events and developments occur which begin to shake and change the journeyer's former
world. He enters a place between worlds in which he is no longer who he
was when he embarked upon the journey but is not yet who he will become. This is not a total state of being. From outward appearances, life
goes on much as before. But the journeyer's center is shifting within. He

gradually lets go of his ego's certainty about who he is and what he knows and opens himself to transformation.

In specifically Christian terms, the first stage of the journey is a deep-level experience of the call to follow Christ. "If anyone wants to be a follower of mine, let him renounce himself and take up his cross every day and follow me." Once the journeyer has made this acceptance and surrender and has begun to allow his or her center to shift from the ego to the Self, the next stage of the journey begins in earnest.

The second stage of the individuation journey is centered around shadow work, which means integrating the contents of the personal unconscious. Shadow work actually begins at the outset of the journey and is never really finished. But from about the second year, when the problem of accepting the guidance of the unconscious has been largely resolved (assuming that it has been), through about the fifth year, shadow work is the primary focus of the journey.

During this period the journeyer is gradually shown the more obvious ways in which he or she is off center from his or her true self. The underlying causes of these imbalances are exposed, leading one to a clearer understanding of one's personal, inherited, family-based issues. The emphasis from the unconscious is on bringing the journeyer's conscious, same-sex self into fullness of being. During this period, a woman faces issues having to do with her feminine reality and is gradually led toward a more complete and satisfying embodiment of the woman she was born to be. A man is led toward a more conscious embodiment of his masculine reality.

The growing consciousness that comes from shadow work ramifies through a journeyer's personal world, bringing about fundamental adjustments in relationships, work, and social life. This is a difficult period of storm and change, but the process can both be felt from within and seen from without to be moving toward health and wholeness and a truer life in God. By about the fifth year the greater part of this change has been effected and the journeyer has begun to settle into the new reality of the more centered person he has become through the integration of a large part of his shadow.

There is no clear division between the stages of the individuation journey, but rather a gradual shift in focus. The third and final stage has to do with the broadening of one's personal context through the integration, to a limited degree, of the collective unconscious. This brings with it the discernment and acceptance of vocation, which is not necessarily a matter of career, although one's career might be involved. Vocation is a deeper and higher calling than a mere career choice. It is the specifically God-centered work in the world for which the journeyer is uniquely suited and toward which his journey gradually guides him. There are hints of one's emerging vocation from the very beginning of the journey, but the true shape of it usually does not appear until the second half of the ten-year individuation cycle, and even then it only appears in its initial phases. Its full scope takes a lifetime to unfold.

Issues having to do with the opposite sex, both in outer-world relationships and in the inner-world dynamics of anima and animus, are present from the very beginning of the journey. In the third stage, however, these issues come more and more to the forefront as the growth toward wholeness progresses and brings with it an ever more satisfying and fruitful union with the contrasexual element, both within and without.

Ten years is an arbitrary ending point for this stage. The individuation journey never ends. Its stages continue to cycle through our lives as our experience of God grows ever richer and deeper. Individuation does not do away with suffering—life always contains pain and difficulty. But it balances life's pain with an awareness of continually revealed meaning, an openness to surprise, joy, and wonder, and an ever deepening experience of love, both human and divine.

## A Context and Guide for the Journey

IF THE INDIVIDUATION JOURNEY is all about God, it might be expected that a person who needed and wanted to deepen his or her life in this way could go to any church and find there a context and guide for the journey. But at the present time this opportunity is offered only rarely within the domain of organized Christianity. Church-based dream groups are becoming more common, but they still are few and far between. Jungian study groups in churches are not quite as rare, but while a study group is valuable for preparing the ground for a journey, it is not in itself a context for the journey. A study group provides what this book provides, an intellectual framework for thinking about the inner life. But ideas alone are not enough. Individuation requires a context in which a person's own dreams and synchronistic experiences can be examined for meaning on a regular basis over a long period of time. The Church as a whole does not yet recognize as a part of its mission the provision of a context for individuation.

Where, then, does this leave a potential pilgrim who wants to embark on an individuation journey? There are many more dream groups outside the context of the Church than within it. Most people could find one of these groups in their area. But more often than not these have the disadvantage that has already been noted of not being firmly connected to a traditional religious framework. While they may have value, they are likely to be off balance toward the feminine side of the spirit.

One could seek out a Jungian analyst as a guide, but there are not many of these available. For the most part they are found only in cities, and wherever they are found, they are costly. Furthermore, they do not necessarily provide a traditional religious orientation, although some of them do.

A questing pilgrim who can afford to do so might participate in some of the Jungian short courses that are regularly offered around the country. Journey Into Wholeness, for example, is an organization oriented toward traditional religion which every year offers a week-long conference and several weekend conferences. (See SOURCES, Appendix A.) These short courses feature lectures and workshops led by Jungian analysts and authors. But while these conferences are valuable as mountain-top experiences, they do not provide the context for a sustained individuation journey. When a seeker returns home, he is on his own again.

The only other option for a would-be pilgrim is to read deeply in Jungian literature, pay attention to synchronicity, try to analyze one's own dreams, attend to one's traditional religious devotions, and hope that the Holy Spirit will guide one into and through an individuation journey. I can testify to the fact that this kind of journey is possible for some people, having traveled that path myself. But I also know that of those who are capable of taking an individuation journey, few can do it in this way. Most people need the help of someone more experienced.

There has not arisen, then, any real alternative to the Church as context and guide for the individuation journey. And why should such an alternative have arisen? The journey is God's business. It belongs in God's house, where the feminine spirit of God should be as well-tended as the masculine spirit and as freely and universally available.

## Natural Spirituality in Scripture

THE FEMININE SPIRIT has not always been neglected by the Church. Its inclusion in Christian life is strongly supported by Scripture. There are several different ways in which both the Old and New Testaments include natural spirituality within their framework and assume it to be an important aspect of our life with God.

The most obvious way in which natural spirituality is carried in the Bible is *straightforwardly.* Present throughout Scripture, to a much greater degree than in Christian life today, is the understanding that dreams and visions play a vital role in the human experience of God. Looking at some of the most well-known examples, we begin with Jacob on his way to the country of Laban.

"He had a dream," says the twenty-eighth chapter of Genesis. "A ladder was there, standing on the ground with its top reaching to heaven; and there were angels of God going up it and coming down. And Yahweh was there, standing over him. . . ." In the dream Yahweh reaffirmed for Jacob the covenant Yahweh had made with Abraham, and He gave Jacob the special assurance that He would be with him through his coming trials and would never desert him until until His promises to him had been fulfilled. The very image of angels moving up and down a ladder between heaven and earth is an image of the dialogue with God that is available to us through attention to our inner life.

The most gifted and reknowned dream interpreters in the Old Testament are Joseph and Daniel, both of whom are also portrayed as towering men of God. In the stories of each of these men a very clear understanding is put forward that dreams come from God and are best interpreted by persons who are especially devoted to the service of God. Soothsayers, sages, and magicians who do not know and worship Yahweh are unable to interpret adequately the images of the inner world.

In the story of Joseph, for example, which is found in the book of Genesis, we are told that the king's cup-bearer and baker, who are imprisoned with Joseph, are distressed because they have had dreams which they cannot interpret. "'Are not interpretations God's business?' Joseph asked them. 'Come, tell me.'" The point is made that because Joseph is a man of God, he can interpret their dreams.

As this story goes on, Pharaoh hears of Joseph's reputation for dream interpretation and summons him to unravel the mystery of his own troubling dreams. He says to Joseph, "I have heard it said of you that when you hear a dream you can interpret it."

Joseph answers, "I do not count. It is God who will give Pharaoh a favorable answer." In this it is made explicit that the wisdom revealed by dreams comes from God, not from the dream interpreter.

Pharaoh goes on to relate to Joseph two dreams which were dreamed in the same night. "Pharaoh's dreams are one and the same," says Joseph, showing us something of what he knew about the regular structure of the inner world—in this case, that dreams that come in the same night are often different images of the same truth. He then adds, "God has revealed to Pharaoh what He is going to do." In this Joseph makes clear his understanding that the God of Abraham, Isaac, and Jacob speaks through dreams to all persons, regardless of nationality or religious consciousness.

Much later in Jewish history, during the exile in Babylon, Daniel makes this same point when dealing with a dream that came to the Babylonian king, Nebuchadnezzar. Daniel, to whom God has given "the gift of interpreting every kind of vision and dream," explains to the king:

> O king, on your bed your thoughts turned to what would happen in the future, and the Revealer of Mysteries disclosed to you what is to take place. This mystery has been revealed to me, not that I am wiser than any other man, but for this sole purpose: that the king should learn what it means, and that you should understand your inmost thoughts.

This understanding that dreams come from God and that their interpretation is God's business is firmly embedded in the spiritual reality put forward and upheld by the Old Testament. There are places where Hebrew Scripture seems to speak against dreams, but an examination of context reveals that in most cases such warnings are against dream interpretations by persons who are not devoted to God.

The firm belief that dreams and visions come from God is carried into the New Testament through the gospel story of Joseph and the Wise Men. Jesus himself does not speak directly about dreams. However, there are many places in the Gospels where there are definite permeations of the veil between consciousness and the unconscious, as for example, when Jesus sees Nathaniel under the fig tree, when he walks on water, when he appears with Moses and Elijah in the Transfiguration, and in his Resurrection appearances. Whether dream, vision, or synchronicity, experiences of inner reality are essentially the same and require the same response from us if we are to gain from them the gifts they offer. That response is to stand firmly in rational consciousness while opening to the nonrationality of the unconscious, using rationality to look for a meaning from God in nonrational events. The Gospels carry at their very heart this approach to the nonrational expression of the unconscious.

Moving on beyond the Gospels to the book of Acts, we can see that natural spirituality was central to early Christianity's life in God. This account of the beginning years of the Church was written several decades after the events portrayed, and it therefore has the same problem with factuality of historical detail that all oral tradition has. But while Acts may not always be reliable for events of time and place, there is no reason to doubt that it gives us an accurate portrayal of the assumptions of spiritual reality by which the earliest Christians were guided. The portrait given is of a people who are intensely focused on being led and taught by God day and night through compensatory events from the unconscious.

One of the best examples of this is the story of Peter's vision of the sheet that comes down from heaven containing every sort of animal, both within and without the bounds of Jewish dietary restrictions. The voice of God tells Peter to eat, but Peter says he cannot eat animals forbidden by the Law. God replies that what God has made clean, Peter has no right to consider profane.

After his vision, Peter contemplates its meaning but is unable to understand it until a Roman centurion, himself prompted by a vision, invites Peter to come to his house and convert his family. This would require

Peter to violate the Jewish prohibition against entering a Gentile home. In a perfect example of how dreams, visions, and synchronicity work together to produce deep and significant meaning from life events, Peter recognizes the symbolic parallel between the vision and the invitation, between the Law's prohibition against eating certain animals and its prohibition against intimate association with Gentiles.

Following the lead given to him by the vision, Peter sets aside the Law's prohibition and goes to the centurion's house. He explains to the people who are there that through dialogue with God (which has come to him from the unconscious), he has been given new understandings that go beyond the rigid code of traditional religious law. He says to them, "You know it is forbidden for Jews to mix with people of another race and visit them, but God has made it clear to me that I must not call anyone profane or unclean." Then he adds, "The truth I have now come to realize . . . is that God does not have favorites."

There is no essential difference between the way Peter's consciousness was expanded in this story and the experience of a modern Christian on an individuation journey. This is exactly how the process works, although modern Christians are usually working with dreams instead of visions. The book of Acts is filled with stories like this which show us that life with God in the early Church included natural spirituality in a straightforward way.

Natural spirituality is also straightforwardly presented in books of the Bible like Ezekiel and Revelation. Here we are given the raw material of visions and dreams, and it is left largely to the reader to interpret them. It is expected that the reader will understand that this obscure symbolic language from the inner world is the language of God and that its interpretation, as Joseph made clear all the way back in the book of Genesis, is God's business.

## Wisdom Theology in Scripture

A SECOND WAY in which Holy Scripture supports natural spirituality is *theologically* through its development of the wisdom tradition. The books of the Bible considered to be "wisdom" books are, from the Hebrew canon: Job, the Psalms (in part), Proverbs, Ecclesiastes, and The Song of Songs (The Song of Solomon); and, from the Apocrypha: Wisdom (The Wisdom of Solomon) and Ecclesiasticus (The Wisdom of Jesus Ben Sirach). Elements of wisdom theology are found in the New Testament in both the Gospels and the Epistles.

Biblical scholar Gerhard von Rad has offered a definitive treatment of the wisdom theology of the Old Testament in his book *Wisdom in Israel*. I draw heavily from this work in the summary I present here.

The earliest recorded Scripture belonging to the wisdom tradition is the proverbial wisdom that begins in the tenth chapter of the book of Proverbs. Also known as sentence wisdom or instructional wisdom, proverbial wisdom consists of such nuggets as, "The wise of heart takes orders, but a gabbling fool heads for ruin," and "Their uprightness sets the honest free, the treacherous are imprisoned by their own desires." This collection was set down around the time of David and Solomon, 1000–800 B.C.

Central to proverbial wisdom is the observation based on long experience that righteous behavior, which belongs to the moment and is to be found in the context of each situation, supports a man and brings him into a sphere of blessing. This basis of *experience*, rather than ideals or speculation, is characteristic of wisdom literature. The assumption behind proverbial wisdom is that experience teaches that creation contains inherent natural laws and that one must learn about these and conform to them in order for things to go well both for the individual and the community. At the heart of the inherent laws is the fundamental principle that goodness is a life-promoting force: life thrives when goodness is done.

The Hebrew wisdom writers found no conflict between the inherent laws in creation and the Law of Yahweh given down from above. They understood that it is Yahweh who delegates truth to creation. Faith in inherent laws and faith in Yahweh are the same thing.

By the time the book of Job was recorded, around the sixth century B.C., the wisdom theologians had begun to go deeper and address the question of the nature of this inherent order that comes up out of the world. "Where does wisdom come from?" asks the twenty-eighth chapter of Job, which puts forth the understanding that wisdom is not a human quality, but rather is something far removed from humankind. God had to do with it at the creation of the world. From the very beginning it has been a reality that is in the world and subject to God's ordering activity. And yet it is separate from the works of creation and cannot be acquired and possessed like the precious metals of the earth. It is something in between created life and heavenly life. Wisdom is the order given to the world by God, but the world never reveals the mystery of its order.

In the eighth chapter of Proverbs, which is believed to have been written around the fourth or third century B.C., the wisdom theologians begin to personify the mysterious order of the world. Personification is a development based on the emerging understanding that wisdom *calls* to humankind. This idea that wisdom calls us was unique to Israel. Other ancient cultures shared the idea of an inherent order in the world, but only Israel perceived that the inherent order was turned toward humankind.

This understanding was not based on speculation but on the actual human experience of being called by wisdom. It is something that happens to a person in the world, something that is actually brought upon us by the world. The wisdom writers are speaking of the active influence on us of the environment itself—an ordering power which affects us and corrects us. This mysterious attribute of the world, this wisdom, is variously characterized by Gerhard von Rad as primeval order, mysterious order, world reason, meaning, or the self-revelation of creation. Because the primeval order turns toward us and calls us, the wisdom writers found personification to be indispensable to the expression of its reality. In Proverbs 8, we read:

> Is not Wisdom calling?
>     Is not Understanding raising her voice?
> On the heights overlooking the road,
>     at the crossways, she takes her stand;
> by the gates, at the entrance to the city,
>     on the access roads, she cries out,
> "I am calling to you, all people,
>     my words are addressed to all humanity."

We are told that the call of the primeval order is not hidden or esoteric. She stands on the heights, by the roadside, where the paths cross. (In other words, her call is in the synchronistic events of our daily lives and in our nightly dreams.) What she says is clear and precise: that people should listen to her and learn from her; that she will lead them out of ignorance and idle talk and teach them intelligence and truth; and that she will show them the way to fullness of life, to divine favor and security. "For whoever finds me finds life," she says.

Another astonishing attribute of the primeval order put forward in these later wisdom writings is that she not only calls us, but *loves* us. The relationship into which she summons us is a relationship of love. "I love those who love me," she says in Proverbs. Jesus Ben Sirach, the author of Ecclesiasticus, which was written around 180 B.C., tells us:

> Court her with all your soul,
>     and with all your might keep in her ways;
> go after her and seek her; she will reveal herself to you;
>     once you hold her, do not let her go.
> For in the end you will find rest in her
>     and she will take the form of joy for you.

Wisdom is presented as a woman who calls to men quite openly in the streets and squares and invites them to come into her house. She is the true partner who calls men to herself—the true lover. The primeval order moves toward us and seeks our ear, loving us, endeavoring to draw us into a sublime bond of love—a bond beween humankind and the divine mystery of creation.

In the book of Wisdom, which was written in the last half of the first century B.C., only a few decades before the birth of Jesus, a decisive step is taken in the development of wisdom theology: wisdom begins to move toward deification. "For within her is a spirit intelligent, holy, . . . so pure, she pervades and permeates all things. . . . She is a breath of the power of God . . . a reflection of the eternal light."

Gerhard von Rad does not extend his discussion beyond Old Testament Scriptures, nor does he look forward toward New Testament developments. And so we leave von Rad as we look at this last of the Old

Testament writings in terms of the easy passage it provides to the gospel events. "What man indeed can know the intentions of God?" asks the book of Wisdom. "It is hard enough for us to work out what is on earth, . . . who, then, can discover what is in the heavens? As for your intention, who could have learned it, had you not granted Wisdom and sent your holy spirit from above?"

In these words are familiar echoes of the Gospels and the Epistles. In John's Gospel, Jesus says to Nicodemus,

> If you do not believe me when I speak about things in this world, how are you going to believe me when I speak to you about heavenly things? No one has gone up to heaven except the one who came down from heaven, the Son of man. . . .

Over and over in the gospel story, Jesus speaks of having been sent down from above to make known the Father's will. In the eleventh chapter of Matthew he says, "No one knows the Father except the Son and those to whom the Son chooses to reveal him." Then, echoing the words of another Old Testament wisdom writer, he says,

> Come to me, all you who labour and are overburdened, and I will give you rest. Shoulder my yoke and learn from me, for I am gentle and humble in heart, and you will find rest for your souls. Yes, my yoke is easy and my burden light.

This is an unmistakable parallel to a passage in the book of Ecclesiasticus, in which Jesus Ben Sirach writes of wisdom,

> Put your neck under the yoke,
> and let your souls receive instruction;
> it is to be found close by.
> See with your eyes that I have labored little
> and found for myself much rest.

In the Gospels Jesus speaks as wisdom incarnate. In him the primeval order that loves us and calls us is made flesh before our eyes. Wisdom's presence in created life is no longer partly veiled, no longer hidden and esoteric. Speaking as wisdom, Jesus tells us that to live in the kingdom of

God we have only to believe in wisdom's reality and follow its continually revealed teachings.

Like the authors of the Gospels, the Apostle Paul recognized Christ as the incarnate wisdom of God. It was Paul who understood what to do with this revelation in the wake of the death, resurrection, and ascension of Jesus. He knew that we must relax our grip on the outer-world, historical Jesus and look for the eternal Christ within ourselves. "Even if we did once know Christ in the flesh," wrote Paul, "that is not how we know him now." He could see that the incarnation had made wisdom visible as a living inner reality, present in everything and available to everyone.

According to Paul, Christ permeates all of creation, just as wisdom was said to do in Hebrew Scriptures. He spoke of the Holy Spirit in the same way. In 1 Corinthians he speaks of "a Christ who is the power and the wisdom of God." Elaborating further, he says,

> But still we have a wisdom to offer to those who have reached maturity. . . . The hidden wisdom of God which we teach in our mysteries is the wisdom that God predestined to be for our glory before the ages began. . . . These are the very things that God has revealed to us through the Spirit, for the Spirit reaches the depths of everything, even the depths of God.

## Natural Spirituality as Underlying Meaning in Scripture

THERE IS, then, a scriptural development of wisdom theology that begins at the time of David and Solomon and extends through the Gospels and the letters of Paul. Thus does the Bible give theological as well as straightforward support to natural spirituality. Beyond this there is a third way in which Holy Scripture lends it support, and that is *inherently*. Reference to the spiritual realities in human life which arise from a conscious, God-centered dialogue with the unconscious can be seen to underlie almost every aspect of both the Old and New Testaments.

This inherent presence of natural spirituality in the Bible becomes obvious once we have a framework of understanding by which it can be perceived. A person who is able to see it in this way finds himself or herself in something of the same position as the disciples to whom Jesus said, "To you it has been granted to know the secrets of the kingdom of God; but for others they are in parables."

This does not mean, however, that there is any competition between this deeper level of understanding the Bible and the more common level at which it is traditionally interpreted. An individuating person continues to hear Scripture at both levels of meaning, sometimes drawing from the deeper level, sometimes from the "parable" level. Both ways of experiencing Biblical truth have their own value and neither negates the other.

The inherent presence of natural spirituality in the Bible does not require that its authors consciously understood this deeper level in the same terms in which we understand it today. The unconscious expresses itself through human lives and human words in layers of meaning that none of us can fully fathom. Just as we could see deeper layers in the lives of the Beatles than they themselves were able to see, so can we see in Scripture aspects of its truth of which its authors may not have been aware.

The deeper level that reflects natural spirituality is found virtually everywhere in the Bible. The stories of the Old Testament, for example, can be seen as stories of individuation. Abraham's call to leave the land of his fathers and follow the promise of God into a new, completely unknown world is a symbolic picture of the call to individuation.

A further illustration can be seen in the story of Saul and David. Saul, in this view, symbolizes the first half of life, when the personality is centered around the ego. Like Saul's kingship, this is a state of being that is ordained by God at the outset, but that ultimately falls short of what God requires of us. David represents a new kingship that can come into being in the second half of life if one learns to put God at one's center. Like David, one's new self must refrain from seizing its day too early, but rather it must bide its time and wait for the slow but sure developments that arise from the inner journey.

Besides its inherent presence in the stories of the Bible, natural spirituality can also be found underlying individual passages of Scripture. For example, Old Testament images of the coming of the Messiah, as well as New Testament depictions of Christ, can be seen as symbolic pictures of what is experienced in the life and being of a person who comes into a conscious relationship with the unconscious. The following passage in Isaiah illustrates this point:

> A shoot springs from the stock of Jesse, . . .
> on him the spirit of Yahweh rests,
> a spirit of wisdom and insight,
> a spirit of counsel and power,
> a spirit of knowledge and of the fear of Yahweh. . . .
> He judges the wretched with integrity
> and with equity gives a verdict for the poor of the land.
> His word is a rod that strikes the ruthless,
> his sentences bring death to the wicked. . . .
>
> The wolf lives with the lamb,
> the panther lies down with the kid . . .
> with a little boy to lead them. . . .
> The infant plays over the cobra's hole;
> Into the viper's lair
> the young child puts his hand.
> They do no hurt, no harm,
> on all my holy mountain,
> for the country will be full of knowledge of Yahweh
> as the waters swell the sea.

When viewed through the lens of natural spirituality, these familiar words become a beautiful picture of the individuation process. They offer a symbolic description of what it is like to come to know the wisdom of the unconscious ("a spirit of wisdom," etc.), to do shadow work ("verdict for the poor," "death to the wicked," etc.), and to experience the gradual transformation of the conflicting aspects of one's life into balance, wholeness, and peace ("the wolf lives with the lamb," etc.). This process is shown to spring forth from earlier faithful living ("the stock of Jesse"). The Messiah when viewed through this lens is understood to be the Self, the divine guidance that arises from within and becomes the new inner center of the individuating person.

Thus it can be seen that Holy Scripture supports natural spirituality in at least three different ways: straightforwardly, theologically, and inherently. There is no reason, therefore, why the wisdom tradition in its modern form should not be fully incorporated into the life of the Church.

Natural spirituality is in fact already coming into the Church, and it will continue to come in as we move into the twenty-first century. Members of the rising generation, those born since the Beatles, are especially open to the feminine side of the spirit of God. So ready are they to understand it that they almost seem to have an inborn knowledge of it. Today's young people are the fruit of the expansion of consciousness that took place in the chaos of the twentieth century. Those of their elders who gained a higher wisdom from that time are the ones now beginning to introduce natural spirituality into the life of the Church. But it is the new generation who will embrace it more fully and who in due time will take over and complete the work.

# CHAPTER FIFTEEN

# *Natural Spirituality*
# *as Church Program*

IN MY OWN CHURCH I have overseen the development of a natural spirituality program that has proven to be of great value to a significant number of individuals as well as to our church community as a whole. Ours is a fairly large parish, but there is nothing particularly unusual about it. I can easily imagine similar programs elsewhere, and indeed several others have been started since this book became available in a preliminary form. Although every program must evolve in its own way, I offer here a description of our program as an example and possible model. Beyond that, I offer this book as an introductory text to be used in the teaching phase of other programs. I offer some advice for beginning a program in situations where no individuated leaders are yet present. And in so doing, I shall name some of the possible pitfalls I can foresee in the development of natural spirituality programs at the local level.

As this book goes to press, our Natural Spirituality Program is beginning its ninth year. Since its establishment in 1991, it has become the strongest spiritual-growth program in our parish. Our program is composed of three separate but interrelated parts: an introductory seminar, an ongoing dream group, and a library. All meetings take place at the church. None of the leaders are paid. Although individuals make voluntary contributions to the library, no fees are charged for any aspect of the program. This absence of monetary exchange seems right and good.

The introductory seminar, or study group, is offered once or twice a year, depending on demand. Enrollment is limited to fifteen in order to allow effective discussion. Classes are held one night a week for twelve weeks, and they cover the material presented in this book. Participants must either purchase a book or borrow one from a friend. Every week the seminar participants read a designated portion of the text, which we then discuss at length in the class. In addition, each group member selects an introductory-level book from our Natural Spirituality Library to read at his or her own pace during the weeks of the course. The class periods begin with informal reports on points of interest from this ongoing outside reading. This gives the entire class some exposure to a fairly wide range of Jungian literature, and it gives each member an opportunity to read more deeply about a topic of particular interest.

We have found that the most effective way to engage people in the natural spirituality material is to center class discussion on the questions, observations, and arguments that each participant brings to class from the assigned textbook reading for that week. The group leader is not a lecturer but a moderator. Even when I myself teach, I try to refrain from lecturing. The participants do a better job of keeping up with the reading, and they appropriate the material more thoroughly, when they are given responsibility for the class discussion. Because people are reading and thinking for themselves, it is not necessary for the discussion to touch on every point contained in the reading assignments.

The seminar is meant to be an introduction to the basic ideas of natural spirituality. Although it is a prerequisite for membership in our program's dream group, it is not itself a forum for dream analysis. This is an important point. Not only would it be premature to begin dream analysis during the seminar, but there would be no time for it with all the material there is to be covered in the course. Even more important is the fact that the seminar needs to be a friendly environment for the merely curious. People must feel free to participate in it without the concern that they might be asked to throw open their inner lives to general scrutiny.

More than half of those who take the seminar do not go on to further stages of the program. This is to be expected and is not at all regrettable. Most of these people still feel that they have received something of value from the course. They go back into the church community with a greater understanding of the nature of the program, and this helps to create a supportive climate for it. All seminar graduates know that that they are welcome to join the dream group at any time in the future, no matter how much time has passed since they completed the seminar.

## The Journey Group

ABOUT A THIRD of those who complete the seminar do go on to join the dream group. We call this the Journey Group, and it is the heart of our Natural Spirituality Program. With its weekly two-and-a-half hour meetings, year around, the Journey Group provides a long-term context for individuation.

No one is allowed to join the Journey Group without first having come through the seminar. This requirement insures that everyone in the group will be drawing on the same conceptual framework for working with the unconscious, and it saves us from having to spend group time explaining basic concepts to newcomers. It also gives everyone a shared initiation experience. This helps the old members feel more comfortable with new members who come in, and it helps new members feel they have gained the right to be in the group. Because of the preparation the new members have received in the seminar, they do not feel they are entering a completely foreign land.

The Journey Group has proven to be an especially strong and durable vehicle. Every seminar class from the very beginning is still represented in its membership. Part of its strength and durability comes from the fact that it is quite fluid. Journeyers flow into it and out of it according to the demands of their individual lives. Some people attend every week, some every few weeks, some every few months. Some come early and stay for the entire session, some come early and leave early, some come late and leave late. Even those who only attend occasionally can walk in at any time and feel at home. Because of its fluid nature, the group has never gotten too big to meet together in a single circle. Currently we have more than thirty regular members. During the course of any one meeting there may be as many as sixteen or eighteen in attendance, but seldom are there more than twelve or fourteen seated in the circle at one time. Sometimes we have a total of only eight or ten at a session, sometimes even less.

The format of the Journey Group is simple. Although we meet as friends in an informal atmosphere, each session has a designated leader who has signed up for that role ahead of time. We try to stay on task, moving to our agenda after a short period of initial conversation and friendly catching up. We open and close our sessions with prayer, for which we have a printed format drawn from *The Book of Common Prayer* and from Scripture. Most of the session is devoted to dream work, except for a fifteen minute period given over to announcements, a brief report on current reading, and the passing around of a sign-up sheet for those who will lead sessions and give reading reports in the coming weeks. We have found that this "business" segment is best placed midway through the session, when attendance for the meeting is at its peak.

In dream work our goal, not often attained, is to examine at least one dream from every person who has a dream to present. This formidable task is made easier by the fact that not everyone brings a dream every week. But we still have plenty of work to do, covering as many as six or eight dreams in a session. This means that we cannot do a thorough analysis of all the symbols in any particular dream, except when the dream is especially short. We spend an average of twenty minutes on each dream.

It can be seen from the brevity of time spent on each person's dream that the members of the group are largely responsible for their own inner work. The Journey Group is not a therapy group. It is a regular meeting place for persons who are on individual journeys, each trying to follow his or her own guidance from within. The group members help each other keep track of their developing themes. They remember each other's earlier dreams and pick out threads of continuity that the dreamers themselves often overlook. As the group asks a dreamer about his or her associations with different aspects of the dream, particular lines of development begin to clarify. Intuitive insights arise in the listeners as well as in the dreamer. Suggestions of meaning are variously offered, to be accepted or rejected by the dreamer. The leader keeps the discussion from ranging too far afield from the dream. "Let's get back to the dream," the leader often says. Or, "What does the *dream* say?"

The discussion proceeds until the dreamer feels he or she has gained some insight, even though we may not reach the point of fully understanding the dream. Sometimes, in fact, we have to give up with no insight at all, admitting that we are stumped. This might be because there are personal issues which the dreamer has preferred not to share with the group, thereby withholding information we need to understand the dream. This is an unavoidable limitation of the group setting. Another reason for failing to get anywhere with a dream might be that the dreamer is in a resistant phase and is not ready to see the real truth of things. (Such resistance is always respected. We may test it a little, but we never push hard against it.) Or it could be that the dream is so much about a future event or development that its meaning simply cannot yet be known.

There are also different reasons for the fact that not everyone in attendance at a particular session shares a dream. A person who declines to tell a dream might be having a dry spell, with no remembered dream from the past week. Or he might feel he has a good enough understanding of his recent dreams and does not need help from the group at the present time. Or it may be that the only dream he remembers is one that refers to an area of his life that he would rather keep to himself and work on alone or in private with another member of the group. And along that same vein, it may be that the only dream he has had in the last week is one with imagery that is so sexually explicit that he would not feel comfortable sharing it with the group.

Members of the group differ in their willingness to tell dreams with sexual imagery. What is shared is up to each person. The group will accept any dream, however sexually explicit. We deal with this imagery at a symbolic level that removes the sexual charge and almost always makes the discussion feel as matter-of-fact as if we were discussing any other aspect of life. Because of this climate, people are more forthcoming than might be imagined. But the group also accepts without question anyone's reluctance to share anything of any nature whatsoever.

It is worth repeating that the Journey Group is not a therapy group. People are not expected or encouraged to lay their lives totally bare. Each person guards his own boundaries and decides for himself how much he wants to share. The discussion is centered more on the unconscious lives of the members than on their conscious lives, which means that the members tend to know more about the progress of each other's souls than about the details of their personal lives. Of course, developments from the unconscious are meaningless unless linked to conscious developments, but often the journeyer is left to make those links for himself after the group has helped him shine the light in roughly the right direction.

Group members benefit as much from the work that is done on the dreams of others as they do from work on their own dreams. In fact, some of the more advanced group members seldom feel a need to tell a dream of their own. They come to participate in the growing wisdom of the group as it discerns more and more clearly from the experiences of its members what life in God is all about.

## Seasonal Meditation Booklets

AN EXTREMELY IMPORTANT DEVELOPMENT in the life of the Journey Group occurred after we had been in existence for several years. The rector of our parish asked if we would be willing to produce a booklet of reflections on the Scriptures given in the daily lectionary for the coming Advent season. The booklet was to be made available without cost to the congregation at large.

The members of the Journey Group agreed to the project with some trepidation. They were not at all sure that they would be able to say anything about their assigned scriptural passages that would be of value to others. Most of them had never done this kind of thing before. They could talk about spiritual matters in the language of dreams and synchronicity, but could they talk about them in the language of traditional Christianity?

As it turned out, they were more than adequate to the task. Because of their experience of learning about God from their own inner lives, they found that they were able to see more deeply into the Scriptures than they had expected to be able to do and that they could convey their insights with a surprising inner authority. Most pleasing of all was their discovery that they could find within themselves the ability to speak their truths in the conventional language of traditional Christianity. Their pieces were deep, rich, and insightful and were written in language that was completely accessible to their fellow Christians (see Appendix C).

This outright union of traditional Christianity and natural spirituality—of the masculine and feminine aspects of God—produced an unexpected florescence of the Holy Spirit in the Journey Group as a whole and in the individual lives of its members. So valuable was this development that the group now includes in its mission the yearly production of scriptural reflections for the seasons of Advent and Lent. This helps us maintain the balance of the masculine and feminine aspects of God in our own lives and in the group as a whole, while at the same time it gives us a way to offer fruits of our shared journey to the congregation that supports us. Our booklets are popular, and because parishioners often give them to friends, they are gaining a modest fame beyond our parish. Our print runs are now up to seven hundred copies and climbing.

It should be noted that not every member of the Journey Group is a member of our congregation. Several are from churches of other denominations in our community. A few are from other towns. And some are not regular members of any church. Interestingly, most of the latter eventually find their way into a church community, their own dreams leading them in that direction when the time is right.

## The Natural Spirituality Library

THE THIRD ESSENTIAL ELEMENT of our Natural Spirituality Program is our Natural Spirituality Library. Because participants in the program are largely on their own as they make their journeys, they must each become as knowledgeable as possible about the life of the inner world. This makes the library an important part of the program. We have several hundred books ranging from simple introductory works to the dense but rewarding writings of Carl Jung himself. We also have a large number of audiotapes and a few videotapes. (Much of our collection is listed in the SOURCES section in Appendix A.) Our library has been financed by individual contributions from group members and by grants from an endowment fund in our parish.

The library is located in the same vicinity as our meeting place and is heavily used. We have a check-out system that allows the borrower to keep a book or tape for two months before being notified that it is time to return it or renew it. Despite the library's heavy use, very few books or tapes have been lost from our collection.

## Establishing New Programs

A NATURAL SPIRITUALITY PROGRAM such as ours would be easy to implement in any church community in which there is a willing leader who has been through the individuation process in a conscious and authentic way. The dynamics of the Holy Spirit that carry our program forward are very strong. This seems to be a version of Christian community that wants to exist and only needs the support of the minimal structure I have outlined. The greatest problem for new programs is that of leadership, for there are at the present time very few people anywhere who have consciously individuated. I feel intuitively, however, that the Holy Spirit is so much at work in this development within the Church that true leaders will begin to emerge on a widespread basis.

The question for the present time is how to get a natural spirituality program started in a church community in which there is no one present with enough experience of the inner world to be an authoritative leader and guide. Fortunately, as we have learned from new groups that were instituted using a preliminary version of this book, what is needed from a leader is not so much authoritative wisdom but the willingness to initiate and coordinate the process that sets the program in motion. Authority itself arises in, and is spread among, the individual members of the program. If there is any single authority, it is this book, but only insofar as it gives people a sound orientation to the inner world and thereby enables them to gain access to their own inner guide and authority.

Wherever there are a handful of people in a church who are interested in starting a natural spirituality program, I would advise them to begin by setting up a study group to read and discuss this book. The group should meet for weekly sessions that run for no less than eight weeks and no more than twelve. Outside readings drawn from the SOURCES in Appendix A might also be used—either all the group reading and discussing the same material or each participant reading and reporting on something different.

A dream group should be initiated as soon as the study group ends. Natural spirituality is meant to be *experienced*, not just studied. It is likely that one of the greatest stumbling blocks for new natural spirituality programs will be the tendency to get stuck at a purely intellectual level of involvement. The group members will go on reading all about Jungian psychology, and they will go out and attend all the conferences that are out there to attend, and with all this outer activity they will avoid a full engagement with the dynamic process in their own inner lives. In so doing they will miss the true dialogue between God and the individual which alone can sustain a natural spirituality program over a long period of time.

It is important, then, to start dream work immediately. There is no denying, however, that a dream group begun by novices after eight to twelve weeks of study will at first be a situation of the blind leading the blind. Starting a dream group is an act of faith—faith that a group of people who want to learn how to listen more closely to God will gradually learn how to do so. Experience has shown that the Holy Spirit is present to help a new group if they will simply begin to try. Their level of insight will not be as great in the beginning as it will be after they have gained more experience, but then they are not ready in the beginning to take in a higher level of insight. The process, which is living and dynamic, works itself out in its own terms.

In our program we have produced some guidelines for dream work which we find helpful. These rules of thumb, given here in figure 17, are posted on a chart and read aloud at each session.

It is essential for good dream work that the members of the group keep on reading and studying after the introductory class is over. Continuing education should be a formal part of every dream group, although it should not deflect the group from its primary business of inner work. I suggest that ten to fifteen minutes of each meeting be devoted to a discussion of what people are currently reading. The purpose is more to encourage continued reading than to convey any great amount of information. In our program one person a week presents a brief report on something he or she has recently read or listened to on tape.

## GUIDELINES FOR DREAM WORK

1. Dreams early in the journey are often about:
    a) the dreamer's awakening experience of the inner journey;
    b) areas of the dreamer's life in which development will be taking place in coming months.
2. Everything in the dream belongs to the dreamer.
3. Everything in the dream is a symbol—of aspects of personality, attitudes, situations, experiences of the divine, etc.
4. *Listen* to what the dreamer says in connection with the dream. He or she will at some point give voice to what lies at the heart of the dream. *Be alert.* This will be like a hidden jewel, easily overlooked among the many words. *Listen!*
5. Beware of guidelines. Be open to the guidance of the Holy Spirit.

Figure 17. Guidelines for Dream Work

It is important that the wisdom of the group be grounded in the writings of Carl Jung himself. Jung's vision was deep and true. He knew the inner world and understood its ways and its requirements. And, most importantly of all, he understood how much the inner journey is a journey with God, toward God. Though other Jungian writers might be easier to read, none can give a group as sure a foundation as Carl Jung can give through his own writings. Therefore, I advise members of a new dream group, as well as new members coming into an established group, to begin their continuing education with particular works by Carl Jung. We have found that Jung's writings are not as formidable as is commonly believed. Most of our new members can wade in without great difficulty. Although not everyone has an equal aptitude for reading Jung, even those who find it hard going are encouraged to stay with it as long as possible, drawing from it whatever they can manage to glean.

I recommend the following reading schedule, although the order I suggest need not be strictly maintained. All new members of a dream group should be able to read Jung's autobiography, *Memories, Dreams, Reflections.* This is the book with which most people would do well to begin. Next should come *Analytical Psychology: Its Theory and Practice,* which is a series of lectures Jung gave to a group of doctors in London. Most of the doctors were not Jungians, and so Jung had to explain everything to them from scratch. He is more immediately intelligible here than in most of his other writings.

The next book to read is *The Portable Jung,* a collection of Jung's writings put together for the general reader by Joseph Campbell. This volume gives a full range of Jung's thought, providing a good overall foundation. Any who are still standing after that should read *Dreams,* a volume of collected writings in the Bollingen Series, published by Princeton University Press. This will be an important book for the work of the dream group—at least one person in the group needs to have read it. It contains valuable examples of recurrent archetypal images and motifs that appear in some form in the dreams of everyone who engages in a conscious individuation journey.

These four books will provide a sound Jungian foundation for any dream group. Further reading in Jung is always worthwhile. More titles are listed in the SOURCES.

After their initial grounding in the works of Jung himself, dream group members should read books about dream interpretation written by Jungian analysts. A number of these are listed in the SOURCES.

Next, in order to better understand the issues being put forward by their dreams, journeyers should read books written by Jungians about masculine and feminine issues, the shadow, and any other relevant topic to which the Holy Spirit guides them. To facilitate this wider reading, a new dream group will need to begin assembling a natural spirituality library.

At the same time a group is familiarizing itself with Jungian psychology, it should also strengthen its grounding in traditional Christianity. Another likely stumbling block for new natural spirituality programs will be the tendency to see natural spirituality more as an alternative to traditional spirituality than as a complement to it. Hostility toward the masculine spirit of traditional Christianity is not a healthy component of a natural spirituality program. Nor is intellectual discomfort with the traditional expressions of Christian faith. Natural spirituality fills out and balances traditional Christianity, providing a crucial element that has been missing from it. It is the bride of the masculine spirit, not its replacement.

Many of the people coming into any dream group will bring with them their own reservations about Christianity as they understand it to be practiced in the world today. There is nothing wrong with this. It is to be expected. As people make their journeys, these issues will gradually be brought forward by the unconscious and resolved, and a new level of understanding will be reached. However, this resolution is less likely to take place as it should if this higher level of understanding is missing from the ethos of the group. Therefore it is especially important that individual members of the group take responsibility for strengthening their involvement in traditional spirituality. This includes regular participation in public worship and conscious attention to Scripture and prayer.

The members of the group will differ in their readiness for this kind of spiritual practice. Some people at the beginning of their journeys have the problem of being too conscientious, and they may actually need to decrease their traditional spiritual practice for a while in order to get that side of the Spirit balanced with the feminine side. Others may feel alienated from traditional practice because of earlier negative experiences and will not be able to feel open to the masculine spirit in the beginning— sometimes not for several years. No one should be pressured to go against his or her strong inner feelings. Everyone is on an individual journey, each beginning from a different point and directed toward the goal along a different route. Those members who *are* able to deepen their involvement in traditional spirituality will strengthen the spirit of godliness that is present in the group as a whole.

The reason traditional religion is important to the inner journey is that it provides the necessary guidelines for shifting the center of consciousness from the ego to the Self. The ego's world is the world at the surface of life, while the Self's world is the deeper reality of the kingdom of God. The principles of that deeper reality are not obvious in the everyday world in which the ego lives. The surface-of-life world clamors loudly with its countervailing principles.

While a part of our ego might want to put God at the center of our being, another part is always at work trying to keep itself, with its own goals and desires, enthroned in that central place. The ego can be devious in the way it works to keep its power. No matter how well-intentioned we are, we all need help in shifting our center from the ego to the Self. That help comes to us in part through the wisdom of the ages that is preserved and carried by traditional religion. In taking this eternal wisdom into ourselves, we are strengthened against the otherwise overpowering voice of the world around us.

For this reason I further recommend that members of a dream group make regular, individual use of the *I Ching*, the Chinese book of wisdom. Like the Bible, the *I Ching* gives us the Self's perspective and teaches us about its principles. Through the phenomenon of synchronicity, regular use of the *I Ching* can shed light on the specific circumstances of one's life. Of even more value, however, is the teaching it provides, in the process of consultation, about the principles of the kingdom of God, principles that are often at odds with the more narrowly focused collective consciousness of our time.

For example, Reading 2 in the *I Ching* is about The Receptive, which is the feminine principle, the principle of earth, nature, darkness, the unconscious, and so on. In the interpretive text we are told about the relationship of the Receptive to the Creative, which is the masculine principle, the light-giving, strong, and active spirit of heaven. The *I Ching* tells us that the Receptive does not compete with the Creative, but completes it. A primal attribute of the Receptive is devotion. In the text we read:

> In itself of course the Receptive is just as important as the Creative, but the attribute of devotion defines the place occupied by this primal power in relation to the Creative. For the Receptive must be activated and led by the Creative; then it is productive of good. Only when it abandons this position and tries to stand as an equal side by side with the Creative, does it become evil. The result then is opposition to and struggle against the Creative, which is productive of evil to both.

This particular lesson is an especially difficult one in our time, a time in which extreme feminist values have attempted to replace the historical excesses of the masculine principle. The idea that masculine and feminine are meant to relate in a certain way that we are free to discover, but not to define, goes against "what everybody says" in our world today.

In Reading 11, Peace, the *I Ching* makes it clear that while the feminine principle must be devoted to the masculine principle, the masculine principle, for its part, must not take a position above the feminine but must, from its position of strength, place itself beneath the feminine—at its service—and stay in communion with it. Says the text:

> Heaven has placed itself beneath the earth, and so their powers unite in deep harmony. Then peace and blessing descend upon all living things.

In such readings as these we find guidance not only for our own personal relationships, but for the relationship in our lives between masculine consciousness and the feminine unconscious, and for the relationship in the Church between the masculine spirit of the tradition and the feminine spirit of nature. The *I Ching* is invaluable for the way it complements, illuminates, and further explains the Judeo-Christian principles that come to us through Scripture and tradition. (Detailed instructions for using the *I Ching* are given in Appendix B.)

These, then, are the four recommendations I would offer to the members of a new natural spirituality group. 1) Read Jung. 2) Read Jungians. 3) Strengthen traditional spiritual practice. 4) Make regular use of the *I Ching*.

I once had a dream that said, *"Every community has its shaman."* I took this to mean that there will always be present in every fully constellated group at least one person who is particularly gifted in the way of the inner world and who can help shine a light in that world for others. The same is true for individuals. We each have a shaman in the inner community of our psyches. But that gift of wisdom, whether it be at the community or individual level, must be given a chance to develop effectively. The inner world continually tries to make itself known, but if there is no understanding of it or value ascribed to it in the greater culture, its attempts to become known are likely to miscarry, and its gifts of healing, creativity, and renewal of life will not be received by either the individual or the surrounding group.

Christianity is beginning to reclaim its mission as the nurturer of inner life. It can provide the understanding and value that are required to bring the feminine spirit back into human consciousness in a balanced way. As it becomes more intentional about this and finds ways to institute programs that make natural spirituality available to those who need it, the Church will become a stronger and more effective presence in the human community, proving itself more than ever to be an authentic source of healing, wholeness, and newness of life.

# APPENDICES

# *Natural Spirituality Sources*

THE INNER JOURNEY cannot be taken without maps, charts, and accounts by earlier travelers. Study is required to gain competency in the inner world just as it is required for the outer world. Concern about the inner world, however, usually comes at midlife, when a potential journeyer has enough capability and self-discipline to educate himself. Indeed, the most effective study for the individuation journey is individual study, for it is then that the Holy Spirit has the greatest freedom to guide a person to the book or tape he or she needs next, according to that person's individual development.

The following natural spirituality sources are arranged in categories which move from entry-level material to long-range, continuing education. While the books listed are available through public libraries and bookstores, the audio tapes must be ordered by mail. A library containing a large selection of these sources would be an important component of any natural spirituality program in a local church.

The lists given here are by no means exhaustive and are meant only to be a starting point.

## Foundation Sources

THE FOLLOWING are basic, entry-level sources that are especially effective in presenting the central themes of natural spirituality. Taken all together they offer a solid foundation for the early stages of the individuation process.

### *Works by C.G. Jung*

Jung's writings can be difficult, but they are important for a well-grounded orientation to the unconscious. More than any of his followers, Jung understood the serious, God-centered nature of the individuation journey. The works of later Jungian writers are usually helpful and worthwhile, but they often contain distortions of the truly God-centered way. By beginning at the source— with Jung himself—one becomes better equipped to judge the value of the works of later Jungians.

When reading Jung, one must not expect to understand everything. The reader must take from it what he can and leave the rest for return readings. The further along one goes on one's individuation journey, the more comprehensible Jung becomes. The following works have been chosen for their ease of entry, as well as for the thorough grounding they offer in Jungian thought when taken all together.

C.G. Jung. *Memories, Dreams, Reflections.* Recorded and edited by Aniela Jaffé. Translated by Richard and Clara Winston. 1961. Reprint. New York: Vintage Books, 1965. Jung's autobiography, as told to his trusted assistant Aniela Jaffé in the last years of his life. Free of scientific language, it tells as much about Jung's inner journey as about his outer one.

————. *Analytical Psychology: Its Theory and Practice.* The Tavistock Lectures. New York: Pantheon Books, 1968. A series of lectures Jung delivered in his sixtieth year to a group of physicians in London. A clear and lively exposition of his basic ideas in nontechnical language.

————. *The Portable Jung.* Edited by Joseph Campbell. Translated by R.F.C. Hull. 1971. Reprint. New York: Penguin Books, 1976. A collection of Jung's more accessible scientific writings. A comprehensive overview of his life's work.

## Dreams

C.G. Jung. *Dreams.* Translated by R.F.C. Hull. Bollingen Series. Princeton, N.J.: Princeton University Press, 1974. A collection of Jung's scientific writings on dreams. Dense reading, but valuable for gaining a foundation in the archetypal elements of dreams.

Morton T. Kelsey. *Dreams: A Way to Listen to God.* New York: Paulist Press, 1978. A short, comprehensive, easy introduction to the world of dreams. Written from a Christian perspective.

John A. Sanford. *Dreams: God's Forgotten Language.* 1968. Reprint. HarperSanFrancisco, 1989. A clear and easily comprehensible introduction to dreams. Written from a Christian perspective.

## Synchronicity

Robert Aziz. *C.G. Jung's Psychology of Religion and Synchronicity.* Albany, N.Y.: State University of New York Press, 1990. An excellent systematic, scholarly study of synchronicity in terms of Jung's psychological framework. Looks at synchronicity in both scientific and religious terms.

Jean Shinoda Bolen. *The Tao of Psychology: Synchronicity and the Self.* San Francisco: Harper and Row, 1979. A short, easy introduction to synchronicity by a Jungian analyst.

## Masculine and Feminine

Gertrud Mueller Nelson. *Here All Dwell Free: Stories to Heal the Wounded Feminine.* New York: Fawcett Columbine, 1991. An excellent, highly readable book about the feminine principle in human life. Uses two fairy tales—"The Handless Maiden" and "Briar Rose" (Sleeping Beauty)—as symbolic vehicles for the wealth of insight offered by the author. Incorporates a Christian perspective.

Robert Bly. *Iron John: A Book about Men.* Reading, Massachusetts: Addison-Wesley, 1990. An interesting, readable book about the masculine principle. Uses a fairy tale—"Iron John"—as a vehicle for discussion.

John A. Sanford. *The Invisible Partners: How the Male and Female in Each of Us Affects Our Relationships.* New York: Paulist Press, 1980. A clear introduction to the problem of anima and animus in human psychology. Incorporates a Christian perspective.

## Natural Spirituality and Christianity

Morton T. Kelsey. *God, Dreams, and Revelation: A Christian Interpretation of Dreams.* Revised and expanded edition. Minneapolis: Augsberg, 1991. An excellent overview of the dream in religious life from Biblical times to the present. Includes a lengthy appendix of writings by early Church Fathers on the subject of dreams.

John A. Sanford. *The Kingdom Within: The Inner Meaning of Jesus's Sayings.* Revised edition. HarperSanFrancisco, 1987. A readable book that explores the teachings of Jesus in terms of inner life and growth. By a Jungian analyst who is also an ordained clergyman.

*Short Courses on Audio Tape*

Morton T. Kelsey. "The Christian Interpretation of Dreams." 13 tapes. Available by mail from Dove Publications, Pecos, New Mexico, 87552. Lectures delivered at a workshop at Pecos Benedictine Monastery, a retreat center in New Mexico. A rich survey of natural spirituality and Christianity by a pioneer in the field.

Morton T. Kelsey and John A. Sanford. "Christianity and Depth Psychology." 17 tapes. Available by mail from Dove Publications, Pecos, New Mexico, 87552. Lectures delivered at a workshop at Pecos Benedictine Monastery. Some overlap in exposition with the set above, but nothing that does not bear rehearing. These two leading Christian writers and lecturers discuss the basic elements of Jungian psychology as it relates to Christianity.

# Christian Sources

THE CHRISTIAN SPIRIT and the Jungian spirit are not the same, although they overlap. Some Jungian works fall entirely outside the overlap and seem foreign to the Christian spirit. Other works fall entirely within the overlap and are especially trustworthy sources for readers with a Christian perspective. Foremost among the latter are the works of three authors:

MORTON T. KELSEY. A former professor at the University of Notre Dame and an Episcopal clergyman. The preeminent pioneer in introducing the Jungian perspective to Christianity.

JOHN A. SANFORD. A Jungian analyst and Episcopal priest who has worked closely with Kelsey in introducing Jung to the Christian community.

ROBERT A. JOHNSON. A Jungian analyst who has been closely affiliated with Journey Into Wholeness, an ongoing series of Christian retreats for exploring Jungian psychology.

There are two mail-order sources for books and tapes which fall within the overlap of Christianity and Jungian psychology:

DOVE PUBLICATIONS. Pecos, New Mexico, 87552. Dove Publications is an arm of Pecos Benedictine Monastery, a retreat center that includes an emphasis on natural spirituality. Their own publications and the tapes of their workshops are relatively inexpensive. Other publications in "Religious Psychology" are also available from Dove Publications, including many listed in the Extended Sources section below.

JOURNEY INTO WHOLENESS, INC., P.O. Box 169, Balsam Grove, North Carolina, 28708. Journey Into Wholeness conducts workshops and seminars that explore Jungian psychology in a Christian context. Tapes of their sessions are available.

## *Direct Ordering of the Natural Spirituality Textbook*

*Natural Spirituality: Recovering the Wisdom Tradition in Christianity* may be purchased through local bookstores or ordered directly from JRH Publications, P.O. Box 942, Danielsville, GA, 30633. Telephone/Fax 706-789-3400.

The price of the book is $16.95. Quantity discounts are available for direct orders as follows: 1 copy, no discount; 2–5 copies, 10% discount; 6 or more copies, 20% discount.

Shipping rates are as follows: 1 copy, $3.00 (Special Standard Mail) or $5.00 (Priority Mail or UPS); each additional copy, $.50. Shipping is free for orders of 12 or more copies.

Add sales tax to orders from within the state of Georgia. Payment is by check or money order (no credit cards). Credit terms are available for church groups. Prices and rates are subject to change.

Write to JRH Publications for a free booklet, "Guidelines for Starting a Natural Spirituality Program."

## *The Wisdom Series*

Whole-chapter excerpts from *Natural Spirituality: Recovering the Wisdom Tradition in Christianity* are reprinted in booklet form in the Wisdom Series, available from JRH Publications at the address given in the section above. These inexpensive booklets are intended for church tract racks, for study groups, and as a way for individuals to give samples of *Natural Spirituality* to friends.

The five booklets in the series are: No. 1, "Nature and Spirit in Christianity Today" *(Chapters 2 & 14)*; No. 2, "Consciousness and the Unconscious" *(Chapters 3, 4 & 5)*; No. 3, "Dreams and Synchronicity," *(Chapters 6 & 7)*; No. 4, "Masculine Wholeness and the Beatles," *(Chapters 10 & 11)*; and No. 5, "Feminine Wholeness and Psyche and Eros," *(Chapters 12 & 13)*. Chapters 1, 8, 9, and 15 are not available in booklet form.

Booklets may be ordered individually or as a set. The price is $2.00 per booklet ($10.00 for a set). To help churches offer booklet *No. 3,* "Dreams and Synchronicity," free in their tract racks, a "track rack" discount of 20% is available *for that booklet only* on orders of 10 or more copies sent to a church address. No other discounts are available for the Wisdom Series.

Shipping rates for booklets are as follows: 1–10 booklets, $.20 per copy *plus* $1.00; over 10 booklets, $.10 per copy *plus* $2.00. Orders of three or more booklets are sent by Special Standard Mail: add $2.00 per order for Priority Mail.

Add sales tax to orders from within the state of Georgia. Payment is by check or money order (no credit cards). Prices and rates are subject to change.

## A Chinese Source

*The I Ching* or *Book of Changes.* Translated by Richard Wilhelm and Cary F. Baynes. Foreword by C.G. Jung. Third Edition. Bollingen Series XIX. Princeton, N.J.: Princeton University Press, 1967. (Other translations are available, but not all are as spiritually trustworthy as this one.) Like the Bible, the roots of this Chinese book of wisdom go back three to four thousand years. Through the principle of synchronicity, the *I Ching* can be used as an oracle to shed light on the way of God in specific situations. Three coins are used to direct one to particular readings, giving voice to the unconscious to an astounding degree. The wisdom of the *I Ching* is not in conflict with Christian tradition. Rather, it is in many essential ways the same wisdom we meet in the Gospels, although cast in a different form. The *I Ching* can be a valuable teacher and companion for the early years of the individation journey, although an intuitive sense and some knowledge of oneself is required to understand the readings. Frequent use of the *I Ching* over a period of several years gives one a strong foundation in the wisdom of the way of God.

(See Appendix B for instructions for using the *I Ching.*)

## Extended Sources

IN ADDITION to the basic sources given above, a traveler on the path of individuation should read widely and continually. Most of the sources listed below have been written with the layman in mind. Though of varying degree of value, all are worthwhile. (See also the Foundation Sources listed above.)

## Reference Books

J.E. Cirlot. *A Dictionary of Symbols*. Routledge, 1983.

J.C. Cooper. *An Illustrated Encyclopedia of Traditional Symbols*. 1978. Reprint. New York: Thames and Hudson, 1987.

Robert H. Hopcke. *A Guided Tour of the* Collected Works *of C.G. Jung*. 1989. Reprint. Boston: Shambhala, 1992.

J.E. Zimmerman. *Dictionary of Classical Mythology*. 1964. Reprint. New York: Bantam Books, 1971.

## Works by C.G. Jung

C.G. Jung. *Aion: Researches into the Phenomenology of the Self*. Translated by R.F.C. Hull. 2d ed. Bollingen Series XX. Princeton, N.J.: PrincetonUniversity Press, 1968.

———. *Analytical Psychology: Its Theory and Practice*. The Tavistock Lectures. New York: Pantheon Books, 1968.

———. *Aspects of the Feminine*. Translated by R.F.C. Hull. Bollingen Series. Princeton, N.J.: Princeton University Press, 1982.

———. *Aspects of the Masculine*. Translated by R.F.C. Hull. Bollingen Series. Princeton, N.J.: Princeton University Press, 1989.

———. *C.G. Jung: Psychological Reflections: A New Anthology of His Writings, 1905–1961*. Selected and edited by Jolande Jacobi. 2d ed. Bollingen Series XXXI. Princeton, N.J.: Princeton University Press, 1970.

———. *C.G. Jung Speaking: Interviews and Encounters*. Edited by William McGuire and R.F.C. Hull. Bollingen Series XCII. Princeton, N.J.: Princeton University Press, 1977.

———. *Dream Analysis: Notes of the Seminar Given in 1928–1930 by C.G. Jung*. Edited by William McGuire. Bollingen Series XCIX. Princeton, N.J.: Princeton University Press, 1984.

———. *Dreams*. Translated by R.F.C. Hull. Bollingen Series. Princeton, N.J.: Princeton University Press, 1974.

———. *The Essential Jung*. Selected and introduced by Anthony Storr. Princeton, N.J.: Princeton University Press, 1983.

———. *Four Archetypes: Mother/Rebirth/Spirit/Trickster*. Translated by R.F.C. Hull. Bollingen Series. Princeton, N.J.: Princeton University Press, 1970.

———. *Memories, Dreams, Reflections*. Recorded and edited by Aniela Jaffé. Translated by Richard and Clara Winston. 1961. Reprint. New York: Vintage Books, 1965.

————. *Modern Man in Search of a Soul.* Translated by W.S. Dell and Cary F. Baynes. San Diego: Harcourt Brace Jovanovich, 1933.

————. *The Portable Jung.* Edited by Joseph Campbell. Translated by R.F.C. Hull. 1971. Reprint. New York: Penguin Books, 1976.

————. *Psyche and Symbol: A Selection from the Writings of C.G. Jung.* Edited by Violet S. de Laszlo. Garden City, N.Y.: Doubleday Anchor Books, 1958.

————. *The Psychology of the Transference.* Translated by R.F.C. Hull. Bollingen Series. Princeton, N.J.: Princeton University Press, 1969.

————. *Selected Letters of C.G. Jung, 1909–1961.* Selected and edited by Gerhard Adler. Bollingen Series. Princeton, N.J.: Princeton University Press, 1984.

————. *The Undiscovered Self* with *Symbols and the Interpretation of Dreams.* Translated and revised by R.F.C. Hull. Bollingen Series. Princeton, N.J.: Princeton University Press, 1990.

## *Overviews of Jungian Psychology*

E.A. Bennet. *Meetings with Jung.* Zürich: Daimon, 1985.

Barbara Hannah. *Jung: His Life and Work.* Wilmette, Illinois: Chiron Publications, 1997.

M. Esther Harding. *The 'I' and the 'Not I': A Study in the Development of Consciousness.* Bollingen Series LXXIX. Princeton, N.J.: Princeton University Press, 1965.

Carl G. Jung, and M.-L. von Franz, Joseph L. Henderson, Jolande Jacobi, and Aniela Jaffé. *Man and his Symbols.* New York: Dell Publishing, 1964.

Eugene Pascal. *Jung to Live By.* New York: Warner Books, 1992.

Marie-Louise von Franz. *Psychotherapy.* Boston: Shambhala, 1993.

Robin Robertson. *Beginners Guide to Jungian Psychology.* York Beach, Maine: Nicholas-Hays, 1992.

Murray Stein. *Jung's Map of the Soul: An Introduction.* Chicago: Open Court, 1998.

Anthony Stevens. *Archetypes: A Natural History of the Self.* New York: Quill, 1983.

Marie-Louise von Franz. *C.G. Jung: His Myth in Our Time.* Toronto: Inner City Books, 1998.

Edward C. Whitmont. *The Symbolic Quest: Basic Concepts of Analytical Psychology.* 1969. Reprint. New York: Harper and Row, 1973.

## *Dreams*

Fraser Boa. *The Way of the Dream: Conversations on Jungian Dream Interpretation with Marie-Louise von Franz.* Boston: Shambala, 1994.

Kathrin Asper. *The Inner Child in Dreams.* Translated by Sharon E. Rooks. Boston: Shambhala, 1992.

Robert Bosnak. *Tracks in the Wilderness of Dreaming: Exploring Interior Landscape through Practical Dreamwork.* New York: Delta, 1996.

Donald Broadribb. *The Dream Story.* 1987. Reprint. Toronto: Inner City Books, 1990.

Jean and Wallace Clift. *The Hero Journey in Dreams.* 1988. Reprint. New York: Crossroads, 1991.

Edward F. Edinger. *The Living Psyche: A Jungian Analysis in Pictures.* Wilmette, Illinois: Chiron Publications, 1990.

Robert A. Johnson. *Inner Work: Using Dreams and Active Imagination for Personal Growth.* San Francisco: Harper and Row, 1986.

Morton T. Kelsey. *Dreams: A Way to Listen to God.* New York: Paulist Press, 1978.

James Kirsch. *The Reluctant Prophet.* Los Angeles: Sherbourne Press, 1973.

John Layard. *Lady of the Hare: A Study in the Healing Power of Dreams.* Boston: Shambhala, 1988.

Mary Ann Mattoon. *Understanding Dreams.* 1978. Reprint. Dallas, Texas: Spring Publications, 1984.

John A. Sanford. *Dreams: God's Forgotten Language.* 1968. Reprint. HarperSanFrancisco, 1989.

————. *Dreams and Healing: A Succinct and Lively Interpretation of Dreams.* New York: Paulist Press, 1978.

Jeremy Taylor. *Where People Fly and Water Runs Uphill: Using Dreams to Tap the Wisdom of the Unconscious.* New York: Warner Books, 1992.

## Synchronicity

Robert Aziz. *C.G. Jung's Psychology of Religion and Synchronicity.* Albany, N.Y.: State University of New York Press, 1990.

Jean Shinoda Bolen. *The Tao of Psychology: Synchronicity and the Self.* San Francisco: Harper and Row, 1979.

Allan Combs and Mark Holland. *Synchronicity: Science, Myth, and the Trickster.* New York: Paragon House, 1990.

Marie-Louise von Franz. *On Divination and Synchronicity: The Psychology of Meaningful Chance.* Toronto: Inner City Books, 1980.

## Natural Spirituality and Christianity

Wallace B. Clift. *Jung and Christianity: The Challenge of Reconciliation.* New York: Crossroad, 1993.

Edward F. Edinger. *The Bible and the Psyche: Individuation Symbolism in the Old Testament.* Toronto: Inner City Books, 1986.

————. *The Christian Archetype: A Jungian Commentary on the Life of Christ.* Toronto: Inner City Books, 1987.

————. *Ego and Archetype: Individuation and the Religious Function of the Psyche.* 1972. Reprint. Boston: Shambhala, 1992.

————. *The New God-Image: A Study of Jung's Key Letters Concerning the Evolution of the Western God-Image.* Wilmette, Illinois: Chiron Publications, 1996.

Fred Gustafson. *The Black Madonna.* Boston: Sigo Press, 1990.

Lawrence W. Jaffe. *Liberating the Heart: Spirituality and Jungian Psychology.* Toronto: Inner City Books, 1990.

Morton T. Kelsey. *God, Dreams, and Revelation: A Christian Interpretation of Dreams.* Revised and expanded edition. Minneapolis: Augsberg, 1991.

————. *Reaching: The Journey to Fulfillment.* Minneapolis: Augsburg, 1989.

————. *Transcend: A Guide to the Perennial Spiritual Quest.* Rockport, Massachusetts: Element, 1981.

Robert L. Moore, ed. *Carl Jung and Christian Spirituality.* New York: Paulist Press, 1988.

Elaine Pagels. *The Gnostic Gospels.* 1979. Reprint. New York: Vintage Books, 1989.

John A. Sanford. *The Kingdom Within: The Inner Meaning of Jesus' Sayings.* Rev. ed. HarperSanFrancisco, 1987.

————. *The Man Who Wrestled with God: Light from the Old Testament on the Psychology of Individuation.* New York: Paulist Press, 1987.

————. *Mystical Christianity: A Psychological Commentary on the Gospel of John.* New York: Crossroad, 1994.

Gerald H. Slusser. *From Jung to Jesus: Myth and Consciousness in the New Testament.* Atlanta: John Knox Press, 1986.

Murray Stein and Robert L. Moore, eds. *Jung's Challenge to Contemporary Religion.* Wilmette, Illinois: Chiron Publications, 1987.

Ann Belford Ulanov. *The Wisdom of the Psyche.* Cambridge, Massachusetts: Cowley Publications, 1988.

Ann and Barry Ulanov. *Religion and the Unconscious.* Philadelphia: Westminster Press, 1975.

Gerhard von Rad. *Wisdom in Israel.* Valley Forge, Pennsylvania: Trinity Press, 1972.

Allen Whitman. *Fairy Tales and the Kingdom of God.* Pecos, N.M.: Dove Publications, 1983.

## Personality Types

C.A. Meier. *Personality: The Individuation Process in the Light of C.G. Jung's Typology.* Einsiedeln, Switzerland: Daimon, 1995.

Isabel Briggs Myers, with Peter B. Myers. *Gifts Differing: Understanding Personality Type.* 1980. Reprint. Palo Alto, California: CCP Books, 1993.

Daryl Sharp. *Personality Types: Jung's Model of Typology.* Toronto: Inner City Books, 1987.

Marie-Louise von Franz and James Hillman. *Lectures on Jung's Typology.* 1971. Reprint. Dallas, Texas: Spring Publications, 1986.

## The Shadow and Evil

Mario Jacoby, Verena Kast, and Ingrid Riedel. *Witches, Ogres, and the Devil's Daughter: Encounters with Evil in Fairy Tales.* Translated by Michael H. Kohn. Boston: Shambhala, 1992.

Robert A. Johnson. *Owning Your Own Shadow: Understanding the Dark Side of the Psyche.* HarperSanFrancisco, 1991.

C.G. Jung. *Jung on Evil.* Selected and introduced by Murray Stein. Princeton, N.J.: Princeton University Press, 1995.

Morton T. Kelsey. *Discernment: A Study in Ecstasy and Evil.* New York: Paulist Press, 1978.

Mary Ann Mattoon, ed. *The Archetype of Shadow in a Split World.* Proceedings of the Tenth International Congress for Analytical Psychology, Berlin, 1986. Zurich: Daimon Verlag, 1987.

William A. Miller. *Make Friends with Your Shadow: How to Accept and Use Positively the Negative Side of Your Personality.* Minneapolis: Augsburg, 1981.

John A. Sanford. *Evil: The Shadow Side of Reality.* New York: Crossroad, 1994.

———. *The Strange Trial of Mr. Hyde: A New Look at the Nature of Human Evil.* San Francisco: Harper and Row, 1987.

## Masculine and Feminine

Robert Bly. *Iron John: A Book about Men.* Reading, Massachusetts: Addison-Wesley, 1990.

Jean Shinoda Bolen. *Goddesses in Everywoman: A New Psychology of Women.* New York: Harper and Row, 1984.

———. *Gods in Everyman: A New Psychology of Men's Lives and Loves.* New York: Harper and Row, 1989.

Irene Claremont de Castillejo. *Knowing Woman: A Feminine Psychology.* 1973. Reprint. New York: Harper and Row, 1974.

M. Esther Harding. *The Way of All Women.* Rev. ed. 1970. Reprint. Boston: Shambhala, 1990.

Robert A. Johnson. *Femininity Lost and Regained.* New York: Harper and Row, 1990.

————. *He: Understanding Masculine Psychology.* Rev. ed. New York: Harper and Row, 1989.

————. *Lying with the Heavenly Woman: Understanding and Integrating the Feminine Archetypes in Men's Lives.* HarperSanFrancisco, 1994.

————. *She: Understanding Feminine Psychology.* Rev. ed. New York: Harper and Row, 1989.

————. *Transformation: Understanding the Three Levels of Masculine Consciousness.* HarperSanFrancisco, 1991.

————. *We: Understanding the Psychology of Romantic Love.* San Francisco: Harper and Row, 1983.

Morton T. Kelsey. *Sacrament of Sexuality.* Warwick, N.Y.: Amity House, 1986.

Linda Schierse Leonard. *Meeting the Madwoman: An Inner Challenge for Feminine Spirit.* New York: Bantam Books, 1993.

————. *The Wounded Woman: Healing the Father-Daughter Relationship.* 1982. Reprint. Boston: Shambhala, 1985.

Helen M. Luke. *Kaleidoscope: 'The Way of Woman' and other Essays.* Edited by Rob Baker. New York: Parabola Books, 1992.

Robert Moore and Douglas Gillette. *King, Warrior, Magician, Lover: Rediscovering the Archetypes of the Mature Masculine.* HarperSanFrancisco, 1990.

Gertrud Mueller Nelson. *Here All Dwell Free: Stories to Heal the Wounded Feminine.* New York: Fawcett Columbine, 1991.

Erich Neumann. *The Great Mother: An Analysis of the Archetype.* Translated by Ralph Manheim. 2d ed. Bollingen Series XLVII. Princeton, N.J.: Princeton University Press, 1963.

John A. Sanford. *The Invisible Partners: How the Male and Female in Each of Us Affects Our Relationships.* New York: Paulist Press, 1980.

John A. Sanford and George Lough. *What Men Are Like.* New York: Paulist Press, 1988.

Laurie Layton Schapira. *The Cassandra Complex: Living with Disbelief: A Modern Perspective on Hysteria.* Toronto: Inner City Books, 1988.

Ann Belford Ulanov. *The Feminine in Jungian Psychology and in Christian Theology.* Evanston, Illinois: Northwestern University Press, 1971.

————. *Receiving Woman: Studies in the Psychology and Theology of the Feminine.* Philadelphia: Westminster Press, 1981.

Ann and Barry Ulanov. *Transforming Sexuality: The Archetypal World of Anima and Animus.* Boston: Shambhala, 1994.

Marie-Louise von Franz. *The Feminine in Fairy Tales.* Rev. ed. Boston: Shambhala, 1993.

————. *The Golden Ass of Apuleius: The Liberation of the Feminine in Man.* Rev. ed. Boston: Shambhala, 1992.

————. *Puer Aeternus.* 2d ed. Sigo Press, 1981.

Edward C. Whitmont. *Return of the Goddess.* New York: Crossroad, 1982.

Marion Woodman. *Addiction to Perfection: The Still Unravished Bride.* Toronto: Inner City Books, 1982.

## Stages of Life, Aspects of Wholeness

Janice Brewi and Anne Brennan. *Celebrate Mid-Life: Jungian Archetypes and Mid-Life Spirituality.* New York: Crossroad, 1988.

Allan B. Chinen. *Once Upon a Midlife: Classic Stories and Mythic Tales to Illuminate the Middle Years.* New York: Parigee Books, 1993.

Barbara Hannah. *The Dog, Cat, and Horse Lectures.* Wilmette, Illinois: Chiron Publications, 1992.

Robert Johnson. *Balancing Heaven and Earth.* HarperSanFrancisco, 1998.

Verena Kast. *Letting Go and Finding Yourself: Separating from Your Children.* New York: Continuum, 1994.

————. *A Time to Mourn: Growing through the Grief Process.* Einsiedeln, Switzerland: Daimon, 1982.

Linda Schierse Leonard. *Witness to the Fire: Creativity and the Veil of Addiction.* Boston: Shambhala, 1989.

Helen M. Luke. *Dark Wood to White Rose: A Study of Meanings in Dante's Divine Comedy.* Pecos, New Mexico: Dove Publications, 1975.

————. *Old Age.* New York: Parabola Books, 1987.

Carol S. Pearson. *The Hero Within: Six Archetypes We Live By.* San Francisco: Harper and Row, 1989.

Marie-Louise von Franz. *The Interpretation of Fairy Tales.* Boston: Shambhala, 1996.

————. *The Psychological Meaning of Redemption Motifs in Fairytales.* Toronto: Inner City Books, 1980.

# How to Use the
# I Ching

IT IS SUGGESTED that you use the Princeton University Press edition of the *I Ching*, Richard Wilhelm, translator (see Appendix A: A Chinese Source).

Familiarize yourself with the book. Read the introductory material. Be sure to take note of the images associated with the eight trigrams. This will help you work with them. On the chart that folds out from the back (Key for Identifying the Hexagrams) it is helpful to label the trigrams with their natural images— Heaven, Thunder, etc.

## The Coin Oracle

Get three coins. (Pennies will suffice.)

Center yourself. Remember that you are seeking dialogue with God.

There are two approaches to the oracular wisdom of the *I Ching*. The first, and perhaps the best, is an open approach in which no specific question is asked. After centering yourself, you cast the coins and find your reading. As you read, you use intuition and feeling to discern the area of life to which the reading applies. This approach reduces the ego's opportunity to subvert the process by trying to use the *I Ching* as a tool of personal power. The *I Ching* cannot be used in this way, but your understanding of the readings can be undermined when this motive is present, consciously or unconsciously.

There is also value, however, in asking a specific question before you throw the coins, provided you proceed in a reverent manner. With this approach, think about the life issue you are addressing. Talk to God about your feelings and your present understanding. Then ask for further understanding. Your question might be: "Please tell me what I need to understand about so-and-so."

CASTING THE COINS

Coin sides: masculine (heads) = 3
               feminine (tails) = 2

Cast the coins and add the total.

A total number which is *even* (6 or 8) is feminine. It is represented by a broken line – –.

A total number which is *odd* (7 or 9) is masculine. It is represented by an unbroken line ——.

Write down the number and its symbol beside it.

Cast the coins again. This should be done a total of six times, forming a hexagram. For example:

$$
\begin{array}{ll}
6 & \text{– –} \\
7 & \text{——} \\
8 & \text{– –} \\
7 & \text{——} \\
9 & \text{——} \\
6 & \text{– –}
\end{array}
$$

The hexagram you are given will direct you to the reading that most aptly applies to your particular situation. If the numbers are all 7s and 8s, this reading of your situation is an unchanging one. If there are any 9s or 6s, a changing situation is indicated, as will be explained below.

IDENTIFYING THE HEXAGRAM

The hexagram is made up of two trigrams. The top three lines form the upper trigram. The bottom three lines form the lower trigram.

To identify your hexagram by its number, look up the trigrams on the chart in the back of the *I Ching*.

In the example given above, ☵ is the upper trigram. This is the middle son, Water. Locate it on the top row.

The lower trigram in the example above is ☴. This is the oldest daughter, Wind or Wood. Locate it on the left hand side.

Find the point where the two columns merge. This is the number of your hexagram. Turn in Book I to the reading that has this number. Check to make sure that the hexagram in the reading matches the one you have written down. It is easy to make a mistake.

In the example given above, the number is 48, which leads to the reading for The Well.

### THE READING

Read your hexagram's introduction, Judgement, and Image, with related material (not including the Lines). This is a general picture of your situation. You must use your intuition to perceive its connection and meaning in regard to your present life. As with dreams, you must feel around until something clicks. Sometimes you are unable to see what the meaning is. Other times it is very clear. Often it is somewhere in between.

The six Lines give more specific meaning about your particular situation. These are "moving lines" and are indicated by a 6 or a 9. If you have any 6s or 9s in your hexagram, read the corresponding lines. NOTE: The lines are numbered from the bottom. In the example given above, we have 6 at the beginning, 9 in the second place, 7 in the third place, 8 in the fourth place, 7 in the fifth place, and 6 at the top. The first, second, and sixth lines would be read.

(The fact that the lines are *read* from the bottom up does not mean that the coin throws have to be *written* in that order. Your first throw can be written as the line at the top, your second throw as the line in the fifth place, and so on. Or you can go from bottom to top if you wish. All you have to do is be consistent. Synchronicity will handle the rest.)

THE CHANGE

If you have 6s or 9s and have read your lines, it is now time to let the hexagram change. Each moving line (6 or 9) changes into its opposite: − − to —, − − to —.

The hexagram in the example given above would change as follows:

```
6 – –    ——
7 ——     ——
8 – –    – –
7 ——     ——
9 ——     – –
6 – –    ——
```

In this new hexagram ≡≡ is the upper trigram. This is the oldest daughter, Wind or Wood. The lower trigram is ⚎, the middle daughter, Flame.

THE NEW READING

Locate your new hexagram on the chart to find its number. Find the reading in Book I and check to make sure the hexagram in the reading matches the one you have written down. (In the example, the number is 37, The Family.)

This reading tells you where your situation is headed. You only read the introduction, Judgement, and Image. The Lines do not apply in the new hexagram.

BOOKS II AND III

Book II, The Material, and Book III, The Commentaries, provide more information about the readings. It is up to you how much or how little use to make of them. It is not necessary to refer to them when casting the I Ching.

# Scriptural Reflections by Members of a Natural Spirituality Dream Group

THIS IS A SAMPLING of reflections on Holy Scripture written by members of the Natural Spirituality Journey Group of Emmanuel Episcopal Church in Athens, Georgia (see Chapter Fifteen). They are based on readings for the season of Advent in the Daily Office Lectionary of *The Book of Common Prayer*. The readings for the day are listed at the bottom of each piece.

## MONDAY, *Second Week of Advent*

*Let integrity and uprightness protect me, for I have waited for thee, O Lord.*
PSALM 25:21

Elie Wiesel tells the story out of the Hasidic tradition of a quiet rabbi named Zushia. Near the end of his life he stood before the members of his synagogue and said, "When I die and face the celestial tribunal, I do not fear that they will ask me, 'Zushia, why were you not Moses?' For I would tell them, 'Moses was a great leader, and I am not.' Nor do I fear they will ask me why I was not Jeremiah, or why I was not Rebbe Akiba—for I was neither a great prophet nor a great teacher.

"The single question I do fear they will ask me is, 'Zushia, why were you not Zushia?'"

That single question focuses on an important part of the protection that the psalmist requests or expects of God in today's reading. When we live out of our very core self, where our thinking, feeling, and doing are in harmony, we connect with God and ourselves in a powerful way.

Integrity, in its original sense, means living in harmony with oneself. Others may have expectations for us, but the significant question is: Are we being who we have been created to be? Dis-stress and dis-ease may occur when we live without integrity. A life lived with integrity is characterized by wholeness— how we live outside reflects who we are inside.

Who we are is constantly unfolding. Through our daily decision-making we are given the chance to grow into that unique person inherent in our creation.
PS 25; ISA 5:8 – 12, 18 – 23; I THESS 5:1 – 11; LUKE 21:20 – 28

## WEDNESDAY, Second Week of Advent

*But Jesus bent down and started to write on the ground with his finger.*
JOHN 8:6

One of the great themes of Advent is the Judgement, the end of the world, and Christ coming again with an army of angels in glory. Those of us who look for the eyes of Christ in a stranger and who listen for the voice of God in our dreams know that our world today, as in the day of the ancient Hebrews, is in desperate need of a Savior.

Being good, doing the right thing, obeying the law, even making more laws, is not enough to save us. The Pharisees were very concerned with the Law, knew it backwards and forwards, knew how very necessary laws are for the protection and development of a society. They were good people who practised their religion diligently, like our parents did, like we try to do, and like we try to teach our children to do. But Jesus told these Pharisees, as he tells us, that God is too good to be pleased with a magnificent religious performance if we are wrong on the inside.

We do not know what Jesus was writing on the ground that day as he thought through the heady problem the Pharisees had presented him with that poor woman. He did not jump up to ask revealing questions, nor did he declare that adultery is okay under certain circumstances. He stooped down and engaged in direct relationship with the earth. ("He came down to earth from Heaven, Who is God and Lord of all.") And when he spoke, he spoke from Wisdom, which includes and integrates, whereas Law differentiates.

This Advent, pray for God's judgement every day and give thanks that through our Lord Jesus, we know the beating of God's great heart.
PS 38; ISA 6:1 – 13; 2 THESS 1:1 – 12; JOHN 7:53 – 8:11

## FRIDAY, 2nd Week of Advent

*May our Lord Jesus Christ himself, and God our Father who has given us his love and, through his grace, such ceaseless encouragement and such sure hope, encourage you and strengthen you in every good word and deed.*

2 THESSALONIANS 2:16

I recently observed two elderly homeless people interacting in a fast food restaurant. The woman listened to the frail old man's story for a while. He had been released from the hospital that day, had no money, no place to live, and was hungry. At one point the old woman got up from her chair, walked away from the man, and with her back turned to him, carefully removed a handkerchief from her skirt pocket. She purposefully untied the handkerchief and thoughtfully picked through her money: some coins and a one dollar bill. She selected the bill to give to him. He purchased a hamburger and a cup of water. What formidable power and joy and capacity for action slumbers in the human spirit!

Christmas is the season of giving. How many of us will select the greater portion of our wealth (money, time in prayer, talents, service) to give to those around us who are truly in need? It is easy to give some small portion of our material wealth toward meeting the needs of others and feel a sense of self-righteousness. Almost never do we give away what we actually need for our own well-being, trusting that, "In as much as you have done it unto the least of these, you have done it unto me."

Let each of us during this Advent season ask prayerfully what it is that God asks of us for others. "Love one another as I have loved you."

PS 31; ISA 7:10 – 25; 2 THESS 2:13 – 3:5; LUKE 22:14 – 30

## MONDAY, Third Week of Advent

*But this is your hour — the triumph of darkness.*

LUKE 22:53

These are Jesus' words to Judas after the betrayal in the garden. Jesus has spent the night alone in prayer, agonizing over what he knows is to come, asking his Father to spare him this, and yet praying, "Not my will but yours be done." To Judas he acknowledges two essential things — the absolute darkness that has prevailed and the temporality of that darkness. An hour is only an hour, it passes, is replaced by other hours. Implicit in the statement is the promise of light. And yet, like the disciple who cut off the soldier's ear, we rebel against the darkness, determined that it should not triumph, even for an hour.

Many of us have been overcome by darkness—evil has prevailed within and around us. Our response is often to resist evil and deny it, until it overtakes us in the form of an illness, the death of a loved one, injustice, lost ideals, or betrayal. Then, in the face of what cannot be denied, we are tempted towards cynicism and despair, crying out that life is nothing but a swindle after all.

This Jesus did not do. He neither denied the darkness nor collapsed into despair. He bore the darkness, but maintained his relationship to his Father. He saw that the darkness would not last forever. He healed the soldier's ear and in so doing confirmed his allegiance with wholeness, health, and life. And because he faced into the void and was not consumed by it, we can say with Isaiah: "Those who have dwelt in darkness have seen a great light."

PS 41,52; ISA 8:16 — 9:1; 2 PETER 1:1—11; LUKE 22:39 — 53

## TUESDAY, 3rd Week of Advent

*While he was still speaking, the cock crowed, and the Lord turned and looked straight at Peter, and Peter remembered the Lord's words when he had said to him, "Before the cock crows today, you will have disowned me three times." And he went outside and wept bitterly.*

LUKE 22:60 — 62

How can I live a truly grateful life? When I try to look at my past and see so many sad and hurtful events in my life, the good and the bad things easily divide themselves up. With my past thus divided into the good things to be grateful for and the bad things to be forgotten, then the future and the new challenges that it holds seem unavailable. As my friend Henri says, "With many things to forget we can only limp toward the future."

All of what has brought me to this moment (the bad as well as the good) happened under God's guidance and didn't happen outside of the loving presence of God. How is it that Jesus' own suffering, passion, and death, brought on by the forces of darkness, are still spoken of as his way to glory?

There are so many things from my past that I feel guilt and shame about, wish had never happened, much less feel a sense of gratitude toward. Yet each time I have the courage to accept the entirety of "my story," I am rewarded with a deeper recognition of His tender mercy, the conviction of His guidance, and commitment to a life in His service.

Once my past awakens in gratitude, I am free to pass on this good news to others. Peter's denials didn't paralyze him. However painful and humbling his betrayal, once forgiven it became for him a source of his faithfulness. So all my failures and shortcomings can be transformed into gratitude and enable me to bring hopefulness to the essential meanings revealed in my life.

PS 45; ISA 9:1–7; 2 PETER 1:12–21; LUKE 22:54–69

## *FRIDAY, 3rd Week of Advent*

*Sacrifice and offering you do not desire, but you have given me an open ear. Burnt offering and sin offering you have not required.*

PSALM 40:6

What happens when I stop listening to God with an open ear? What happens when I decide I have heard enough?

I begin to forget (Did I ever really know?) that God is whole and I am partial. And by forgetting this, I cannot help but judge God. I cannot help but see Him in my own image. I cannot help but assign my motives to Him. I cannot help but imagine that what pleases my "best self" pleases Him. All this because this is all I can know without listening to God.

And yet, I never tire of listening to the "God" I have made. He confirms my reality. He justifies me. Even if I should hate myself, this "God" stands by my judgements. And now I am really trapped, because I can swear that I listen to "God" with a hungry ear. And I will try to prove this by proclaiming what I believe I know.

I have thus fallen into a pit I would have missed if I never knew anything of God. Why? Because I wanted so badly to know my God; and yet, I was unwilling to set aside my pride and wait upon God for the rest of my life. I was unwilling to keep listening, keep listening, keep listening as God reveals Himself to me.

God is whole. I am partial. If God needs anything from me, I must admit I do not know what that may be. But I do know that by His goodness it pleases Him that I should become whole. It pleases Him that we help each other become whole.

PS 40,54; ISA 10:5–19; 2 PETER 2:17–22; MATT 11:2–15

## TUESDAY, *December 24*

*The wilderness and the solitary place shall be glad for them; and the desert shall rejoice, and blossom as the rose. . . . They shall see the glory of the Lord, and the excellency of our God. Strengthen ye the weak hands, and confirm the feeble knees. . . . And a highway shall be there, and a way, and it shall be called The way of holiness; the unclean shall not pass over it; but it shall be for those: the wayfaring men, though fools, shall not err therein.*

ISAIAH 35:1—3,8

"A highway shall be there, and a way; . . . the wayfaring men, though fools, shall not err therein." These words haunt me. I cannot read them without feeling a stinging behind my eyes, an aching constriction in my chest, as I am overtaken by the tenderness and love offered in their promise. We, the "wayfaring men"— soul travelers, long tired from our journey and bound by a flawed humanity, are seen and forgiven by merciful God, a benevolent father who sets us upon a path from which we can no longer stray. Such love He holds for us in His promise.

And yet even with a promise like this ahead—we struggle. How can I be worthy of such divine love when I cannot even fulfill my own expectations of leading a Christian life? My head is ever spinning with reminders of how I have fallen short: things I could have done, what I should have been, paths I might have chosen. And so I ask, what is the solution? How can I live with my flawed humanity and go on seeking God's path? As usual, God provides: He tells us, "Strengthen ye the weak hands, and confirm the feeble knees." With this guide-post I profess my fears and inadequacies to God and ask for strength to carry on, courage to be better, and grace to feel the way.

PS 45,46; ISA 35:1—10; REV 22:12—17,21; LUKE 1:67—80

# Notes

### CHAPTER ONE. *Beginnings*

p. 13   "I don't need to believe . . ." *C.G. Jung Speaking: Interviews and Encounters,* William McGuire and R.F.C. Hull, eds. (Princeton, N.J.: Princeton University Press), 428.

### CHAPTER TWO. *Nature and Spirit*

p. 16   "There is only Christ . . ." *Colossians 3:11.*

p. 18   "The coming of the kingdom . . ." *Luke 17:20−21.*
      "Follow me" *John 1:43.*
      "I am the Way" *John 14:6.*
      "Foxes have holes . . ." *Matthew 8:20.*
      "Once the hand is laid on the plow . . ." *Luke 9:62.*

p. 19   "has seen the Father . . ." *John 6:46.*
      "If you know me . . ." *John 14:7.*
      "The Father is greater . . ." *John 14:28.*
      "The Father and I are one" *John 10:30.*
      "I am in my Father . . ." *John 14:20.*
      "The Spirit reaches the depths . . ." *1 Corinthians 2:10.*
      "fills the whole creation" *Ephesians 1:23.*

p. 20   "Yahweh created me . . ." *Proverbs 8:22−31.*
      "All that is hidden . . ." *Wisdom 7:21−28.*

p. 21    "Hear, O Israel . . ." *Deuteronomy 6:4–5* (*The New English Bible* © 1961,
         1970 by the Delegates of the Oxford University Press and the Syn-
         dics of the Cambridge University Press).

p. 22    "The Lord is my shepherd . . ." *Psalm 23:1,4* (King James Version).


CHAPTER THREE. *Consciousness*

p. 31    "Our consciousness . . ." C.G. Jung, "The Psychology of Eastern Medi-
         tation," in *Collected Works*, vol. 11 (Princeton, N.J.: Princeton Univer-
         sity Press, 1958), par. 935.


CHAPTER FOUR. *The Unconscious*

p. 49    "Just as conscious contents . . ." C.G. Jung, "Approaching the Uncon-
         scious," in *Man and His Symbols*, C.G. Jung, ed. (London and New
         York: Dell Publishing, 1964), 37.

p. 58    "The Father is greater . . ." *John 14:28.*
         "If you know me . . ." *John 14:7.*
         "I am the Way" *John 14:6.*
         "I am the gate" *John 10:9.*
         "come . . . through me" *John 14:6.*
         "believe in me" *John 10:38.*

p. 61    "We know that the mask . . ." C.G. Jung, *Psychology and Alchemy, Collected
         Works*, vol. 12 (Princeton, N.J.: Princeton University Press, 1944),
         par. 29.
         "'Speak to us yourself' . . ." *Exodus 20:19.*


CHAPTER FIVE. *The Language of the Unconscious*

p. 63    "The unconscious is the only . . ." C.G. Jung, "The Undiscovered Self,"
         in *Collected Works*, vol. 10 (Princeton, N.J.: Princeton University Press,
         1954), par. 565.

p. 64    Lincoln's inauguration. Carl Sandburg, *Abraham Lincoln: The War Years*, vol.
         4 (New York: Harcourt, Brace, and World, 1939), 91–94.
         Lincoln's last dream. Ibid, 265–66.

p. 65    "old women and by young men and maidens . . ." Ibid, 244.

## CHAPTER SIX. *Dreams*

p. 79    "The dream is often occupied . . ." C.G. Jung, "On the Psychology of the Unconscious," in *Collected Works*, vol. 7 (Princeton, N.J.: Princeton University Press, 1953), par. 24.

Nativity story. *Matthew 1:18–2:23.*

## CHAPTER SEVEN. *Synchronicity*

p. 99    "Since psyche and matter . . ." C.G. Jung, "On the Nature of the Psyche," in *Collected Works*, vol. 8 (Princeton: N.J.: Princeton University Press, 1960), par. 418.

p.106    "She is so pure . . ." *Wisdom 7:24–25.*

p.107    "The Spirit's power . . ." *The Hymnal 1982: according to the use of The Episcopal Church* (New York: The Church Hymnal Corp., 1985), Hymn 296.

p.108    "river of life . . ." *Revelation 22:1.*

## CHAPTER EIGHT. *Carl Jung and Christianity*

p.110    "If Christian doctrine . . ." C.G. Jung, *Mysterium Coniunctionis, Collected Works*, vol. 14 (Princeton, N.J.: Princeton University Press, 1970), par. 455n.

p.111    "Even the enlightened person . . ." C.G. Jung, *Answer to Job*, in *The Portable Jung*, Joseph Campbell, ed., (New York: Penguin Books, 1976), 650.

"I falter before the task . . ." C.G. Jung, *Memories, Dreams, Reflections* (New York: Pantheon Books, 1961), 353–54.

p.112    "The Christ image as we know it . . ." C.G. Jung, *Letters*, vol. 2 (Princeton, N.J.: Princeton University Press, 1975), 121.

"I have a certain picture . . ." Ibid, 94.

"You see, this is the crux . . ." C.G. Jung, *Letters*, vol. 1 (Princeton, N.J.: Princeton University Press, 1973), 236n.

p.113    "On the whole my illness . . ." Ibid, 357–58.

p.117    The dark side of Jung's relationship with Toni Wolff is reported in Paul Stern, *C.G Jung: The Haunted Prophet* (New York: Braziller, 1976). Stern does not name his sources for what seems to be insiders' gossip, leaving it up to the reader to believe it or not.

p.119   "the devil left him . . ." *Luke 4:13.*

p.122   "I still have many things to say . . ." *John 16:12—13.*

p.123   "Enter by the narrow gate . . ." *Matthew 7:13—14.*

"with an exactness . . ." C.G. Jung, *Aion, Collected Works*, vol. 9, pt. 2 (Princeton, N.J.: Princeton University Press, 1959), par. 79.

p.124   "The religious person . . ." C.G. Jung, *The Undiscovered Self*, in *Collected Works*, vol. 10 (Princeton, N.J.: Princeton University Press, 1970), par. 562.


CHAPTER NINE. *The Opposites*


p.129   "Alleluia! The reign of the Lord . . ." *Revelation: 19—22*


CHAPTER TEN. *Masculine Wholeness*


p.143   Jung's four stages of the anima. C.G. Jung, *Psychology of the Transference*, in *Collected Works*, vol. 16 (Princeton, N.J.: Princeton University Press, 1954), par. 361. These ideas are recapitulated by Marie-Louise von Franz in C.G. Jung, et al., *Man and His Symbols* (New York: Dell, 1968), 195.

Robert Moore and Douglas Gillette's version of the masculine quaternity is laid out in their book, *King, Warrior, Magician, Lover: Rediscovering the Archetypes of the Mature Masculine* (HarperSanFrancisco, 1990). It is elaborated in four further volumes, each of which is devoted to one of the quarters: *The King Within: Accessing the King in the Male Psyche* (New York: Avon Books, 1992); *The Warrior Within: Accessing the Knight in the Male Psyche* (Avon, 1992); *The Magician Within: Accessing the Shaman in the Male Psyche* (Avon, 1993); and *The Lover Within: Accessing the Lover in the Male Psyche* (Avon, 1993). Each of these books contains an appendix in which Toni Wolff's feminine quaternity is discussed.

CHAPTER ELEVEN. *The Beatles and the Masculine Quaternity*

p.162 "The thing is, we're all really the same person. . . ." Hunter Davies, *The Beatles: The Authorized Biography* (New York: McGraw-Hill, 1968), 322.

p.166 Jung on psychedelic drugs: Marie-Louise von Franz, *Psychotherapy* (Boston: Shambhala, 1993), 297.

p.171 "There's four of us . . ." *The Lost Beatle Interviews*, Geoffrey Giuliano and Brenda Giuliano, eds. (New York: Dutton, 1994), 41.

p.187 Jung's Liverpool dream: C.G. Jung, *Memories, Dreams, Reflections*, 197–199.

CHAPTER TWELVE. *Feminine Wholeness*

p.200 "Sophia is the woman wisdom of God." C.G. Jung, *Jung on Alchemy*, ed. Nathan Shwartz-Salant (Princeton, N.J.: Princeton University Press, 1995), 148.

p.201 "Happy the man . . ." *Ecclesiasticus 14:20–27.*

CHAPTER THIRTEEN. *Psyche and Eros and the Feminine Quaternity*

p.204 C.S. Lewis, *Till We Have Faces* (New York: Harcourt Brace, 1957); Erich Neumann, *Amor and Psyche: The Psychic Development of the Feminine* (Princeton, N.J.: Princeton University Press, 1956); Robert Johnson, *She: Understanding Feminine Psychology*, revised edition (New York: Harper and Row, 1989); Marie-Louise von Franz, *The Golden Ass of Apuleius: The Liberation of the Feminine in Man* (Boston, Shambhala, 1992).

CHAPTER FOURTEEN. *Individuation as Church Mission*

p.237 "If anyone . . ." *Luke 9:23.*

p.240 "A ladder was there . . ." *Genesis 28:12–13.*

p.241 "Are not interpretations . . ." *Genesis 40:8.*
   "I have heard it said . . ." *Genesis 41:15–16.*
   "Pharaoh's dreams . . ." *Genesis 41:25a.*

"God has revealed . . ." *Genesis 42:25b.*

"the gift of interpreting . . ." *Daniel 1:17.*

"O king . . ." *Daniel 2:29–30.*

p.243  "You know it is forbidden . . ." *Acts 10:28,34.*

p.244  Gerhard von Rad, *Wisdom in Israel* (Valley Forge, PA: Trinity Press International, 1972).

"The wise of heart . . ." *Proverbs 10:8* (*The New Jerusalem Bible*, copyright © 1985 by Darton, Longman & Todd, Ltd. and Doubleday, a division of Bantam Doubleday Dell Publishing Group, Inc.).

"Their uprightness . . ." *Proverbs 11:6* (*New Jerusalem Bible*).

"Where does wisdom . . ." *Job 28:12.*

p.245  "Is not Wisdom calling . . ." *Proverbs 8:1–4* (*New Jerusalem Bible*).

p.246  "For whoever finds me . . ." *Proverbs 8:35* (*New Jerusalem Bible*).

"I love those who love me . . ." *Proverbs 8:17.*

"Court her . . ." *Ecclesiasticus 6:26–28.*

"For within her . . ." *Wisdom 7:22,24–26.*

p.247  "What man can know . . ." *Wisdom 9:13.*

"It is hard enough . . ." *Wisdom 9:16–17.*

"If you do not believe me . . ." *John 3:12–13.*

"No one knows the Father . . ." *Matthew 11:27.*

"Come to me . . ." *Matthew 11:28–30.*

"Put your neck under the yoke . . ." *Sirach 51:26–27* (*The New English Bible*).

p.248  "Even if we did once know . . ." *2 Corinthians 5:16.*

"a Christ who is the power . . ." *1 Corinthians 1:24.*

"But still we have a wisdom . . ." *1 Corinthians 2:6,7,10.*

p.249  "To you it has been granted . . ." *Luke 8:10* (*The New English Bible*).

p.250  "A shoot springs . . ." *Isaiah 11:1–9.*


CHAPTER FIFTEEN. *Natural Spirituality as Church Program*


p.264  "In itself of course the Receptive . . ." *The I Ching or Book of Changes*, Richard Wilhelm, trans. (Princeton, N.J.: Princeton University Press, 1967), 11.

p.265  "Heaven has placed itself . . ." Ibid, 48.

# Index

*Abbey Road* (Beatles), 167, 180–85, 186–87.
  For *specific songs see* Beatles music
Abbey Road (street), 181–82
Abraham: and individuation, 249
Accident: as symbol, 76
Active imagination, 63, 114–15
*Aion* (C.G. Jung), 116
Airplane: as symbol, 69
Alchemy, 115, 116–17
*Amadeus* (motion picture), 101
Amor, 204
Analogy, 74–75
Analyst, Jungian, 239
*Analytical Psychology* (C.G. Jung), 262
Anima, 90–91; and Beatles 174, 184; and
  individuation 238; Jung's quaternity
  for 143; and Psyche and Eros, 204–05;
  and Wise Man, 203
Animal: as symbol, 70, 89
Animus, 91; and individuation, 238; nega-
  tive, 199; and Sophia, 203; as surrogate
  father, 152
Annunciation, 223
Anxiety, 9, 62, 100, 228
Aphrodite, 205–32
Apollo, 205
Archetype, 54–60; defined, 54; king as,
  55–56; mother as, 54–55; Self as, 56–
  60; Zeus as, 55–56. *See also* Collective
  unconscious; Self; Unconscious

Athena quarter, 191, 197–200; and God,
  203; and Psyche and Eros, 222–24

Baptism, 100
Ball: as symbol, 71
Ball field: as symbol, 72
Basement: as symbol, 69, 88–89
Bathroom: as symbol, 73
Bear: as symbol, 89
Beatles, 160–89; breakup of, 180–85; and
  "concept" albums, 179; and drugs, 166,
  179; and feminine principle, 187; gen-
  eration of, 181; and inner world, 233;
  and India, 163, 167, 171; and Linda
  Eastman, 185; and love, 168–69, 182,
  185; music of, 165–85; and "Paul is
  dead," 186–87; and Self, 187, 188–89;
  and shadow, 183, 184; and synchronic-
  ity, 167, 186; and unconscious, 166; and
  Yoko Ono, 179–80, 183. *See also* Beatles
  music (individual works); Harrison,
  George; Lennon, John; McCartney,
  Paul; Starr, Ringo
*The Beatles* (album). *See* White Album
Beatles music (individual works): *Abbey
  Road*, 167, 180–85, 186–87; "All You
  Need is Love," 176; "And My Bird
  Can Sing," 170; "Baby You're a Rich
  Man," 177; "Because," 184; *The Beatles*,
  178–80; "Being for the Benefit of Mr.

Beatles music (*continued*)
Kite," 172; "Blackbird," 180; "Blue Jay Way," 177; "Carry That Weight," 185; "Come Together," 182; "A Day in the Life," 173, 174–75, 186; "Doctor Robert," 170; "Don't Pass Me By," 180; "Eleanor Rigby," 168, 185; "The End," 185; "Fixing a Hole," 174; "Flying," 178; "The Fool on the Hill," 175; "For No One," 169; "Getting Better," 174; "Golden Slumbers," 185; "Good Day Sunshine," 169; "Good Morning Good Morning," 173; "Got to Get You Into My Life," 169, 186; "Hello, Goodbye," 175; *Help!*, 166; "Here Comes the Sun," 183–84; "Here, There, and Everywhere," 168; "I Am the Walrus," 176, 179; "I'm Only Sleeping," 169; "I'm So Tired," 180; "I Want You (She's So Heavy)," 183; "I Want to Tell You," 171–72; *Let It Be*, 181; "A Little Help from My Friends," 173; "Love to You," 171; "Lovely Rita," 174; "Lucy in the Sky with Diamonds," 172; *Magical Mystery Tour*, 167, 175–78; "Maxwell's Silver Hammer," 183; "Mean Mr. Mustard," 184; "Octopus's Garden," 183; "Oh! Darling," 183; "Penny Lane," 175; "Polythene Pam," 184; *Rubber Soul*, 166; *Sgt. Pepper*, 167, 172–75, 186, 189; "Sgt. Pepper's Lonely Hearts Club Band," 174; "She Came in Through the Bathroom Window," 184–85; "She Said She Said," 170; "She's Leaving Home," 174; "Something," 182–83; "Strawberry Fields Forever," 176, 186; "Sun King," 184; "Taxman," 167, 171; "Tomorrow Never Knows," 170; *Revolver*, 166, 167–72, 171, 187; "When I'm Sixty-Four," 174; "While My Guitar Gently Weeps," 180; White Album, 178–80; "Within You Without You," 173; "Yellow Submarine," 172; "Yesterday," 166; "You Never Give Me Your Money," 184; "Your Mother Should Know," 175. *See also* Beatles

Bird: as symbol, 69, 70, 103
Boundaries, 70, 72; and dream groups, 256; and Eve, 193; and Soldier, 152, 153
Brooks, Noah, 64
Bus: as symbol, 70

Calendar, Church: as cycle, 77–78
Cats: as symbol, 70
Center. *See* Self
Charity: and King, 159
Child: as symbol, 70–71
*Chokhmah*, 200–01. *See also* Wisdom
Christ: and dreams, 79; in dreams, 78; and dream work, 97; and fish symbol, 70; as flower, 71; and individuation, 214; and Jung, 112; and King, 181; limited understanding of, 25; masculine and feminine joined in, 16; in nature, 16, 19, 22, 24, 25; and Self, 56–57, 58, 62, 71. *See also* Jesus; Messiah
Christmas: as symbol, 77–78
Church: as context for individuation, 238–66; in dreams, 87, 88–89; and Jung, 123; natural spirituality program in, 252–66; as symbol, 72
Circle: as symbol, 71
City: as symbol, 87
City of God, 54, 129, 156–57; as symbol, 72
Clergy: and God, 124
Collective unconscious, 53–60; defined, 53; and symbolism, 67. *See also* Archetype; Unconscious
Colors, rainbow: as feminine spirit, 16, 22

Community life: and Athena, 198; and inner world, 231; and King, 156, 159, 181; and Wise Man, 156

Compensation: 60–61, 66; in dreams, 95; and synchronicity, 109

Consciousness, 31–48; cooperation of, with unconscious, 66; defined, 31; ego, 31, 32, 69; four functions of, 34–43; and God, 66; images symbolic of, 69; limitations of, 33; and nature, 66; one sided, 66–67; resistance to, 43–44; and stages of life, 43–48

Courthouse: as symbol, 72

Creative illness, 9

Cross: as symbol, 72

Crystal: as symbol, 72

Cupid, 204

Cycles: in dreams, 93–94; and unconscious, 77

Daniel: and dreams, 240–41

Darkness: as symbol, 69

David, King: and individuation, 249

Death: in dreams, 96; and individuation, 156; symbolic images of, 139

Demeter, 212, 214–15, 217, 226

Depression, 60, 173, 183; images symbolic of, 69

Dove Publications, 272–73

Dog: as symbol, 70, 89

Dream groups, 254–57; and boundaries, 256; and church, 97, 252; continuing education in, 260–66; outside church, 239; and sexuality, 256; value of, 97. *See also* Dream work; Natural spirituality program: dream group

Dream work: in church program, 254–57; guidelines for, 260. *See also* Dream groups; Natural spirituality program: dream group

Dreams, 79–98; and Abraham Lincoln, 63–65; and "Aha!" moment, 98; associations with, 87–93; and Bible, 79–81; collective symbols in, 68–74; cycles in, 93–94; and dream groups, 97; duality in, 60; "flagship," 84–85; fragments of, 84; and future, 96, 178; and God, 79, 81, 98, 240–43; indexing of, 83–84; inner or outer meaning of, 89–90, 92–93; interpretation of, 85–98; proper weight of, 94–96; recording, 83–85, 95; remembering, 82; and Scripture, 240–43; sequence in, 93; settings of, 87; "summary," 94; warnings in, 96. *See also* Dreams (specific)

Dreams (specific): Avoiding the Evil Snake, 122; Body Mind and Spirit Mind, 207; The Dark Self, 59; The Family Side of Life, 87; Freud and Sex, 207; The Giant Mouse, 32; Going Across Is Not Good, 57–58; To Integrate God Is To Integrate the Self, 57; Jacob's Ladder (Genesis), 240; Julian of Norwich Today, 83; Jung's Assassination on Religion, 110; Limits of Inner and Outer Life, 230; Lines to the Center, 57; Liverpool (Jung), 187–88; Living Between Good and Evil, 121; Love Beyond the Universe, 139; Meaning and Life Go Together, 116; Mobsters Want Silence, 120–21; Never Forget the Feminine Vessel, 192; The Other Shore (Lincoln), 64–65; Peter's Sheet of Animals (Acts), 242; Pinning Lace, 141; Sexual Packages, 133–34; Trying on Feelings, 37; Two Levels of Life, 207; The Unresponsive Groundskeeper, 74–75; Whiteness and Color in the Church, 15. *See also* Dreams

*Dreams* (C.G. Jung), 262

Drugs: and Beatles, 179; psychedelic, 166

Duality: in dreams, 60

Eastman, Linda, 185

Ego: and dreams, 86; and God, 235–36; and human quaternity, 146; importance of strength of, 31, 60, 61–62, 86, 236; inflation of, 178; and King, 181; resistance by, 175; and Scarlett, 195; and Self, 235–36, 263–64

Einstein, Albert, 25, 65

Electric light: as symbol, 69

Elements, Four, 142

Elven glens, 94

Epstein, Brian, 162, 184

Eros (principle): defined, 135. *See also* Feminine principle

Eros (mythology). *See* Psyche and Eros

Eucharist, 19, 24, 25, 81

Eve quarter, 190–94; in Jung's quaternity, 143; in Psyche and Eros, 216–18

Evil, 118–22; and the dark Self, 59

Excrement: as symbol, 73–74

Extraversion, 35–36, 70; and King, 156

Father world: and Beatles, 177, 184; defined, 144; elements of, 151; levels of, 145–46; after World War II, 160

Father's daughter. *See* Athena quarter; Feminine quaternity; Scarlett quarter

Father's son. *See* King quarter; Masculine quaternity; Soldier quarter

Feeling. *See* Functions, Four: feeling function

Feminine principle, 130–40; and Beatles, 161–62, 169, 170, 175; and Church, 240, 265, 266; devaluation by masculine principle, 66; domination by, 183; and Eve, 193; and "frilly" feminine, 196–97; and God, 66–67, 126, 131, 204–32, 258; in human life, 66; and *I Ching,*

264–65; misuse of, 180; and natural spirituality program, 258; quaternity of, 142, 190–232; right relationship to, 230–31; and soul, 196; as spirit of earth, 16; and surrender, 213; as vessel, 198–200; and Wise Man, 154–56. *See also* Athena quarter; Eve quarter; Feminine quaternity; Opposites; Scarlett quarter; Sophia quarter; Union of opposites

Feminine quaternity, 190–232; defined, 190–91; and God, 204; and Psyche and Eros, 204–32; of Toni Wolff, 142–43

Feminine spirit. *See* Feminine principle

Fish: as symbol, 70

Flower: as symbol, 71

Flying: as symbol, 69

Foot travel: as symbol, 70

Four functions. *See* Functions, Four

Freud, Sigmund, 25–26, 65; dream about, 207

"Frilly" feminine, 196–97

Functions, Four, 34–43; "divine" function, 42–43; feeling function, 34, 36–37; integration of, 41–43; intuitive function, 34, 35, 36; "power" functions, 41–43; ranking of, 38–41; "salvation" function, 41–43; sensation function, 34, 35, 36; thinking function, 34, 36–37

Gestation: as cycle in psyche, 77

Gillette, Douglas, 143, 149

Gnosticism, 115, 116–17

God: and Athena, 199, 203; child symbolic of, 71; and clergy, 124; and dream work, 97; and dreams, 79, 81, 86, 98, 240–43; and ego inflation, 178; and evil, 118–22; fear of, 102; and feminine principle, 131, 258; and feminine quaternity, 204–32; feminine voice of, 66–67, 126; and human quaternity,

146; and individuation, 60, 214, 237;
and inner world, 234; and King, 154,
157; masculine aspect of, 66; and masculine principle, 131, 258; as mother,
106; and perfection, 157–57, 199–200;
picture language of, 66; redefining of,
235–36; role of, in individuation, 234;
and Self, 56–59; and sexuality, 91–92,
206–08; and Sophia, 201, 203; and
sychronicity, 104, 109; and unconscious, 48, 63, 91; and union of opposites, 129, 258; and wisdom, 244–48;
and Wise Man, 154; and woman, 204–
32, 212–14
God-center. *See* Self
*Golden Ass* (Apuleius), 204
Golden fleece, 219–21
*Gone With the Wind*, 190, 194–95
Grail, Holy, 54
Guidelines for dreamwork, 260

Harrison, George, 163, 167, 171–72, 173,
178, 180, 182, 183–84. *See also* Beatles
Heaven: as ideal, 198; as perfection, 154,
156–57; in Revelation, 156–57
Helen of Troy, 143
*Help!* (Beatles), 166
Hera, 212, 214–15
Hermes, 212, 215, 229
Hierarchy, 70
Hobbits, 94
Holy City. *See* City of God
Holy Spirit, 22; and dream work, 97, 98;
and dreams, 81; limited understanding
of, 24; masculine and feminine aspects
of, 16; and natural spirituality pro-
grams, 259, 260; presence after Jesus,
19, 24; and Self, 59; and shadow, 52; as
teacher, 122; and wisdom, 248. *See also*
Feminine principle; Masculine prin-
ciple; Wisdom

Homosexuality, 133–34
Honeycomb: as symbol, 72
Hotel: as symbol, 87, 88
Hound, three-headed, 225, 228
House: as symbol, 103
Humors, Four, 142

*I Ching*, 264–65, 274, 283–86; and Wise
Man, 155
India, 112. *See also* Beatles: and India
Indians, American, 142
Individuation, 141, 242–43; and Beatles,
164–85, 187; and childhood issues,
175–76; and Church, 233–66; and
death, 156, 185; defined, 46; and God,
234–37; and limitation, 177, 181; and
Scripture, 248–50; stages of, 234–38;
and traditional religion, 235–36; and
weeping, 213; and Wise Man, 156; and
woman, 204–32
Inner life: limits of, 230–31
Instinct: symbols of, 70
Introversion, 35–36
Intruder: as symbol, 73
Intuition. *See* Functions, Four: intuitive
function

Jesus: nativity of, 79–81; and Self, 71;
teachings of, 17–19, 23–24, 103, 108,
122, 124, 146, 207–08, 228, 237, 247. *See
also* Christ
Johnson, Lyndon B., 121
Johnson, Robert A., 204, 272
Joseph (Old Testament): and dreams,
240–41
Joseph, Saint: and dreams, 79–81
Journal: in dream work, 83, 85
Journey Group, 13, 254–57; *See also* Dream
groups; Natural spirituality program:
dream group
Journey Into Wholeness, Inc., 239, 273

JRH Publications: ordering information, 273

Judaism, 19, 21

Julian of Norwich, 83, 203

Jung, Carl Gustav, 13, 65, 81, 110–26; autobiography of, 7, 8; and Beatles, 187–89; and Christ, 112; and drugs, 166; and evil, 118–22; and feminine quaternity, 143; and four functions, 34; and Freud, 26–27; and the inner world, 8; intellectual development of, 26–27; near-death experience of, 113; problems with, 114–18; and quaternities, 142; and religion, 26–27, 110–26; and Sophia, 200; and stages of life, 44; and synchronicity, 100, 104; and Toni Wolff, 117; and unconscious, 26–27; writings of, 269–70; writings of, in natural spirituality programs, 261–62

Jung, Emma, 117

Kelsey, Morton T., 272

Kennedy, John F., 121

Kennedy, Robert, 121

King quarter, 143, 147, 156–59; and Beatles, 163–64, 167, 169, 172, 173, 178–79, 180–85; and blessing, 158–59; and Christ, 181; and community, 156, 181; and ego, 181; and love, 149; and order, 158; after World War II, 160; and reality, 179; and Self, 181; and woman, 190

Kingdom of God, 17–18; and *I Ching*, 264–65; and Self, 263–64

Lennon, John, 161, 162–63, 166, 169–71, 172–73, 174, 176–77, 178, 179–80, 181, 182–83. *See also* Beatles

Lent: as symbol, 77–78

*Let It Be* (Beatles), 181

Lewis, C.S., 204

Light: as symbol, 69

Lincoln, Abraham, 63–65

Liverpool: and Beatles, 161, 162, 164, 181, 187–89; Jung's dream of, 187–89

Logos: defined, 135. *See also* Masculine principle

*Lord of the Rings,* 94

Love: and Beatles, 177, 187; two streams of, 206–32

Lover (masculine quaternity), 143, 149. *See also* Poet

Lover, Divine, 140

Loyola, Ignatius, 115

McCartney, Paul, 161, 162, 163, 166, 168–69, 170, 174–76, 178, 179, 180, 182, 184–85. *See also* Beatles

*Magical Mystery Tour* (Beatles), 167, 175–78. *For specific songs see* Beatles music

Magician (masculine quaternity), 143. *See also* Wise Man

Mafia, 120–21

Mandala, 71

Marriage: of Lamb, 129; mystical, 129, 139–40, 141; of Psyche and Eros, 231–32; as symbol, 141. *See also* Union of opposites

Mary, Virgin, 54, 79, 199, 214, 223; as flower, 71; in Jung's quaternity, 143

Masculine principle, 130–89, 190; abstract quality of, 66–67; and Church, 265; and consciousness, 152; and God, 16, 131; in *I Ching,* 264–65; and natural spirituality, 262–63; in natural spirituality program, 258; quaternity of, 142, 146–89; as supporter of feminine, 196. *See also* King quarter; Masculine quaternity; Opposites; Poet quarter; Soldier quarter; Union of opposites; Wise Man quarter

Masculine quaternity, 146–89; and Beatles, 160–89; defined, 146–48; levels within quarters of, 150; of Moore and Gillette, 143, 149

Masculine spirit. *See* Masculine principle

Meditation, 63

Meditation booklets, 257–58; 287–92

*Memories, Dreams, Reflections* (C.G. Jung), 262

Messiah: and Self, 249–50. *See also* Christ; Jesus

*Metamorphoses* (Apuleius), 204

Metaphor: and unconscious, 65–66, 68

Midlife. *See* Stages of Life

Mob. *See* Mafia

Money: as symbol, 88

Monotheism, 21–23, 24, 235–36

Moon: as symbol, 69, 71, 134–37

Moore, Robert, 143, 149

Moses, 61

Mother: as archetype, 54–55; as symbol, 150

Mother world: and Beatles, 161, 169; defined, 144; gifts of, 151; levels of, 145–46

Mother's daughter. *See* Eve quarter; Feminine quaternity; Sophia quarter

Mother's son. *See* Masculine quaternity; Poet; Wise Man

Mustard jar: and Eve, 192

Myers-Briggs Type Indicator, 35

Natural spirituality: as church program, 252–66; and dreams, 79; origin of term, 3; and Pan, 213; and Psyche and Eros, 213; and Scripture, 240–51; as teacher at the heart of life, 23–24; and wisdom, 3; and Wise Man, 155

*Natural Spirituality* (book): purpose of, 14; ordering information for, 273

Natural spirituality program, 252–66; in Athens, Georgia, 3, 11–14, 252–61, 287;

continuing education in, 260–66, 269–82; dream about, 15; dream group in, 254–57, 260–66; establishment of, 259–66; and Holy Spirit, 259, 260; and *I Ching*, 264–65; leadership of, 259; library for, 252, 258–59, 262, 269; and masculine principle, 262–63; meditation booklets in, 257–58, 287–92; study group in, 252–54, 260; traditional religion in, 262–64; and writings of Jung, 261–62

Nature: amorality of, 22; as "colors," 22; and consciousness, 66; in dreams, 87; and God, 23, 66, 154; as inner life, 233; and scientific rationalism, 25; spiritual aspects of, 16, 18, 19, 23, 63, 155, 145; and Sophia, 201; and synchronicity, 106; unconsciousness of, 66; and Wise Man, 155

Nazis, 119, 122

Neumann, Erich, 204

Nightmares: purpose of, 234

Octopus: as symbol, 183

Ono, Yoko, 179–80, 183

Opposites, 129–40; and Beatles, 175, 185; and sexuality, 133–34; and stages of life, 137–39; as sun and moon, 134–37; as yin and yang, 129–31. *See also* Union of opposites

Oracular devices, 63; *See also I Ching*

Pan, 211, 213, 230

Park: as symbol, 72

Paul, Saint, 16, 19, 24, 27, 248

Perfection: as heaven, 154; and King, 156–57

Persephone, 224–26

Peter, Saint, 242–43

Physics, 25, 132; and synchronicity, 106

Plate: as symbol, 71

Play on words, 75

Poet quarter, 143, 147, 148–51, 153; and Beatles, 162, 163, 167, 167–72, 174–75; and Eve, 194; and King, 158; after World War II, 160; and woman, 190

Poisidon, 205

*The Portable Jung* (C.G. Jung), 262

Primeval order, 245, 247. *See also* Wisdom

Primitive life, 78

Projection: on opposite sex, 92–93; and shadow, 52

Psyche (in mythology), 204–32; and ants, 216–18; betrays Eros, 210; and box, 224, 225–26, 229, 230–31; and crystal urn, 221–24; and coins and cakes, 224–25, 227, 228; and Demeter and Hera, 212, 214–15; four tasks of, 215–31; and golden fleece, 219–21; and Pan, 211; and rams, 219–21; and River Styx, 221–24; sacrifice of, 205; and sexuality, 206–08; surrenders to Aphrodite, 212, 215; and tower, 224, 226; and underworld, 224–29; wedding of, 229–32; and weeping, 213

Psyche and Eros, 115, 204–32. *See also* Psyche (in mythology)

Psychological types. *See* Functions, Four

Psychosis, 61

Quantum mechanics, 25

Quaternities: 142; balance in, 194; competition in, 194; feminine, 142–46, 190–232; human, 144–46; masculine, 142–89; and shadow, 150–51; as Wise-Man system, 155. *See also* Feminine quaternity; Masculine quaternity

Rain: as symbol, 68

Rebel: as Soldier, 153

Religion: primitive, 78; traditional, 262–64, 235–36

Repetition: in dreams and synchronicity, 75–76

Resistance: to consciousness, 43–44, 81–82, 86, 100; in dream work, 256; to unconscious, 175

*Revolver* (Beatles), 166, 167–72, 151–56, 171, 187. *For specific songs see* Beatles music

Ring: as symbol, 71

Ritual: and King, 159

"River of life," 108, 156–57

*Rubber Soul* (Beatles), 166

Sanford, John A., 272

Satan: and God, 118

Saul, King: and individuation, 249

Scarlett quarter, 190–91, 194–97; in Psyche and Eros, 219–21

Scientific rationalism, 25, 105

Scripture: levels of meaning in, 248–50; and natural spirituality, 240–51

Sea: as symbol, 67

Self, 56–60; and Beatles, 187, 188–89; and Christ, 56–57, 58, 62, 71; dark side of, 59–60; dreams about, 57–59; and ego, 263–64; and God, 56–59; and *I Ching*, 264–65; images symbolic of, 71–72, 183; and individuation, 214, 235–37; and King, 181; and kingdom of God, 263–64; in Liverpool dream, 188–89; and Messiah, 249–50; overbalance of, 236; and synchronicity, 107, 186

Seminar. *See* Natural spirituality program: study group

Sensation. *See* Functions, Four: sensation function

*Sgt. Pepper* (Beatles), 167, 172–75, 186, 189. *For specific songs see* Beatles music

Sexuality: and dream groups, 256; and Freud, 207; and "frilly" feminine, 196; and God, 91–92, 206–08; and human quaternity, 146; levels of, 206–08; and opposites, 133–34; and Scarlett, 195; and stages of life, 91–92

Shadow, 51–53, 124–25; and Beatles, 174, 183, 184; defined, 51; in dreams, 90; and human quaternity, 150–51; and individuation, 237; and King, 159. *See also* Shadow work

Shadow work: and human quaternity, 150–51; images symbolic of, 73–74. *See also* Shadow

Shamanism, 9, 63, 265

Short courses, Jungian, 239

Sky: as symbol, 69

Snake: as symbol, 70

Soldier quarter, 143, 147, 151–54; and Beatles, 162, 167, 169, 169–71, 172–75, 176, 179, 181; and King, 158; after World War II, 160; and woman, 190

Sophia. *See* Sophia quarter; Wisdom

Sophia quarter, 191, 200–03; in Jung's quaternity, 143; in Psyche and Eros, 226–29.

Sorcery, 226

Soul: as anima, 90; and man, 204–05; and Psyche and Eros, 204–32; and woman, 196, 204–05

Spirit: as animus, 91. *See also* Holy Spirit

Square: as symbol, 71–72

Stages of life, 43–48; childhood in, 44–45; mature adulthood in, 46–47; midlife turn in, 46; and opposites, 137–39; and sexuality, 91–92; young adulthood in, 45–46

Starkey, Richard. *See* Starr, Ringo

Starr, Ringo, 161, 163–64, 172, 173, 178, 180, 183. *See also* Beatles

Stranger: as symbol, 73

Study group. *See* Natural spirituality program: study group

Styx, River, 221, 224

Sun: as symbol, 71, 69, 134–37, 184

Sun circle (American Indian), 142

Sutcliff, Stu, 162

Swimming: as symbol, 68–69

Symbol: collective, 67–74; as God's feminine voice, 66; personal, 67; and unconscious, 65–66. *See also* Symbols (specific)

Symbols (specific): accident, 76; airplane, 69; animals, 70, 89; ball, 71; ball field, 72; basement, 69, 88–89; bathroom, 73; bird, 69, 70, 103; cats, 70; child, 70–71; Christmas, 77–78; church, 72, 87, 88–89; circle, 71; city, 87; City of God, 72; courthouse, 72; cross, 72; crystal, 72; darkness, 69; dog, 70; electric light, 69; excrement, 73–74; flower, 71; flying, 69; fish, 70; foot travel, 70; honeycomb, 72; hotel, 87, 88; house, 103; intruder, 73; Lent, 77–78; light, 69; Mafia, 120–21; marriage, 141; money, 88; moon, 69, 71, 134–37; mother, 150; nature, 87; octopus, 183; opposite sex, 90–93; park, 72; plate, 71; rain, 68; ring, 71; sea, 67; sky, 69; snake, 70; square, 71–72; stranger, 73; sun, 69, 71, 134–37, 184; swimming, 68–69; table, 72; toilet, 73; tree, 103, 201; underground, 69; urination, 74; vacation house, 87, 88; vehicles, 69–70; water, 68; wedding, 139; well, 68

Synchronicity, 99–109; and A. Lincoln, 63–65; and Beatles, 167, 186; and God, 104, 109; and *I Ching*, 264; and stages of individuation, 236; and Jung, 27; origin of term, 64; and Self, 107, 186; and unconscious, 63

Table: as symbol, 72

Tao, 17, 18, 19, 27, 28, 129–30. *See also* Yin and yang

"Teacher at the heart of life," 23—24, 122

Temenos, 72

Terms of Endearment, 4

Themes: and unconscious, 76—77

Thinking. See Functions, Four: thinking
    function

Till We Have Faces (C.S. Lewis), 204

Toilet: as symbol, 73

Tradition, 72; and father world, 152

Train: as symbol, 70

Tree: of Life, 188; as symbol, 103, 201

Truck: as symbol, 70


Uhsadel, Walther, 112

Unconscious, 49—62; and archetypes,
    54—60; and Beatles, 166; collective, 53—
    60, 238; compensation by, 60—61, 175;
    and cycles, 77; danger of, 61; and
    dreams, 79—98; and drugs, 166; duality
    in, 60; Freud's understanding of, 25—
    26; images symbolic of, 49—50, 68, 69,
    70; Jung's understanding of, 26—27;
    language of, 63—78, 93; methods of
    contacting, 63; model of, 50; moral re-
    sponse to, 27, 61—62, 166; overempha-
    sis on, 114—17; personal, 50—53, 67,
    237; resistance to, 61; right relationship
    to, 230—31; and themes, 76—77. See also
    Archetype; Collective unconscious

Underground: as symbol, 69

Union of opposites, 67, 105—06, 258; and
    Aphrodite, 208—09; defined, 129; in
    Genesis, 131; as goal, 140; and God, 129;
    and heaven, 157; and individuation, 141,
    233; levels of, 206—08; in Psyche and
    Eros, 231—32. See also Opposites

Urination: as symbol, 74


Vacation house: as symbol, 87, 88

Vehicle: as symbol, 69—70

Vision quests, 63

Vocation, 223, 238

Von Franz, Marie-Louise, 204

Von Rad, Gerhard, 244


Warrior (masculine quaternity), 143. See
    also Soldier quarter

Water: as symbol, 68

Way, The, 17, 18, 27

Weapon: and Soldier, 153

Wedding: in dreams, 96; as symbol, 139.
    See also Marriage; Union of opposites

Well: as symbol, 68

White Album (Beatles), 178—80. For spe-
    cific songs see Beatles music

Will: and Beatles, 162, 170, 172—73, 177;
    and father world, 150—51

Winds, Four, 142

Wisdom: biblical theology of, 243—48;
    equivalence to natural spirituality, 3; and
    God, 106, 244—48; and Holy Spirit,
    248; and Jesus, 247—48; personification
    of, 245—46; proverbial, 244; in Scrip-
    ture, 20, 243—48; and sexuality, 206—
    08; and Sophia quarter, 200—03; as tree,
    201; and Wise Man, 155

Wisdom in Israel (von Rad), 244

Wise Man, 143, 147, 154—56; and anima,
    203; and Beatles, 163, 167, 169, 171—72,
    173, 175—78; and King, 158; and love,
    149; and passion, 171—72, 182; after
    World War II, 160; and Sophia, 203;
    and woman, 190

Wise Men, Three, 79—80

Wolff, Toni, 117, 142—43


Yin and yang, 129—31. See also Opposites


Zeus: as archtype, 55—56; and Athena,
    197; eagle of, 221—24; and Eros, 229